THE ADVENTURES OF A HAPPY HOMOSEXUAL

Memoirs of an unlikely activist

Terry Sanderson

Published in 2016 by FeedARead.com Publishing
Copyright © Terry Sanderson.

A CIP catalogue record for this title is available from the
British Library.

Terry Sanderson, PO Box 130, London W5 1DQ

DISCLAIMER

The problem with invoking the past is that memory doesn't always serve us accurately; it can play mischievous tricks. It can be modified by wishful thinking, and we may be tempted to fill in the gaps with dreams.

I am reaching back to a time before the internet and before the advent of personal computers and mobile phones. In those days, before blogs and social media were ubiquitous, only the most important people had the minutiae of their daily lives recorded. For the rest of us, the only place from where it can be recovered now is inside our heads.

I've done my best and searched out as many verifiable facts as I can from old newspaper clippings and archives, but a lot of it rests entirely upon my fallible ability to recall. So, if you were involved in any of this and your recollections are different, I apologise and promise to change anything that I haven't got right. Just let me know.

For Keith – love always

~ *1* ~

How did I - an ill-educated, poverty-stricken lad from a Yorkshire mining town - get swept up in the creation of two of the most amazing and unexpected social revolutions of the past century – gay rights and secularism? How did I manage to propel the grimy industrial town of Rotherham on to the front line of the struggle for homosexual emancipation? I still pinch myself when I recall I was an agony aunt on a leading woman's magazine, that I was responsible for the longest-running column in any gay magazine and that I wrote and published what was to become one of the most influential gay self-help books of the eighties. How did all that happen?

After that came the organisation of the biggest demonstration against a papal visit ever seen and an epic struggle to protect free speech from blasphemy law.

At the beginning of this story I, along with every other gay man in the country, was a sexual outlaw. If I had expressed my sexual preference for those of my own sex I could have ended up in prison. Now, six decades later, I am about to exercise my option to be married to my male partner.

During that same period, religion has staged a revival that could conceivably reverse everything that gay people have achieved. In Europe, only a few short years ago, religion was regarded as being in its death throes. Now it is renewing itself in new and more frightening forms, with the potential to threaten us all.

How did we get here from there in such a relatively short time? And how did I, a most unlikely activist, play a part in this tumultuous period of change?

We have to go back to the winter of 1946 – 47, one of the coldest on record. Snowdrifts were piled high throughout the country, food and fuel distribution were restricted. Coal stocks were running out.

I was born in the middle of all this on 17th November 1946 at 13 Burns Road in Maltby, a coal mining town in South Yorkshire, just down the road from Rotherham and within an hour of Sheffield and not all that far from Doncaster.

Not long after I had popped out, I'm told I developed dysentery and it was touch and go for a time as to whether I was to become part of the nation's infant mortality statistics.

But I survived, and my childhood in Maltby was happy and sheltered, surrounded by a big, loving family. We were poverty-stricken, as was everyone around us. At the end of the street the pawn shop, or "pledge office" to give it its posh name, did a roaring trade.

If we ran out of money during the week (pay day was on Friday), my mother would occasionally take up the stair carpet and lug it down to the pawn shop where it would reside until Friday when we could retrieve it. It seems the stair carpet was the most valuable item in the house.

My father, Fred (not Frederick, and known to one and all as Sandy) worked on the coal face at Maltby Main Colliery for fifty years. At the end of it he got a certificate signed by Derek Ezra, chairman of the National Coal Board, which was framed and proudly displayed on the wall. He also got a good pension which he enjoyed for another twenty years – far longer than any of his contemporaries, all of whom dropped off the peg at a relatively early age.

I think my father survived so long because he didn't smoke. Nearly all the other colliers did and in combination with the coal dust inhaled throughout their working life, few had fully functioning lungs when the time came for them to hang up their helmets and snap tins for the last time.

My father had been in the pit since he was fourteen and had worked diligently there on the coal face until he was sixty-five. At the time I took little notice – it was just what he did and he didn't complain much. The only time I showed an interest in his work was when he occasionally brought home a piece of coal with a fossilised creature embedded in it. It was only then that I got an inkling of the nightmare world he was working in.

It never occurred to me as a child just how terrible that gruelling half century must have been for him.

Because of the inhuman shifts he had to work, he wasn't around much except when he got Sundays off, then he would go out to the British Legion at lunch time, get blind drunk, come home very angry and voluble, talking intoxicated rubbish, and then sleep it off during the afternoon.

Mi Dad was often grumpy and unapproachable, but I was never afraid of him. Although Mi Mam would occasionally administer a slap on the bottom or a clout round the head when I deserved it, my father never raised a hand to me or even raised his voice.

He also prided himself on never swearing. He claimed that he had never uttered a single profanity of any kind in his entire life. All this despite working in an extremely macho environment where swearing was a way of life and cussing was continuous.

Needless to say, laughter and joy didn't figure highly in my father's working life. It was only later when he had retired and the burdens of the pit were lifted from him that he started to lose some of the anger at his lot in life and become a likeable person. He even started to take holidays abroad and blossomed in a way that he had never been able to in his working life. Who knows what he might have been had he not been put into the pit at such a young age?

Mi Mam had five sisters. As well as Jean there was Rhoda, Celia, Mae and Rose - all of them formidably independent-minded and feisty, and all living within walking distance of our house. Her mother, "Mi Granny", lived immediately across the road and was a frequent visitor – maybe three or four times a day. Mi Granny had been a young widow, her husband perishing in one of the many accidents at the pit long before I arrived on the scene.

My mother, and other women on our street, also worked on farms in the summer, picking peas or potatoes or weeding carrot fields to supplement the family income. My mother loved this because it got her away from the house and enabled her to be herself for a few hours, to have her own friends and express her own personality away from the family. She kept up this work, even though it was backbreaking labour, right up until it began to be mechanised.

The rest of us all knew that our path in life was pre-ordained - as either pitworkers, factory workers, steelworkers or, if you were lucky, office workers. There was no world beyond Maltby as far as I was concerned or indeed most of the residents were concerned. The only person who seemed to have escaped into a world of glamour was Freddie Truman, the famous cricketer, whose mother still lived on the next street to us.

There was a considerable age gap between me and my two elder brothers which later led me to conclude that I had been an accident, an unintended addition to the family. This, I suspect, led to my mother indulging me in ways that she had not done with my brothers. I was her bonus prize – the cuddly toy.

So my older brothers were well ahead of me, and as I grew up they resented the inconvenience of often having this mardy kid as they called me, hanging round, cramping their style. I was glad later that I had two elder brothers who were going to provide my parents with the grandchildren they regarded as their due. That relieved me from a duty that I knew I could never fulfil.

It wasn't until much later that I heard the theory of the third son in a family.

In 2013, scientists from Brock University in Ontario published some research showing that for each older brother that you have, the odds that you will be gay rise by a third.

The theory is that when a mother is pregnant with a boy, she produces antibodies which attack the part of the unborn baby's brain that controls sexuality. The strength of this 'immune response' is said to increase with each son, raising the odds of homosexuality.

I don't know how much credence to give to this theory, but it would have been comforting to know when I was young because at that stage homosexuality had not yet, apparently,

7

been invented. Or so I thought. I certainly didn't have any conception of such a thing.

But I did have thoughts and feelings that indicated to me that I wasn't quite like the other boys in my school. I must have been incredibly effeminate. I hated football, preferred girls as playmates. I was attracted by theatricals and play-acting. What a stereotype!

When my mother was out shopping and I was in the house alone, I began to experiment with drag, buying outlandish clothes from the local jumble sales and telling everyone that it was for the school concert, something in which I was always intimately involved.

My favourite was an extravagant multi-layered flamenco dress I had found at the church hall. I adored it and when no-one was looking would don it and swan around the room like a film star, swishing and twirling. I also bought a mangy fox fur stole that I liked to put on and, when the house was empty, pretending I was an important lady.

I was petrified of the reaction if anyone found out what was going on in my head. Even so, I couldn't resist doing my Old Mother Riley impersonation at every opportunity (Old Mother Riley – played with manic energy by Arthur Lucan in dozens of films - was the first drag act I ever saw, and then only in old films on the telly. I found it exceedingly liberating to see a man dressed as a woman even though the end result was grotesque).

But the drag-wearing had to be kept, literally, in the closet.

As puberty approached, I was a mass of confusion and acne. The skin eruptions were pretty severe and left me scarred not only physically but emotionally.

As my school mates were off doing sport or smoking behind the bike-sheds, I was at the Saturday kids' matinee at the local fleapit cinema feeling very odd about my reaction to the weekly Tarzan serial. I was strangely obsessed by this scantily-clad man who not only occupied my Saturday mornings at the matinee, but invaded my dreams and tormented my daytime fantasies.

Everyone else in the place was amused by Cheetah the chimpanzee and gripped by Tarzan's hand-to-paw struggle with a tiger (yes, I know, tigers/Africa – I didn't know about the geographic spread of wild animals and neither, apparently, did Hollywood).

My attention was not on the jungle creatures but almost exclusively on Tarzan's loincloth. When not staring at this small, but irritatingly efficient cover-up, I would be gazing adoringly at his gleaming pectorals or rippling thighs. I would sit there in the dark casting myself in the role of the heroine when, inevitably, she sprained her ankle due to fleeing through the jungle in high heels. I could almost feel Tarzan gathering me up in his arms, as he did her, and carrying me off.

But unlike my boyish schoolmates, I didn't want to *be* Tarzan, I wanted to be *rescued* by Tarzan, enveloped in those strong arms and taken to his tree house. And then what? My imagination did not stretch that far – yet.

But, oh to untangle the thrilling mysteries of what lay beneath that loincloth.

This was not hero worship, this was my budding sexuality. I had no idea why I felt this way, but of one thing I was certain - I must keep it to myself. No-one would understand. *I* didn't even understand.

After a few weeks, the Tarzan epic ended and was replaced by a new serial, Jungle Girl.

Week after week I would hurry to the fleapit (or The Grand Cinema to give it its official name) to see my new heroine, Nyoka. She was one tough cookie, although pretty and nice with it. She could do judo and throw aggressive men over her shoulder with incredible ease. Her tree-swinging skills were as good as anything Tarzan could manage. She even did a little somersault between vines. She was surely the prototype for Emma Peel in the *Avengers*, much later.

In fact, rather than the usual story of the girl having to be rescued from peril by the hero, Jungle Girl was always rescuing the heroes from either being eaten by lions or sacrificed by sadistic 'natives'.

This time I *did* want to be Nyoka. She had all the qualities that I desired. She could do all the things that boys wanted to do – fight, climb trees, wrestle crocodiles, overcome a giant gorilla – the lot. But she was also romanced by a handsome young man. She wore a skimpy leather skirt and had long eyelashes that she fluttered at her admirer, even though she was totally self-reliant and didn't actually need him for anything.

What was going on with me? At that stage my only concern was to become Nyoka, the motive for my ambition deeply buried in my subconscious.

This gender confusion continued throughout my school years and I was often treated by my schoolmates at the all-boys school as if I was a girl. Sometimes they teased me about it, sometimes they offered to carry my satchel and some of them were simply attracted because I was a relief from the relentless expectation of boyishness that the culture of an all-boys school imposes.

In fact, I made quite a few friends who followed me through the school system and looking back I think some of them might have been on the same wavelength as me but equally unable as yet to accurately tune in to their troubling feelings.

Once or twice there would be a fumble in the dark in the school hall when we were being treated to a catatonically boring film show about tractors or the Kalahari Desert. I would always sit with my best friend Evan Cresswell because, like me, his mother was still making him wear short trousers when all the other lads in the class were graduating to long ones.

This was a humiliation in one sense but a God-send in another as it permitted easy access for semi-exciting fumblings.

At this time, and without realising it, I was developing a protective shell, too. I was becoming expert at distracting attention, making sure I never said or did anything that would give the game away. No-one must have the slightest inkling of the unconventional, topsy-turvy world that existed in my head. I could control the expression of my internal life, but there was no controlling the effeminacy that put the truth up there in neon lights.

Anyone with an iota of sense could have seen what was happening, but I still lived in dread of the consequences if my mother knew that I had such thoughts.

As part of the wall of self-preservation I had erected, I had become the class clown, always ready with a funny remark or a silly impersonation of the teachers. "Acting daft" it was called, and I became very adept at finding what amused the roughest boys and ensuring that they were treated to variations on that theme if ever they were in my vicinity. This often disarmed any latent aggression that they might otherwise have felt towards me.

It's a technique that I now know is quite common among more obvious gay men. The comedian Julian Clary used a similar method in his Catholic school and became so good at it that he went on to put it to professional use later in life.

But not just gay men. The American comedy actor Paul Rudd revealed he had used the same technique in his own childhood. Being raised in Kansas by English parents had left him feeling like an outsider. He said in an interview with *The Guardian*:

"I was always in new schools and had British parents, which was not the norm, and I think there was also ... I'm not particularly religious, but I was born Jewish and I always felt like the outsider because I wasn't Christian or Catholic. So I learned early on that I could be accepted if I made people laugh when I turned the joke on myself and, particularly in Kansas, if I made a joke about being Jewish, my friends would laugh really hard, harder than they perhaps should have."

I think that if I had been in Paul Rudd's or Julian Clary's class at school, we would have been the best of pals.

At school we had all been encouraged to have penfriends abroad. This was supposed to be a means of widening our horizons. I chose two girls in America, one in Minnesota, Linda, and one in New England, Carla.

Linda was the more conventional of the two, but not without interest. It was her intention to "come to Europe" one day and investigate her Spanish ancestry. Carla, from the photo she sent, was prettier and more interested in culture and music.

I was astonished that we managed to keep the correspondence going over three decades, but there always seemed some news to share. These days, of course, it would all have been done through email, which tends to be brief and lacking detail, and it is unlikely that the intimacy we managed would have been achieved.

Meanwhile, my preferred friends were almost all girls, Sandra and Margaret, Lorraine and Sylvia. And they liked me as a companion. Or they did until puberty arrived, when I began to notice that their attention was turning elsewhere. Once the hormones kicked in I became even more isolated.

The boys in my class turned their attention from companionable things like going for walks in the woods or re-enacting scenes from Jungle Girl (with me as Jungle Girl). Suddenly they were spending all their playtime at the fence that separated the girls' school from the boys' school. On the other side, the girls would giggle and scream and show off because the boys were watching.

I felt utterly unable to join those boys at the fence because although we had never had any form of sex education, I knew that their fascination with the screeching girls was something that didn't interest me.

However, I would have been very interested if I had been on the other side of the fence, and felt it was so unfair that I was in the boys' school and not with the girls where I belonged.

But then came an incident that set me off on the road to self-knowledge. It was a Sunday evening and, given that we had one of the only two television sets on the street, Mi Gran and two of the younger aunties who were as yet unmarried (Mae and Rose) would gather to watch *Sunday Night at the London Palladium*.

They would arrive loaded with sweets and I would sit between them, being cuddled and spoiled rotten. We all sat round munching our Rolos or KitKats and staring at the tiny screen. Our favourite programmes were *Wagon Train* and for a while we were held spell bound by *Quatermass*.

This particular week the star of the Palladium show was the American crooner-with-a-sob-in-his-voice, Johnny Ray. While he was singing one of his numbers, Aunty Rose leaned over to Aunty Mae and whispered: "You know he's one of them homosexuals?"

I was not supposed to have heard, and I gave no reaction, but I made a mental note of the word and decided to look it up in my dictionary at the first opportunity. Like all my friends, I had pored through the dictionary looking for dirty words, but I had never come across this one. The fact that they'd felt the need to whisper meant it must be particularly bad.

As soon as I had the chance, out came the dictionary and there was the word. "Homosexual: A person who is sexually attracted to people of their own sex."

Bingo.

There it was.

There *I* was.

This confirmed to me that what I was feeling with increasing intensity was a real phenomenon, an actual emotion that other people had experienced, not something that was unique to me, invented by my perverted imagination. It had happened to someone else at some time, otherwise how could it be in the dictionary?

This at least explained why, when my mother's Littlewood's mail order catalogue arrived, I would immediately turn to the men's underwear pages.

All the same, I had no idea what to do about it. These other people who were "sexually attracted to members of their own sex" must be very rare. I'd never heard of another one. Well, not until Johnny Ray, that is. And he lived in America.

I was feeling further and further separated from my contemporaries. It seemed I was becoming shyer and more introvert in some ways, yet with this protective façade of humour and niceness. I couldn't see a way out of my loneliness.

~ 2 ~

My schooldays were coming to an end. Despite in some senses feeling like an alien – particularly towards the end - I hadn't been totally unhappy. By far the best lesson I had learned at school was a self-taught one. I had discovered how to effectively deal with people who might be becoming suspicious. I had ways of sending them off in the wrong direction, deflecting any approach to the truth. I had ways of making them like me so that my secret would be safe and unpursued. I had become an ace deceiver. My disguise was, I thought, complete.

Having failed the eleven plus through lack of application, my formal education came to an end at fifteen. I would now be expected to find a job even though, because of my poor, nerve-wracked performances in exams, I didn't have as much as an O-level.

Nobody - not me or my parents or my school - thought I was going to follow the family tradition and go down the pit. I was too – well, *unusual* for that. My father had reassuringly said: "You're not going down that hell hole. No lad of mine is going down there."

But my elder brother, Our Albert, did, briefly. He soon gave it up and started a job in the steelworks in Sheffield. Our Roy, my other brother, had been involved in a catastrophic road accident as a youth and eventually had his leg amputated (after many years of pain, skin grafts and other operations attempting to save it). His career path took him into engineering.

But what was I going to do? I wouldn't make factory fodder. Too dreamy, too full of silly ideas, too delicate.

Some of my teachers had recognised that I had a creative streak. My English teacher, Mr Bown, encouraged me to tell stories, to write them down. I filled endless exercise books with prototype novels. Whatever I had seen at the pictures would send me into a frenzy of writing to try to recreate it on the page.

I had still by this stage hardly been out of Maltby. The bigger town of Rotherham was only half an hour down the road by bus, but it seemed like a foreign country.

As a result of this, I was naïve and lacking even rudimentary knowledge of how the rest of the world functioned. Everything I knew was second-hand and gained from the television. Even the holidays spent in a caravan at Skegness were always just an extension of being at home, surrounded as I was by protective relatives.

One good friend I had was Kevin Chancellor who lived on the other side of Burns Road. He went to my school but wasn't in the same class, but he was clever and curious, as was his cousin Sylvia who also lived on our street. The three of us would play board games in our front room for hours on end, re-writing the rules to make them ever more complicated. We also went to the cinema together sometimes and Kenny was inadvertently present during my first almost-sexual encounter.

We had gone to the pictures one Sunday evening to see *Devil Girl from Mars* (we always went to the films we hoped would scare us). Almost as soon as the lights went out, a man came and sat next to me on the other side from Kenny. He must have been cruising the joint and spotted me from another seat. How had he known?

His leg touched mine. When I didn't resist, his leg pressed harder. Still I made no move to disengage the contact. His hand touched my knee. He was carrying a large mackintosh which was slung over his lap and my leg to hide his wandering hand.

At first I was alarmed – at Saturday matinees the implacable usherette, who might in a previous life have been a concentration camp guard, was always shining a torch down the row of seats to make sure nothing nefarious was going on. If it was, there'd be a big commotion and you'd be chucked out in no time. But I was willing to risk it. She was less inclined to shine the torch on adults.

As this man's hand reached higher and higher, my heart started pumping so hard that stars were spinning in front of my eyes and a voice in my head was yelling "It's happening! At last, it's happening!"

He took my hand and, pulling it under the folds of his coat, placed it on his crotch. His fly was open and the monster was on the loose. There was the object of my desire in all its rigid, warm and velvety glory. I wrapped my hand around it and just held it – those few moments of intimacy bringing ecstasy beyond compare.

But I had spent a lifetime training myself to restrain any facial expression or body movement that would give anything away. Glances at men's crotches were done so furtively that no-one would ever notice. Despite the hurricane of emotion swirling within, all was calm and still without.

Was Kenny aware of what was going on? He showed no sign and was wrapped up in what was happening on the screen (the Devil Girl from Mars was about to use her ray gun on her unfortunate victims). Then the man got up and quietly walked down the aisle to the gents' toilet. Obviously I was expected to follow.

Could I do that without arousing suspicion? I waited a moment and then got up and made my way to the loo. Inside the man was waiting and immediately started undoing my flies.

I was petrified – suppose someone else came in? I panicked and after copping a farewell feel of his exposed and throbbing manhood, I sprinted for the door and returned to my seat, heart pounding and full of excitement and with Kenny apparently totally oblivious.

It hadn't amounted to much, but it had illustrated to me that I was not alone in my desires. There were even other people in Maltby who were "attracted to members of their own sex".

But it would be a long time before another opportunity arose, and the effeminacy that had become so pronounced, without any effort on my part, made some of my teachers despair.

Sport was a write-off, of course, and eventually the PE teacher simply excused me from all attempts at ball games – much to the relief of the other boys who always groaned if all options had been exhausted and I had to be included in a football team.

There was no question of me joining the cricket team, either. I had problems bowling overarm ("Don't chuck it like a lass, yer daft bugger, bowl it properly"), and my shrieking and cringing when the ball came towards me were tantamount to a straightforward admission that I was a lad-lass, as it was known in local parlance. At the same time, it was all totally involuntary and unconscious and seemed perfectly natural to me.

The woodwork teacher, Mr Smith (who, appropriately, had a wooden leg, presumably from a war injury), sighed loudly as he saw my cack-handedness with bradawls and saws. He looked on with pity at my antipathy to hammering and my half-hearted approach to mortise and tenon joints.

My only achievement under his tutelage was a birdbox, crudely nailed together, which was unlikely to provide a refuge to any bird that didn't want to die from splinter wounds. It was a pathetic disgrace by any standard, and at that point Mr Smith surrendered and invited me spend the woodwork lessons sitting in the corner writing stories. He reasoned that while other boys in his class were fashioning exquisite acoustic guitars or chests of drawers worthy of Chippendale, I was simply wasting resources and time.

It was a mutual relief when I was permanently excused from the work bench.

So then came the round of interviews for jobs.

"Shy and retiring type," the careers officer had said on the phone when he was arranging for me to see the personnel officer in a large firm in Rotherham. That instantaneous summary of my character, made after a three minute acquaintance, stuck with me. Was I really shy and retiring? It didn't feel like that when I was in the classroom or at home. I was regarded there as funny and likeable and sometimes noisy. "Shy and retiring" sounded like somebody who burst into tears at the slightest thing or who daren't talk.

That wasn't me. But I didn't contradict him – I was too shy and retiring to argue with an official sitting behind a desk. My confidence was high when I was with those I knew and with whom I was familiar. But would it survive in the big, wide world of Rotherham?

I had the feeling that 'careers' were not what the careers officer had in mind. His job was to try to find gainful employment for us secondary school boys as soon as possible. Anything. He was just the Job-Finder General, tasked with getting us all off the hands of the state and out of the dole office pronto.

"So what kind of job would you like to have?" he had asked.

Instead of saying "I'd like to be a Tiller girl kicking up my legs on Sunday Night at the London Palladium," I simply said: "I don't know."

The careers officer turned to Mi Mam, who was with me at the interview, and said: "I think clerical work would suit him best."

As far as my mother was concerned being a "clerical worker" was tantamount to being the Prime Minister. It wasn't down the pit and it wasn't in the factory. It was a step up. I, on the other hand, had no idea of what being a clerical worker would involve.

The officer flicked through his card index and said: "There's a vacancy at the British Wagon company in Rotherham. I'll arrange an interview."

~ 3 ~

The British Wagon Company was a finance company housed on Moorgate, the poshest road in Rotherham, in a sparkling new sky scraper (well, ten floors, which was a skyscraper in Rotherham terms).

Rotherham was the go-to place for the things you couldn't get in Maltby (which was just about everything) and a place I discovered that you could mooch around in, looking at the many shops or the market. "Going to Rotherham" was a big deal for us Maltbyites.

But in those days Rotherham was a dirty, grimy place, surrounded by the coal mines on one side and the steelworks of Sheffield on the other. They used to say that even the pigeons in Rotherham flew backwards to avoid getting grit in their eyes. Just breathing the air was the equivalent of smoking 20 cigarettes a day.

Compared to Maltby, though, it was a grand metropolis. Marks and Spencer and Woolworths were there and Boots the chemist as well as the twice weekly outdoor market. There were two picture houses (Essoldo and Odeon) and cafes and modest restaurants. There was even a Temperance Bar that sold Sarsaparilla, Root Beer and Dandelion and Burdock as an alternative to alcohol.

My mother was convinced that I needed a business suit to go to such a job and so she took me to Burton's in Rotherham to be measured up. She insisted on coming with me because she knew that left to my own devices I might order a suit in leatherette, like my current heroine Cathy Gale in the *Avengers*, or something with diamante discreetly incorporated.

The man who was to take my measurements had ginger hair. As my mother leafed through pattern books, seeking a suitable pin stripe material, this man was taking an awful long time measuring my inside leg. So long, in fact, that I soon came to the conclusion that his primary interest wasn't in the length of my leg. When I didn't resist he gave me a comprehensive fondling.

Once again my heart was pounding and once again the fireworks were exploding and the voice in my head was singing an ode to joy. I was being "interfered with" (as the Sunday papers of the time would euphemistically have it). They always made being "interfered with" sound like the worst thing that could happen to a young man. I was loving it.

Seeing how nervous I was that all this was going in close proximity to Mi Mam, he whispered: "Meet me in the square at six o'clock." And with that he once more assumed his professional persona and the suit was ordered.

Of course I didn't meet him at six o'clock. I was far too nervous – perhaps too "shy and retiring" – to go through with it. But it fuelled a million fantasies after that.

By this time, of course, like all my contemporaries, I had discovered masturbation. As far as I was concerned, it was the most momentous discovery since Henry Morton Stanley had found Dr Livingstone in Africa. And like most lads of my age the urge was relentless. My fantasies were pretty restricted, though, as my experience was so limited I had nothing to base them on. I had a crush on an actor who appeared on *Wagon Train* and moonily drew pictures of him in his tight buckskin pants copied from the *Radio Times*, and that was about it.

After my new suit was delivered, I was packed off to the British Wagon Company to be interviewed by a Mr Bennett, the personnel officer. I had never had a job interview before, had no idea of what was expected of me and no idea of what I could offer. There were no CVs or interview training courses for those on the bottom rung of the employment ladder. You just turned up and hoped for the best. This was a finance company and I didn't even know what that was.

But it was beholden on me to "get a job". I was no longer at school and therefore I was expected to pay rent at home.

I have no memory of the interview or what was asked or what I said, but for some reason Mr Bennett gave me a job as a post room clerk. I would put letters through the franking machine and deliver incoming and internal mail throughout the building.

There was a big staff at British Wagon and many offices. In the post room there were lots of other young people starting their working careers 'at the bottom' and I immediately clicked with some of them.

It took me quite a while to get used to the idea that this wasn't school. It was my first taste of being in the adult world where a modicum of discipline and self-restraint was required. If it wasn't exercised, grown-ups would tell you off and, unlike teachers, they had real sanctions at their disposal.

All the same, the exuberance of youth was flowing from me in abundance. The post room was on the ground floor and had a big window that faced out on to the main road. The buses along Moorgate went by at regular intervals. One day at home Mi Aunty Mae said to me: "I saw you from the bus in your office the other day. You were doing high kicks."

Given my sickly start in life I was turning out to be exceptionally healthy and energetic. I don't think I ever took any time off work, and would jump out of bed every morning anxious to get the day started.

One girl who I became very friendly with was called Moira and she worked in the typing pool. She was a very glamorous girl, tall and straight backed, beautifully coiffed blonde hair, immaculate dress sense. She had a slight cast in her eye and wore glasses (lovely, fancy glasses, not pop bottle bottoms). But she had overcome these small flaws by sheer confidence. Unlike the others she spoke quietly and thoughtfully and was obviously a cut above. She often came to work in a red, convertible sports car. She lived with her well-to-do family in the posher part of Maltby (yes, there was such a place) in a detached house.

Sometimes she gave me a lift home in her car, which always thrilled me – no-one in our family had ever had a car. Once, coming home, on a straight stretch of road she revved the engine and I watched as the speedometer briefly reached a hundred miles an hour. She loved it and I loved it, too.

Moira had fallen for the charms I was using to keep everyone on side, but she had seen something else in me that she wanted to cultivate. I think she realised that underneath all the "acting about" there was an intelligence looking for escape.

I think Moira might have been my first experience of the GBF – the gay best friend. This is the unthreatening man who straight women can relate to on a completely equal basis. No game-playing or flirtatiousness required. At that time women were only just beginning to shrug off the straitjacket of expectation. Most of the girls in the typing pool were already engaged to be married and were putting things aside "in the bottom drawer" ready for the time when they would set up their own home and have a family and become just like their mothers.

At British Wagon only women worked in the typing pool (I longed for a job there and taught myself to type during the lunch breaks). Only men were allowed to smoke in the building. I didn't smoke.

Anyway, one lunch hour I was passing the time mooching round the shops in town and ended up browsing through the books in Boots the chemists (they sold books and records in those days). My attention was grabbed by one entitled *Homosexuality: its nature and causes* by DJ West.

The mere sight of this word in print made me swoon a little. My heart started pounding and I was trembling. I desperately wanted this book, it might open a door into the twilight word of the homosexual ("someone sexually attracted to members of their own sex"). But it was 2/6d, an amount that was well beyond my means at that stage of the month.

How was I going to get my hands on it before they sold it to someone else?

I hurried back to the office and headed straight for Moira. I didn't want to tell her the real reason I wanted the book. I just sort of gave her a cock and bull story about wouldn't it be fun to read such a thing, it might be a laugh.

She saw immediately what was going on and reached straight for her purse and gave me the half crown. I promised to pay it back, but she just said: "Keep it."

I shall be ever grateful to Moira for that. She had illustrated to me the concept of unspoken understanding. I didn't need to spell it out and she didn't want to embarrass me with questions. She simply understood what it meant to me and it was a valuable life-lesson that I would try to incorporate into my own future dealings with other people. I heard a few years later that Moira had been felled by breast cancer and died way before her proper time.

Unfortunately, the book, when I got it, failed to provide any reassurance. It was written from a detached perspective that seemed almost pathological. I suppose that was the only way it could have been published in those days. It was certainly not a book for the worried young gay man. I believe it's still available from Amazon, even though it was originally published in 1955. Now it must be simply a museum piece.

Coincidentally, many years later I met the author DJ West at a gay group. He was a very old gentleman by that time. He had been a parapsychologist. I told him of my experience with his book. He said he had heard similar stories many times over the years.

And just in case anyone should get the idea that there might be more reassuring positive images of homosexuality available elsewhere, it was around this time that I saw a story in the Sunday scandal sheet *The People* – one of only two papers that came into our house, the other being the *Daily Herald*. It concerned a gay pub in Leeds called the Hope and Anchor. *The People* reporter described his visit in the most lurid terms:

"A place like the Hope and Anchor might have an adverse effect on curious, impressionable youngsters. I saw men –

DANCING CHEEK TO CHEEK TO THE MUSIC OF A JUKE BOX

KISSING PASSIONATELY on the dancefloor and in secluded corners

HOLDING HANDS, PETTING and EMBRACING unashamedly in the packed room.

There were men heavily made up and smelling strongly of perfume. Others wore women's clothes and charm bracelets and

23

rings on their fingers. They giggled and talked among themselves in high-pitched voices.

I watched effeminate-looking men disappear into the 'Ladies' to titivate their appearance and tidy their waved dyed hair...Girls too danced together and kissed. Many of the girls wore men's hairstyles, suits, shirts and ties."

This was the level of reporting of gay life in the "swinging sixties". It was enough to traumatise any young gay person who was worried about what the future would hold for them. The idea that I would be titivating in the ladies toilet was not entirely horrific for me, but for others the prospect of a life as described in the *People* article might have been pretty depressing. As far as I was concerned, the swinging sixties didn't start until about 1984.

I can honestly say that British Wagon never got its money's worth from employing me. I was utterly indifferent to the business it was conducting and went through as few of the motions as possible in order to retain the job.

Apart from the occasional hopeless and obsessive crush on one or other of the men in the office (and there were a lot of healthy, hunky young men working there), my gay life was not progressing.

It was so easy to get infatuated with the lads I fancied, even when I knew it was pointless. At that time I didn't have a lot of confidence, but I still had a lot of acne (I'd been to the doctors and he had given me an evil-smelling lotion that did my spots no good at all but I'm sure would have brought Mi Mam's chip pan up a treat). It was easy to get obsessed when you are so desperate and when any of these men showed even the slightest hint of a friendly reaction I'd start going off my food and not be able to sleep at night.

Fantasies would conjure in my mind around the latest object of my affection. One day it would be him from the post room who'd offered me a bite of his Milky Way in the coffee break and next day it would be the trainee from Sales and Statistics who'd once given me a lift in his Morris Marina. On days when

24

I was feeling particularly randy, it would be both of them together.

Every move that these fantasy love objects made would be analysed for signs of "response". Was I overestimating the squeeze of the arm or did he subconsciously mean he wanted an erotic encounter? Was that prolonged eye contact simply his roundabout way of telling me that he wanted to get me to bed? Of course, it never was. They always backed off when it came to the crunch, leaving me screaming with frustration. Poor old me, with nowhere to go but to the lav for a quickie.

I was so vulnerable to these hopeless infatuations, falling in love at the drop of a hint. All I asked was that one of them would return the feeling – or was that too much to hope for?

One day when I was walking round the market in my lunch break I saw the man from Burton's, his red hair immediately recognisable. He recognised me, too, and started following me. Again, I was terrified and once more fled from an opportunity that might have opened doors into the other world, the one I was craving to find so badly.

~ *4* ~

Occasionally a group of us from the post room would go out in the evening to the cinema or the bowling alley. I avoided outings to discos and similar events where the emphasis was on pursuing activities that were of no appeal to me (i.e. girl/boy hook-ups). Being in such an environment made me feel even more of a freak and an outsider. I didn't want to dance or snog with girls.

One evening we all went to the pictures and during the film one of the girls, Zena, reached out and took my hand. My reaction was the polar opposite of what it had been when the man at the showing of *Devil Girl from Mars* had made his move. I was mortified, shocked and – I have to say it – slightly repelled by the idea that I would be holding hands with a girl at the pictures.

I wanted to get up and run screaming from the building, but I didn't want to hurt her feelings or cause a commotion that might lead to speculation, so I let her hold my hand without giving any reciprocal indication. She might well have been holding the hand of a corpse for all the response she was getting.

The extremity of my reaction at the prospect of a sexual connection with a woman merely reinforced my fears that I was well and truly "a homosexual".

It took a while, but I had one particular friend at work who was giving signals that he might be a bit like me. His name was David Allen and we were the same age, although he seemed much more mature and worldly than I was. He was a talented musician and had an evening job playing as organist and accompanist to the "turns" at the Trades and Labour Club. He was in show business! However, he made very little of it – to him it was just a means of making a bit more money on the side - and it was never a factor in our friendship.

He was one of my 'fans' in that he seemed to think everything I said was hilarious. We went everywhere together and eventually I came to the conclusion that it might be safe to share with him *the Secret that Must Not be Told.*

So one fateful day when we were alone and the conversation had turned to sexual matters, I blurted out: "I am if you are." He understood this rather obtuse message immediately and without hesitation replied: "I am".

Once more the joyous voices rang out in my head. I had a friend who was like me. A homosexual! A person attracted to members of their own sex! I could say out loud at last what had been buzzing around in my brain, trying to burst out, since before I could remember.

David and I were bosom buddies from then on. Neither of us wanted to have a romantic attachment. We'd be like girlfriends, he said, or sisters.

~ 5 ~

One Christmas my parents bought me a reel-to-reel tape recorder, a fairly rudimentary piece of equipment that nevertheless provided hours of pleasure. I used it to record music from the radio to listen to locked in my bedroom, moping.

One way this tape recorder brought joy to my life was when I accidentally captured a song by Marlene Dietrich. I had recorded it from an edition of *Two-Way Family Favourites*. It was Honeysuckle Rose from the record of her show in London.

I was instantly brought up short by this woman's voice. There was something in it that appealed to me – it was deep, it was suggestive and what she made of the song was like nothing I'd come across before. It was so sexy, so full of promise and yet there was sadness somewhere. It was quite unlike any other female singer I had heard.

I had to find out more about Marlene, who I'd never heard of before. Of course, there was no internet then, only the library. I spent many of my Saturday afternoons at the library in Rotherham. I loved browsing the books, not looking for anything in particular but just coming across interesting things. As long as it wasn't about sport (or woodwork or cars) I was interested to find out more.

I found a few references to Marlene. She had been a big movie star once and now she was giving concerts, singing songs like the one I'd got on my tape recorder. I then went to the record shop and found a disc of hers, the first of many that I hunted down over the years.

Marlene became something of an obsession for me. I listened to her records constantly, looked at pictures, found every reference I could about her. I longed to see her stage show, but that wasn't going to happen. She lived somewhere exotic, over the rainbow, in a place where ordinary mortals could not tread. She was a goddess.

Nobody else I knew liked Marlene's singing. I tried to interest others in my fascination but the usual response was something on the lines of "bloody hell, Terry, give it a rest!" They preferred the other singers of the day - Sandy Shaw or Cilla Black.

But little did I realise that Marlene had confirmed in me another characteristic common in gay men – the worship of divas. It would be many years later that I came to know that many gay men also adored Marlene and, indeed, other singers with equal fervour – usually singers who were prepared to rip open their chests and show us their broken hearts.

I had no way of knowing that Judy Garland had a special meaning for so many gay men at the time. Or what Edith Piaf meant to the French gay community, just as closeted and afraid as we were. Perhaps they were hearing in these songs the anxieties that were common to so many in those days.

I've never got to the real reason why gay men like this kind of chanteuse so much. Perhaps it's a genetic thing, because when my attachment to Marlene began that Sunday afternoon on the Light Programme, I had no idea that she was already the object of worship by so many other young men, just like me, all around the world, and had been for generations.

My attraction was purely subconscious and spontaneous. She had touched something deep and prompted a love and loyalty that persists to this day.

The day I first heard Marlene sing was the day I abandoned my ambition to become Cathy Gale off the *Avengers*. I now wanted to become Marlene Dietrich. I began affecting many of her rather artificial mannerisms – the coquettish downward glances, the fluttering eyelashes, the deep, inviting voice. If the occasion demanded, I also began talking with a vaguely German accent.

If I was in a one-to-one situation with any of the boys at work that permitted me to employ these rather pathetic seduction techniques, they didn't seem to have the desired effect. I cringe now as I think back to it.

My style of dress was becoming equally outlandish, too. That wasn't so much of a problem, though, because we had entered the age of the hippy. Having long hair and wearing fur coats and highly coloured shirts with big collars didn't bring instant crucifixion as it might have done a few years earlier. I had grown my hair very long ,more extreme than the style of the Beatles.

For a time I had a coat with a big fur collar that could be turned up. I would do this at the slightest suggestion of cold and pretend that I was Marlene in *The Scarlet Empress*.

~ *6* ~

My time at British Wagon had helped me into the world of adults and I had enjoyed it immensely. On my 21st birthday I received cards from 60 of my colleagues, which astonished me.

It would be a wrench, but now I wanted to move on. I wanted to try something else. I must be able to find a boyfriend somewhere and it wasn't going to happen at British Wagon, which had become a kind of second home to me and far too comfortable.

So, I scouted round and eventually got a job in a Dolland and Aitchison camera shop on the High Street in Rotherham. It became apparent very soon that I had not been employed for my skills as a salesman. I knew as much about cameras as I did about football, which was absolutely nothing. The manager of the shop who had given me the job, Mr Farrer, was gay and it wasn't long before there was a different kind of developing going on in the darkroom.

Mr Farrer also had some understanding of the way I thought. He didn't consider it unusual or silly for someone like me to be such an obsessive fan of Marlene Dietrich. He was a great admirer of her himself and even had some records – the first other person I had ever met who had even heard of her.

My crush on Mr Farrer was the love affair of the century as far as I was concerned, even though all it amounted to was a few cuddles and a brief fondle. Nevertheless, while I was mooning about humming "I'm in love with a wonderful guy", Mr Farrer was entertaining just about half the gay population of Yorkshire in that shop (which had a handy area at the back that could be screened off and was used for taking passport photos during the day and gawd-knows-what after closing).

Still, even as I recovered from the heartbreak of discovering that Mr Farrer did not reciprocate my passions, he had revealed to me the big, wide, hidden word of the homosexual. I came to

31

see that the "twilight world" existed unseen and in parallel with everyone else's world. The manager of the local department store used to come to the Dolland and Aitchison shop regularly, so did the butcher from three doors up and the manager of the local Odeon cinema.

Mr Farrer seemed to know so many people, and the reason he knew them was because they were gay. I was completely bewildered by the sheer number of people he knew and how unlike me they were, how ordinary and who you would never suspect in a thousand years were "persons sexually attracted to members of their own sex". I had a lot to learn.

But Mr Farrer's many distractions were taking a toll on the business. He was often away at mysterious appointments that were never explained (more to do with monkey business than retail business, one assumes) and my efforts at salesmanship weren't exactly helping. Every time someone came into the shop with a view to a purchase, sometimes a very serious photographer looking for something expensive, and began to ask technical questions about lenses, apertures, single lens reflexes and so on, I would go blank and say: "Have you seen the new Instamatic 5000 with flash attachment? That's very good."

Shoplifters were having a field day. One family in particular were regulars. "I'm just browsing," was their usual refrain as they took it in turns to pay us a call, casually examining the displays until a few customers had come in and the staff were distracted.

The members of this family were, as my mother would say, "right scruffy buggers", oiks of the first order. It was clear the moment they stepped through the door that their intention of buying anything of a photographic nature ranged from minimal to non-existent. They would, however, always bring with them a very large shopping bag which was empty when they came in but looked as though they'd just done a week's shopping at Tesco when they went out.

They were bruisers with calloused fists and shifty eyes and even though I knew they'd slipped another Nikkon into their pocket, I was far too nervous to challenge them. There was no Nikkon on earth that would convince me to mix it with this lot.

So, eventually and inevitably, the shop was closed, Mr Farrer moved back to his native London and I was in the job market again.

Fortunately, a position had arisen again at British Wagon and I applied for it and got it. I stayed there for another couple of years, enjoying the camaraderie before the news came through that the company was to be wound up (if everybody was as unproductive as I was, then there's little wonder). We were to be made redundant and given a pay-off of, perhaps, £2,000.

To me this was like winning the pools. I was sorry to lose the job and my friends, but the money would permit me to travel and see the places that I had always wanted to see.

My brother Roy, by this time, had emigrated to Rhodesia (now Zimbabwe), where his wife Janet had relatives. They had become persuaded by these relatives that life was good and the living was easy in Rhodesia, so they'd decided to give it a go.

Rhodesia's almost all-white parliament had famously declared unilateral independence (UDI) from Britain in 1965 in order to prevent the country being handed over to the black majority. It was ruled by Ian Smith. There were 220,000 white people in Rhodesia at the time and a 4 million black population. But the white people held all the power, and they weren't going to let it go.

I put the politics aside because I wanted to "see Africa" and so it was arranged that I would spend six weeks with my brother and his family (he had two kids by now) in Rhodesia.

I would certainly be in Africa, but how much of it I would see is a different matter. I was no Armand and Michaela Dennis – I wouldn't be brave enough to mix with the dangerous fauna of the Serengeti or its Rhodesian equivalent.

Rhodesia was still practising a kind of apartheid which brought an immediate sense of discomfort. It wasn't as harshly enforced as in neighbouring South Africa, but there was a quite clear delineation between the back and the white population, and it was not an equal divide by any stretch.

My resolution to ignore the politics would be hard to maintain. Injustice was glaring from all sides. Was I colluding in this in some way, simply by being there?

My brother told me stories of some people in the neighbourhood who regularly hit the servants, sometimes with sticks. My stomach churned at this news. How could they? What superiority gave them the right to batter working people – people like my mother and, indeed, me? Many of these white migrants had come from working class backgrounds in England themselves.

All the white people I came across seemed to think it worked well and everyone was happy. If they weren't employed as servants, these black Rhodesians would have no way to earn a living, they said.

But the one valuable lesson that I came away with was that just because some nasty belief or practice was regarded as normal, excused by phrases like "that's the way it is, why change it?" and the "it's the natural order of things", doesn't mean that it is right or has to be accepted at face value.

As a visitor and an outsider in this overtly racist culture, the injustices seemed so glaringly obvious that they didn't need to be pointed out. And yet the people around me were unaware of them because "that's how it is" and "that's how it's always been." The complacency – at least among the white population – was staggering.

I suppose they were donning these blinkers because it was to their advantage and protected their privileged way of life. What I couldn't understand was why there wasn't more resentment and resistance from the black population. Perhaps there was, perhaps they were just good at keeping it under wraps for the purposes of self-preservation, just as I had done for so many years with some of the unreasonable employers I had worked for.

But what could I possibly have known about what was really going on in their minds? I didn't meet the intellectuals and the revolutionaries, but their time would come and, unfortunately, it wouldn't necessarily make things immediately better. The dictator and human rights abuser Robert Mugabe was waiting in the wings.

Zimbabwe is a beautiful country with lovely people, let's hope they can create a society one day that brings justice to all.

But the insight I had gained into the foolishness of allowing unjust conventions to remain unchallenged, excused on the grounds of "tradition", was to motivate my own personal revolution later.

~ 7 ~

When I returned from Rhodesia it was back to reality and the need to find work. For some reason this never proved difficult. I'd go to the Labour Exchange, they would give me a ticket for the next interview, I would pop along to wherever it was – another finance company, a cutlery manufacturer, a stone quarry - and I'd go for a few days and decide I didn't like it (mainly because it wasn't British Wagon and they expected me to buckle down and work).

Where was the fun in these jobs that drearily demanded concentration and application? I was now reaching the age where I couldn't come the cute young lad act any more. People expected me to be the very thing I dreaded most – a grown up!

If I was to avoid the awfulness of real life, I would have to find an occupation that would suit my temperament.

My efforts to become established as a writer had resulted in enough rejection slips to paper the front room (and the backroom. And the bedrooms). The terrible short stories I submitted to women's magazines inevitably came winging back by return post. And no wonder. They wanted stories about an emotional and romantic world of which I had no experience.

I got a job in an office that was occupied by three very elderly people, two women and a man. They had obviously worked there for centuries between them. The office itself was straight out of Dickens with only one tiny widow that seemed to resent the light it was forced to admit. Everything was dusty and there was a telephone switchboard of such antiquity it should have been in a museum of telecommunications.

One day I went out for lunch and while eating my egg sandwich at the local café, dreading the moment I had to return to that dark den of silence, I decided that I wouldn't go back. So, my employment there came to an abrupt end and that soul

36

destroying job joined the long list of others I had flitted into and out of.

Surely there was something more exciting than this I could do, some glamorous occupation that I could simply walk into without any qualifications and without any experience? You could be an actor or a writer without any qualifications – well, except for talent, of course.

Anyway, my literary ambitions had not entirely died. I had written a radio play that was highly derivative but had a few good lines and off it went to the BBC. After a few weeks I received a letter from the Leeds office saying that there was a scheme to encourage promising young northern writers and they would like to invite me over to meet the man who was running it.

This was it, I thought, I've arrived. I'm going to have a play on the wireless. That'll show all the doubters.

So, off I went to Leeds and met the man, Henry Livings. It was his job to make life or death decisions over the plays submitted on spec to the corporation. Mr Livings was a well-known and established playwright himself and had been given the task by the BBC of nurturing talent outside of London.

No, he said, they wouldn't be producing my play, which was set in the "heavily soiled department" of a scuzzy laundry. The heroine was a dreamy girl, Janice, who longed to escape the drudgery of her job, which she regarded as little more than slavery. She wanted something better and more in line with what her imagination told her was possible.

Then she is offered an escape route by the owner of the laundry, who wants to take her to Ceylon as his lover. He is kind and cultured and cosmopolitan. She likes him because he treats her like an equal, talks to her about things that no-one else in the laundry talks about. She wants the knowledge and skills and sophistication that he has. She wants him to be her Svengali.

But he is quite elderly and everyone is telling her she shouldn't do it. In the opinion of her colleagues he's only interested in her because she has a large bosom, that he'll dump her as soon as he gets bored. Can she overcome her doubts in order to fulfil at least some of her dreams?

Does this sound familiar? Well, they always say you should write about what you know. The only difference between me and Janice was that no sugar daddy was offering me a trip to Ceylon and nor did I have any physical attributes with which to allure.

Despite the fact that they weren't going to produce it, Mr Livings said my play showed promise and he would like to see anything else I had written.

I came away thoroughly disheartened. My masterwork was not to see the light of day after all. Janice of the heavily soiled department would have to continue to dream, and such was my disappointment I wasn't sure I could write another word.

But after I had consigned Janice and the laundry to the dustbin, I set about my next opus. This time it was set in an office. The play was portentously called *The Darkness after Dawn* and concerned a young man, Eric, working in a factory office overlooking the shop floor. Working at a tooling machine, is another young man, Roger, with whom Eric has fallen madly in love. Roger, though, is straight and engaged to one of the girls in the typing pool.

Eric and Roger have, somehow, become good friends and Roger is giving Eric all the signals that something more meaningful might come of their friendship. Eric follows Roger round like a pathetic poodle, even going to a football match to please him.

But Roger never delivers. The romance is always on the brink of blossoming only to evaporate at the last moment, and Eric is afraid to be too forthright. (Oh dear, here comes my subconscious, spilling all over the page again).

It was all terribly tortured and naïve. And, of course, it ended tragically, mainly because that's how anything that touched on homosexuality ended in those days. I didn't have the courage to buck the convention.

I sent it off and it came back, this time with a printed rejection slip and no reassuring words about it "showing promise".

So my final attempt to make a breakthrough into the world of broadcast drama was another office epic entitled *Hilary*

Breadghast and the Little People. Hilary was based on a woman I had known at British Wagon. She was a warm and kindly woman whose fiancé had been killed in the war and she had never really recovered. Now she was in late middle-age, still attractive and smartly turned out, but her opportunities for a love life appear to have passed her by.

Then she is courted by and falls for Harold Bailey, a manager at the firm. They start a clandestine affair, but Hilary feels a mixture of enervating guilt and unexpected excitement about it, given an extra *frisson* because Harold is already married. Hilary is a woman with a conventional morality, but also an overwhelming desire to grab this one last opportunity for happiness.

Harold says that he will leave his wife if Hilary wants him to. She is on the brink of saying yes to that when the office Christmas party intervenes and Harold turns up with his wife, Bella. She is severely disabled from a road accident and in a wheelchair – a fact that Harold had never mentioned to Hilary. Bella is a lovely, courageous, uncomplaining woman who Hilary comes to admire and befriend. It is clear how much she depends on her husband for support. Hilary becomes increasingly guilt-ridden that she might cause this blameless woman to be abandoned in her time of great need. Naturally she ends the affair.

This time I sent it to ITV and instead of the usual bulging manila envelope containing more fuel for the living room fire, I was invited to London to meet a script editor.

At this point I was signing on at the dole again and didn't have the train fare to London. But I was determined to go and see what they were planning to do with my play – would it be starring anybody famous? Could I persuade them to get Marlene to take the part of Hilary?

The only option was to hitch hike and so I did. It took a long time to get to London, but when I pitched up at the office of this TV woman she told me again that, no, the play wasn't going to be produced, but that it showed promise and that they wanted to see anything else that I had written…da-di-da.

Trudging once more through London to the M1 slip road to hitch my way back, I was weighed down with a heavy load of disillusion.

This writing lark was proving harder than anticipated. Being told endlessly that your work shows promise but isn't quite up to scratch is demoralising and the constant disappointments hard to stomach.

I hadn't realised that many had trodden this path before me before finding glory. Perseverance is the keyword, but I wasn't sure I had it.

~ 8 ~

I had taken to reading *The Guardian* and *The Sunday Times*. These "posh papers" were revealing to me journalists who wrote wonderful witty and amusing prose. They showed that you didn't have to be deeply earnest and serious every time you put pen to paper, you were allowed to be light-hearted in print. People like Clive James, Jilly Cooper, Nancy Banks-Smith - all with an enviable way with words that inspired me to want to move into that rarefied world they inhabited, the world of newspaper columnists. I thught this would be easier than play writing.

So now I began showering the newspapers with articles that I deluded myself into thinking were just as sophisticated as anything by Bernard Levin or Kenneth Tynan. None was accepted by the *Sunday Times* or the *Guardian*, so I aimed a little lower and started sending stuff to the *Sheffield Star* and the *Morning Telegraph*. It started with regular letters to the editor, many of which were at the head of the page with biggest headline. That always gave me a kick, but what I really wanted was a place among the professionals, with a by-line.

As it was, my regular appearances in the letters columns meant I was stuck among the moaning minnies complaining about the shoddiness of the bus services or asking why the council was spending money on an arts centre when there were dustbins to be emptied.

Occasionally something would take the editor's fancy, and I started to see my name in print over an article on the features page. Other writers have told of the extraordinary excitement at seeing their work published professionally for the first time. Now I knew that feeling myself, even though it was in a very small way.

My articles were sometimes about travel (being such a seasoned traveller) and sometimes they were just little flights of fancy that were mildly amusing. Still, they got into print and small (very small) cheques were received in exchange.

The absolutely magical feeling when I paid the first of these cheques into my bank account was indescribable. It was one of those rare moments in life when optimism trumps a sense of inevitable failure.

Maybe there was a way to escape the round of ghastly routine and crushing boredom in the jobs I was doing after all. If I kept trying, I might make some kind of breakthrough into authorship. That was certainly the advice I was reading in the many books about How to Become a Writer that I borrowed from the library. Keep going, rewrite, try again, don't give up. They would all tell tales of famous authors or famous books that had been rejected at the beginning and only through sheer doggedness had they seen the light of day.

But my successes were few and far between. I was not going to be offered a regular column in any periodical at any point in the near future.

~ *9* ~

My next job was the worst. I needed to generate some kind of income and South Yorkshire Transport were always looking for conductors for their buses and it seemed to pay reasonably well - in my not very ambitious, qualification-less terms. So, I put in for a job, got it and went on the training course which taught us how to use the ticket machine and, most importantly, how to count the cash and reconcile it with the ticket sales at the end of the shift.

The only other thing I can remember learning on the "training course" was that you rang the bell once to signal to the driver to stop and twice to tell him to continue. If there was a disaster that required the bus to halt immediately, it was a continuous ringing of the bell. If the inspector got on the bus (and they did, often) and you had not collected fares from everyone, you were in trouble. I also discovered that it is illegal to display the wrong destination on the front of a bus. Fortunately that was the driver's job.

These were pre-decimalisation days and, given this was the Socialist Republic of South Yorkshire, the bus fares were very cheap, a matter of pennies in most cases. So the bus conductor's satchel was always weighed down with hundreds of these clunky old pennies and threepenny bits.

The buses were widely used, but mostly during the rush hours to transport the miners and steelworkers to their places of employment.

I had hardly any interaction with the driver because these buses were mostly backloaders with an open platform at the rear for people to get on and off. The driver sat in grand isolation in his enclosed cab at the front, with me in the body of the vehicle dealing with the often belligerent or eccentric public.

Running up and down the stairs of the bus at least kept me fit. I still found it difficult to call "Any more fares, please?" in the authoritative manner required.

I received a small amount of homophobic abuse for mincing up and down the aisle demanding to see tickets from those to whom I could not remember issuing one. "Fuck off, nancy," would be the retort of the rough boys when requested to prove that they'd paid.

When all seats were occupied, there was officially room for eight people standing. But when there were big crowds, as on football match days, or the weather was bloody, "the general public" (as I came to regard the passengers, none too affectionately) would crowd on to the bus and there would be twenty or thirty standing. People would be almost piled on top of each other.

"Some of you will have to get off," I would say, in a voice as butch as I could manage, which wasn't very. But I lacked the commanding presence of some of the other clippies, particularly the women, and no-one took any notice.

"We're not moving until some of you get off," I would say. But then some wag near the exit would ring the bell and off we would go.

In those circumstances it was impossible to move around the vehicle to collect the fares, so an added bonus for those defiant riders was that they hopped off without paying.

At the end of my first week I was given a route that I wasn't familiar with. When one of my colleagues asked what I had been allocated. I told him it was to Treeton, one of the mining towns on the periphery of Rotherham.

It was a Saturday and I was on an afternoon shift that ended at around eleven o'clock in the evening. The final return journey would bring us past a notoriously rough pub, the Miner's Arms.

"Oh dear. You want to be careful," said my colleague ominously. "It's not nice at that time of night up there. Especially not on a Saturday. You'll have to watch yourself."

A little shudder of fear passed through me. Could this pub be any worse than some of the other pubs on the routes the buses served? Everyone in the canteen was shaking their heads and looking at me pityingly, in the manner of the peasants in those Dracula films warning the hero not to go anywhere near the castle.

But I had to do it. It wasn't acceptable to refuse a shift and besides which, I needed the money so that I could take another trip somewhere interesting.

The evening passed without incident until we came to the dreaded final journey past the Miner's Arms. As we approached I saw a crowd of about fifty people waiting for the bus, which was already fairly full. They were – what shall we say? – a bit ebullient. There was violent horseplay, with youths trying to push each other into the path of the on-coming traffic, girls were screaming and there were people with blood coming out of their noses. A volcanic sense of threat permeated this mob.

As we pulled into the stop, the drunks piled on to the bus. I tried to put my arm across the entrance once the allotted number had got on board. But this was the last bus to Rotherham and none of them was going to be left behind.

I was elbowed out of the way without ceremony and the rest of the mob somehow squeezed themselves into the bus. I tried the usual: "Some of you will have to get off, the bus is overcrowded." There was then a chorus of "Fuck off, yer puff."

I decided that I could not handle the situation alone and so stepped off the bus to walk round to the driver's cabin. Needless to say, as soon as I was off the platform, the bell was rung and the driver set off, leaving me on the pavement with my ticket machine and satchel of pennies, three miles out of town.

A great cheer went up from the bus as it disappeared over the horizon with arms flailing from all the windows and people swinging from the pole at the back. It was like a scene from an X-rated St Trinian's film.

~ *10* ~

The shift work on the buses was a real burden, getting up at three a.m. in order to get the factory workers and the miners to their jobs on time was torture. By the end of a week of such shifts I would have a tearful breakdown-ette as the alarm went off in the dark and I was forced to haul myself out of bed, exhausted and sleep-deprived in order to face another day at the mercy of the General Public (now a malign entity to be avoided whenever possible).

One day, though, a young man, very good looking, was getting off the bus when he said: "Are you Terry?" I said, yes, and he said "David's told me all about you." Then he was gone.

That night I rang David to see who this mysterious stranger had been.

"Oh, that's Stewart, my new boyfriend. Isn't he cute?"

David had a boyfriend! A proper boyfriend.

"But where did you find him?" I asked.

"We met in a cottage. We hit it off straight away."

Cottaging? David had told me all about cottaging and which lavatories in town were good for it. I couldn't imagine myself doing anything like that, even though on the few occasions I had availed myself of the town centre facilities for legitimate purposes, I had been fascinated by graffiti that decorated the walls. "Wednesday, 7pm, for cock fun". "Young lad wanted for fucking," are two of the memorable inscriptions that stick in my mind.

It had never occurred to me that David would be hanging around toilets looking for sex, but all was now revealed and like the pathetically inexperienced creature that I was, I was shocked. I'd fallen for the mythology that cottagers were all horrible dirty old men looking for young flesh to devour. It never occurred to me that you might meet a dishy young bloke like Stewart.

All the same, I wasn't tempted to take up the cottaging lark. I was far too shy and frightened. The consequences of being caught were unthinkable.

David introduced me to Stewart and we socialised together a lot after that. I got on with them both famously. I just wished I had a boyfriend like Stewart.

I was so relieved when my time on the buses came to an end. I let out a little cheer as I handed in my uniform and ticket machine together with my resignation and then walked out into the fresh air. I didn't say goodbye to any of my colleagues because I didn't like any of them.

Now that I had accumulated a bit of cash, I was anxious to spend it. So I chose to take a trip on the hippy trail to Kathmandu. I would join eleven others and we would drive there and back in a Land Rover. We would pass through Iran, Afghanistan, Pakistan and India along the way – some of which would be very difficult to do now.

It was three months full of adventure and incident and because of the long hours of driving, I was able to do a lot of reading and thinking. I really needed to get an emotional life started. I had made my mind up. When we got back, I would seriously set about finding the kind of life I wanted, and if it didn't exist already, I would create it.

The other conclusion that was formulating in my mind as we progressed through the Islamic and Hindu and Buddhist worlds was about religion and its utter strangeness.

Seeing the women drifting through the streets of Iran and Afghanistan like black ghosts, shrouded from head to foot in what to my eyes were ridiculous garments, made me wonder how a culture had ever come to imagine that obliterating women from public view was in any way desirable.

I had told myself when we set out that I would enjoy the different cultures we would encounter on this journey and, indeed, I had met some lovely people. But the further east we got in Muslim lands, the more extreme the veiling of women became and the more I started to question the thinking of those who could apparently make sense of it.

I had no problem with their being faithful to their religious beliefs, but I was appalled not only by the treatment of women and the refusal to allow them to be part of the wider world, but also – when we got to Nepal – the cruelty to animals in the name of religion. The way that buffalos and goats were sacrificed (i.e. had their throats cut) while tethered to posts in the street and then simply left to bleed to death. Grotesque to my eyes, but simply part of the culture to the people around.

Religion had never played much of a part in my childhood. My parents were supposedly members of the Church of England, but beyond weddings and funerals, I never saw them set foot in a place of worship and certainly I was never encouraged to go.

When I became conscious of religion, I initially fell for the message that you have to believe *something*. Anything. You can't believe nothing – it just isn't possible. So I started exploring the various options.

My best friend Maggie, who lived immediately across the road, was a Catholic and she would go with her mother to Mass every Sunday. One week, out of curiosity, I asked if I could go with her. She took me along and I endured what seemed like hours of this intensely tiresome rigmarole with lots of standing up and sitting down and the priest waving something about and lifting things up and giving out biscuits – something I was not allowed to have.

Margaret explained 'confession' to me and again I was bemused as to how anybody could take such stuff seriously.

Next I went to the Congregationalist Church, mainly because they had a youth club which put on a nativity play that I wanted to be in. I was made to play Joseph, even though I wanted to play an angel with sparkly frock and feathered wings. When the youth club ended, so did my Congregationalism. Soon after, the church was turned into a carpet warehouse.

I went to the Spiritualist Church, which was exciting because it had the potential to be scary and I had always liked scary things. But again rather than ghosts and spirits, it turned out to be just more hymn singing and praising to God (who was doing nothing through all this to persuade me into the fold – any fold).

After that it was the Baptists whose worship really was truly frightening. There was shouting and jumping up and down, people shaking the pews and jabbering as they were 'possessed by the holy spirit'. I couldn't get away fast enough. These people were deranged - or maybe just showing off to each other.

The Salvation Army had its weekly "Joy Hour" for kids. The only joyful thing about it was that you got to play a tambourine with ribbons on it and they gave you a star on your star card for each time you went. If you went 12 times you qualified for a Bible.

They had religious propaganda especially produced for children. Illustrated tales from the Bible had colourful pictures of figures like Moses and Jonah. Then I read the story of Noah's Ark, which in the kiddie's version was all about cute animals going in two by two. It avoided dwelling on the nasty bit about God destroying the whole world and drowning everybody in it except horrible Noah and his family. I asked whether God might get angry again and end up destroying the world a second time, including Mi Mam and Dad and Mi Gran and our Roy and Albert. When the Sally Army bloke said it wasn't beyond the realms of possibility, I was horrified and worried about it for weeks.

The star card bribery didn't work on me, either. I didn't want a Bible. If it had been a Famous Five book I might have kept up my attendances. It was only much later that I came to know just how homophobic the Salvation Army is.

At school we had the usual morning assembly where we were required to sing hymns and say prayers. This means that although I am an out and out atheist, I can still sing a dozen or more hymns from beginning to end, but only the ones with a good tune – *Onward Christian Soldiers, To Be a Pilgrim* and *Green Hill Far Away.*

Our religious education classes were derisory. The RI teacher, Mr Elliot, was clearly uninterested in us boys or the subject he was supposed to be teaching us. Maybe he was worn out, disillusioned and embittered by a lifetime of bashing his head against a wall of indifference. Each lesson was exactly the same – draw a map of the Holy Land. We went through the motions of drawing the Tigris and Euphrates, and then he probably threw it all in the bin.

Maltby was a strange place in that respect. I know in other communities which revolve around a dangerous occupation, such as deep sea fishing or heavy industry, there is often a strong religious undertow. There are endless hymns about those in peril on the seas, but very few about miners (actually, I can't think of any off hand).

There was very little religious feeling among the mine workers that I was aware of. I'm sure some of them had fallen for the blandishments of the many evangelists that infested the town. And certainly the Catholics were more loyal to their church than the Protestants were to theirs. Everyone in the town had an affection for the parish church of St Bartholomew – that was of Saxon origin and very picturesque, sitting in the meadow – but most only visited it on the day of their wedding or their funeral.

I remember one Sunday the Catholic priest, Father Mullaney, arrived at Maggie's house across the road. He had been sent for by Maggie's mother who could not persuade her recalcitrant teenage son, Tommy, to get out of bed to go to Mass.

Later Maggie told me that the priest had stomped upstairs and roughly pulled Tommy out of the sack and forcibly marched him to church.

I was absolutely horrified and outraged by this. Even though I was very young – maybe eight or nine – I had imagined if the priest had come to my bedroom and tried to force me to do something I didn't want, I would resist in some way. I fantasised about stabbing him or pushing him through the window so he fell into the yard and busted his head open. Of course, since then we have all become much more aware of the abusive exercise of authority by priests over young people. The idea that a priest would be allowed into a young boy's bedroom these days is unthinkable.

This incident stayed with me, and from then on I was never tempted to darken the doors of a Catholic Church again. Not only was the Mass an absurd palaver, and the confession a laughable idea, but then you had to put up with bullying priests who pulled you out of bed.

And very soon I had no time for any religion, even the ones with tambourines and youth clubs.

For all the adventures we had on that trip to Kathmandu and all the narrow escapes from disaster, I was now ready to get home, to get back to real life and make a determined start on my search for the Big Dark Man. Or, if he wasn't available, a lesser equivalent.

And so as the marathon drive back began, I was always very aware that the sun was setting in the west and that it was ahead of us. I was returning with a beard, which had been allowed to grow because shaving was such a nuisance on the road.

I've still got it, a souvenir of my brief time as a fake hippy.

~ *11* ~

Of course, the first consideration on getting back home to Burns Road was to find a job so that I could pay my way. It did still seem that jobs were quite easy to come by in the early seventies, even for someone like me who had no real aptitude for practical things and certainly no qualifications. Computers were yet to arrive and so menial tasks still had to be done by human beings.

Aunty Mae was married to George Buck, known to everyone as Tudge. He was working as a porter at Doncaster Gate Hospital in Rotherham, which at the time, was the main hospital in the area. He said they had portering vacancies and I should put in for it.

He and Aunty Mae had four daughters but no sons. I think Tudge briefly thought that I – like the spare part that I was in my own family - would make a suitable surrogate son. He had tried hard when I'd been a child to interest me in war films and football and other masculine pursuits. He wanted me to join him in kick-abouts in the garden, he wanted to train me up for the rugby team.

But I just didn't – couldn't - respond in the way he wanted, and after a while he realised that I was not going to fill the gap in his life that this house full of women had created. In fact, I was rather like another addition to it.

Well, you didn't need any qualifications to wheel trollies around and haul sacks of rubbish, so I went to the hospital and applied.

Quite soon I had been issued with my brown porter's overall and shown the ropes. It all seemed straightforward. If one of the wards needed anything doing involving physical labour like switching the beds round or lugging away unwanted furniture, a porter would be sent for.

I was shown techniques for lifting and carrying heavy objects without ending up as a patient on the orthopaedic ward myself.

Once again, the environment in which I was working was almost completely male. I hated it. The crude matiness, the macho cynicism, the big-headed arrogance – I couldn't abide it then, and I can't abide it now - but I needed the pay cheque. I've never liked having male bosses. I can't get on with men in authority, they frighten and repel me.

I much preferred being with the nurses. There was one sister on the geriatric ward who reminded me of Moira at British Wagon. She was a good-looking woman and all the other porters fancied her like crazy. But she always gave them short shrift if they were cheeky or showed signs of not knowing their place.

I, though, tended to get a different reception. When I came on to her ward she was always friendly and tried to detain me for a while to chat and give me a glass of Robinson's Barley Water with ice in it, much to the disapproval of her sour-faced senior nurse. I suspected that Sister Sheila detected *the Truth*, and maybe she had a *Truth* of her own that she was hiding. If she did, we never got round to discussing it.

If any of the other porters happened to come on to the ward while I was there, sitting in the sister's office, chit-chatting, laughing and tinkling my glass of Barley Water as though I was Noel Coward in some cocktail bar, they would hurry off to tell the other lads. They couldn't work out my magic way with the ladies.

Then came the day that I had to collect my first body to take to the mortuary. Tudge had taken it upon himself to personally show me the ropes on this one and we collected the mortuary trolley – a sort of metal coffin on wheels - and took it to the ward where the deceased was awaiting removal.

The trolley had to be brought on to the ward discreetly so as not to upset the other patients. It was taken to the curtained-off bed where the cadaver lay and we then had to lift the body into the trolley.

I had never seen a dead body before and this whole procedure was beginning to feel surreal, as though it was happening to someone else. The elderly gentleman who had recently "passed away" was lying there with his eyes slightly open in a rather unnerving way.

Tudge took the shoulders and I took the feet and we hauled him (it?) into the trolley. I was shocked to realise that he was still warm, that only an hour or so earlier he had been alive, extant. Now he was this bag of flesh and bone that would never again be conscious, never wake again in the morning to the sound of birdsong, never smile or cry. At that moment the mystery of life and death dawned. The intimation of my own mortality suddenly sent a wave of fear through me.

But I kept it hidden and we took this body to the mortuary and transferred it to one of the refrigerated compartments. I was trying to be matter-of-fact and pretend that this was not affecting me, that it was just part of the job and that once it was done I would move on to the next thing without giving it a further thought.

But I was haunted by the incident for days after. And every time I had to collect a body, the same questions about what had changed in this person between the few moments before they died and the eternity that lay ahead afterwards. Where had they gone?

Of course, religion has had a field day with that one. It's the basis and the strength of all religions that they claim to have the answer to this. You may be dead, and your body might rot but your essence goes on in some other form. To paradise, heaven, nirvana, hell – whatever.

I could see the appeal of that, and the comfort it gives to the bereaved who do not like to think that their loved one is extinct and that what they loved about them no longer exists in any form, not even in dreamland.

Even though the question occurred to me every time I was in the mortuary, the life-ever-after answer never seemed very convincing. I had concluded that death was indeed extinction, obliteration, not "sleep" or "passing over", not reincarnation just nothingness. That was satisfactory as far as I was concerned, preferable even. The real mystery to me wasn't about the end of life but why it had begun in the first place.

After a while I was promoted to being a theatre porter and would be fetching and carrying for those doing the surgical operations. I would bring blood from the blood bank, books from the library when something occurred that the surgeon needed to read up on and take people back and forth to the wards.

The staff in the theatre soon got used to me being around and the assistants decided one day that they would invite me in during an operation to see what it was all about. I knew that they mischievously hoped I was going to faint or become nauseous when I saw the blood and guts. I thought I might, too, but actually I was less squeamish than I realised, and when I approached the operating table someone was having a laparotomy. This is an exploratory operation where a large incision is made in the abdomen and whole cavity is opened up for examination.

A small shock went through me when I first saw the gaping wound with all the organs exposed and being moved around and pulled out for examination. If this had been a road accident I might well have fainted, but I reasoned with myself that it was something that was being done to cure a possible lethal malady. Therefore it was a benign thing and desirable, something good, not a horror show.

When I saw the surgeon on other occasions with hammer and chisel in hand, battering away at diseased hip bones or with hacksaw for the amputations, it never bothered me. If he could bring himself to do it, I could bring myself to watch.

Non-invasive techniques for internal examinations, like scans, were were a rarity in those days and keyhole surgery had not been developed to the degree it is today. There were X-rays and endoscopes and that's about it.

And with each operation I saw, it became easier because I had also seen how quickly people recovered. I would bring people down from the ward, they would have the most traumatic-looking operations and the next day I would go back on to the ward and see them sitting up having a bowl of cornflakes and joking with the nurses. The human body has incredible powers of healing.

It's not the surgeon's knife that is likely to kill you - the anaesthetic is far more dangerous. But the riskiest factor of all is something that you can't even see – some micro-organism that can finish you off just as effectively as a collision with a number 69 bus, but a lot more slowly.

I now understand why so many TV soap operas are set in hospitals. The drama really is non-stop. One of my jobs in theatre was to dispose of amputated limbs. These were taken to the incinerator, which was kept burning day and night, and thrown in with the rest of the rubbish.

One day a below-knee amputation had been performed. The usual plastic container into which the limb was put for disposal was not available, so the theatre assistants popped it into a brown paper bag and gave it to me to take to the incinerator.

The packaging for was insufficient. Fluids were leaking from the leg, weakening the paper, and there were particularly long toenails.

It was just before visiting time and people were queuing in the corridor outside the wards, waiting for the doors to be opened. As I walked past these visitors on my way to the incinerator unit I tried to make the leg as unobtrusive as possible, but by this time the bag that contained it was rapidly disintegrating.

A few people caught sight of what was emerging and gave quizzical looks as though they couldn't quite believe what they were seeing. Eventually the leg did go into the furnace and as I tossed it through the hatch I thought about my brother, Roy, whose own leg had met a similar fate in this very place.

It was during all this, in 1967, that a momentous event occurred which almost passed me by unnoticed.

I was watching the TV news one evening, when the newsreader said that parliament had legalised homosexuality for men over the age of 21 in private. There was more detail than that, of course, but I don't remember it very clearly. But it seemed a very brief announcement, as though the BBC knew it must be included in the news but was rather embarrassed by it.

I had no idea of the long and bitterly contested road that had led to this change. My interest in politics up until that point had been non-existent. I was wrapped up entirely in the happenings (or lack of them) in my own life, the never-ending round of work and small domestic dramas. It was perfectly possible then – as it is now – to shut out the wider world entirely and restrict yourself to a tiny bubble of family and friends, surviving the challenges of each day one at a time.

But the mighty battle that led up to the 1967 Sexual Offences Act had passed me by unnoticed. I hadn't realised that I was illegal, all I knew was that I had to keep silent. I was far more afraid of my mother finding out than the police.

It was only afterwards that I came to know some of the extraordinarily courageous characters who had made a stand in order to bring this about. Antony Grey of the Albany Trust and Alan Horsfall who worked diligently in the north. The history of the campaigns that led up to 1967 has now been well-recorded, so I won't repeat it here.

Little did I know that the item on the news signalled a change that would alter the course of my life and millions of others like me. It would give us the opportunity to abandon the twilight world and step out into the sunshine.

But because the opportunity had arisen didn't mean to say everyone grabbed it with the same enthusiasm that I did. And it was never easy. But there was suddenly a crack in the closet door and a chink of light was shining through.

~ *12* ~

One of the advantages of reading the *Sunday Times* was that it kept me abreast of what was happening in London, that great repository of everything that I wanted. One Sunday I was brought up by a jolt by an advertisement in the entertainment section.

Marlene Dietrich would be appearing for charity at a midnight matinee at the Theatre Royal, Covent Garden, for one night only. Tickets were now on sale and the cheapest was £9.

I thought long and hard about the cost of going to London to see Marlene in the flesh, the hotel that would have to be paid for, the train fare, the ticket for the show.

But nothing was impossible as far as Dietrich was concerned. I would be at that show whatever it cost, whether I had to rob a bank or go into debt. I began saving like mad and bought the cheapest possible ticket in the gods at the Theatre Royal.

No-one else was prepared to make the investment that I was in order to be in the same room, even the same city as my idol. I was going to see Marlene at last, and the fact that I had to go alone made not one iota of difference. I would not have done this for anyone else, of course, but I had to conquer my fear of "getting into trouble" (an ill-defined state about which Mi Mam had a phobic obsession) and doing what needed to be done.

How had I become so timid?

The date was 15 September 1971. I had booked myself into the sleaziest hotel I could find in Kings Cross. I would have to have a taxi back from the theatre, as the show wouldn't end until about 2am.

This all seemed terribly sophisticated. I arrived at the theatre at the allotted time, found my seat very high in the second balcony of this huge theatre and put my shilling into the slot for the opera glasses.

But who was that sitting in the front row of the balcony? From behind it looked like Mr Farrer from the camera shop. I stared at the back of this head intently and eventually it looked round and, yes, it was Mr Farrer, and, naturally, he was accompanied by a young man.

He didn't notice me. He no more expected to see me there than I did him. The question now was whether I would renew acquaintances and see what would happen. (Anything could happen – he knew London and I didn't. He might want to introduce me to the delights of the city.)

Needless to say, I didn't approach him, didn't let him know I was there and yet another opportunity slipped through my frightened fingers.

But then the overture struck up, the curtains opened and on to this huge stage strode the object of so many of my fantasies, Marlene Dietrich. She was wearing a swansdown (as I learned later) coat of prodigious proportions and a dress dripping with bugle beads and rhinestones. She glittered and shimmered in the spotlights. She was everything I wanted her to be. She was everything *I* wanted to be. Commanding, sexy, knowing and by turns warm and icy cold. She told jokes and sang rambunctious songs from her Hollywood pictures.

Then she walked from the stage, divested herself of the swansdown coat and then returned to break our hearts with songs about love and the pain of love.

In that huge theatre this tiny woman held the audience spellbound. When she commanded it, we were silent and when she demanded it we applauded like demented creatures. It was like a magic trick – she had hypnotised us and we did her bidding.

At the end of the show the orchestra struck up the sound of her signature tune, "Falling in Love Again" over and over as she strode the stage absorbing the adulation like a sponge. It went on for what seemed like hours. My hands were aching and raw from applauding and yet still it went on.

Someone in the stalls ran to the stage and threw his dinner jacket at her feet. She casually picked it up and put it on over her silvery, glittering dress. This caused another wave of enthusiasm in the auditorium, which she milked for every second. I believe someone filmed this incident from the auditorium and it can be seen on Youtube.

Eventually the curtains closed, but the applause went on. There was a rustling and movement behind the drapes, deliberately created to keep us on tenterhooks I suspect. It indicated that the vision was still with us somewhere and was not finally gone. Then she pulled the curtains apart to demand more cheering, shouting and stamping. She bowed, they screamed, she bowed again – a deep bow right from the waist – and the noise in the theatre grew louder. It seemed to be verging on hysteria.

My limited experience of theatricals had not prepared me for anything like this.

When she eventually drew the red curtains around her for the final time and the show was ended, I was determined that I would go to the stage door and see her emerge. I wanted to see this mythic creature in the flesh, close up. I wanted reassure myself that the shining personage that had owned the football-pitch size stage at the Theatre Royal was an actual human being.

So, round I went and found myself in the company of hundreds of others, waiting the emergence from the stage door of the legend. Of course, most of those clamouring in the street must also have been gay, but I was unaware of that. Now all I wanted was for Marlene to come out of the theatre and show herself to be mortal.

And so she did. When, eventually, she came through the door she was dressed in a denim suit, with denim cap covering that blonde hair. Her lipstick was bright red and she was very small. On the stage she had seemed tall and domineering. In the street, under the harsh lights, she seemed tiny and not at all like the dream that had drifted about the stage.

But somehow that made her even more fascinating. If this gorgeous creation that had entranced the world could really be just a little old lady, then there was hope for me. Perhaps I could fool the world, too.

~ *13* ~

There were no immediate or dramatic changes after the 1967 Act came into force. Not for me, anyway. All those hunky homosexuals who I imagined had been hidden only just out of sight didn't suddenly reveal themselves on the streets of Rotherham.

My own personal Big Dark Man was still eluding me and even if I'd met him, the trade-off for his hunkiness would probably be arrogance, violence and a desire to control. This had been the way I'd seen so many straight men behave with the women I'd worked with.

And so more years passed, more awful jobs were obtained and endured for a few months before being abandoned.

These were years when feelings of loneliness overwhelmed me. Despite a working life packed with people of varying degrees of congeniality, I felt completely alone with the burden of isolation that fell on me as soon as I got home. I could not bring myself to socialise with my friends from work, because they all wanted to gather in places where the feeling of alienation would be intensified a thousand fold.

These were the places that were, apparently, reserved exclusively for heterosexuals, the pubs and clubs where husbands and wives, men and their girlfriends, lads on the hunt for women and women looking for husbands congregated, and were like torture chambers for me.

So I stayed home and fell into a deep depression each Saturday night as I sat in front of the television with my parents, enduring stupid TV quiz shows and detective stories with crushing boredom. It was their home and their television and their choice.

Soon I was working for another finance company in Rotherham. They gave loans for commercial refrigeration. I got the job on the basis that I had worked for so long at British

Wagon that I must know something about commercial financing. I didn't.

I knew all about doing the splits in the office to get a cheap laugh, but little about interest repayments.

Although it was on a much smaller scale than British Wagon, there were other young people working there and that made it more tolerable. One of the lads was called Bernard and I suspected that he might be a fellow traveller. My novice gaydar was quivering when in his presence.

After I'd been there for a year or so and we had become good friends and I had made a few non-committal coming out noises, he let me know that he wasn't entirely straight himself. But he was married and had two young children – a state that I was naïve enough to imagine qualified a person as an undoubted, 100% heterosexual.

Later experience was to show me that sexuality is not so conveniently delineated for everyone. My own sexual identity was pretty solidly fixed. The the Kinsey scale rates sexuality from 0 – 6 with zero being completely heterosexual and six being completely homosexual, with all the variations in between. I think I'm about 7 on that scale.

I was in no doubt at all about where my preferences lay and imagined everyone else was equally certain. I came to know that isn't true, but it still took a while to get my head round.

Later I was even more bewildered when David Allen, my first gay friend from British Wagon, told me out of the blue that he was engaged to be married to a woman, Sarah. I was staggered by this revelation and not a little hurt that he had said nothing about it until now.

I met Sarah and liked her; she was a pretty, down-to-earth girl, but I was still slightly puzzled about what was going on. David seemed quite happy with the arrangement and offered no explanation. He just assumed I would accept the situation without question. He was having regular sex with Sarah, he said, and the intention was for them soon to be married. It was a mystery beyond my understanding.

But what about Stewart? By this time, Stewart had become the leading official at the Trades and Labour Club where David was making his living accompanying the cabaret acts. Their relationship had turned from a romantic partnership to a business one.

David was, apparently, straight. He and Stewart were still friends and working amicably at the Trades Club.

I struggled with the news, and eventually drifted away from David. I don't know whether he ever married Sarah, but several years later I heard that he had died. I wasn't able to find out the cause of his death, but I was still sad to hear this news.

~ *14* ~

My penfriend Linda who was now living in San Antonio, Texas, where her husband had been posted by the army, asked if I'd like to pay them a visit. She now had three children, but she said there was a spare room and she'd love to see me and introduce me to her husband and family.

Naturally, I started saving madly and soon had enough money for a return flight to the USA. The ticket was bought and I arrived, eventually, in San Antonio full of excitement.

But this was the first time I had lived in a house full of kids since my brother had returned from Rhodesia with his own two. On their return they had moved into the house on Burns Road for a period until they got a new home sorted for themselves. It had been a bit of a nightmare. Not only were we grossly overcrowded, but my sister-in-law and Mi Mam tussled constantly over the right way to bring up the children.

In San Antonio the kids dominated everything. They cried, screamed, demanded constant attention and were rude and defiant. I now know that most children of that age (three, four and six) are like that, but these three just overwhelmed the whole house.

I tried not to say anything, and to tolerate the bad behaviour without comment, but when the time came to write my postcards home I commented on the one to Mi Mam "Linda and Gary are great but their kids are brats".

I said I would pop out to post the cards, but Linda suddenly said that she would pass the Post Office on her way to taking the children to school and playgroup. She would post them for me, she said, and plucked the cards from my hand.

I spent a long period chewing my finger nails wondering whether she would read what I had written about her children.

64

She was tense when she returned and her friendly demeanour had disappeared. It was clear that she *had* read the cards and she wasn't pleased.

"I'm sorry you think my kids are brats," she said eventually.

I tried to make some pathetic excuse about not meaning *brats* exactly, more like exuberant, lively, even noisy. Brat didn't mean the same in English as it did in American, I said. She wasn't convinced. Oh dear, this was awkward. I still had a week to go, and not enough money to stay anywhere else.

After a few hours she broke the silence and said, well, maybe her kids were a bit bratty. She would try to keep them out of my way. And then a pleasant holiday resumed.

It was during this stay that I was questioned about my life back home. Did I have a girlfriend?

To my eternal shame I said that I did. "Oh really, what's her name?" Linda enquired.

Thinking quickly I said "Rita". The Beatles song about "Lovely Rita meter maid" was going round in my head at the time.

There was no way that they could know I was lying, but they didn't ask about "Rita" again, obviously dubious about her actual existence. I was grateful for that because the fib had stuck in my throat and I had wanted very much to tell them the truth.

I couldn't anticipate their reaction, and in the situation where I was more or less dependent on them, having very little cash, I couldn't risk it. An adverse reaction would have spelled disaster – I would have been homeless in a not very friendly city.

When we'd been talking about their friends, they said that two guys living next door were (as Gary put it in his soldierly way) "Fairy nice boys." I wanted to ask them to introduce me. They might add a bit of adventure to this holiday which had turned out to be ultra-domesticated. But I never did see the fairy nice boys.

Gary was a great motorcycle enthusiast and one day he asked if I'd like to take a ride on his pillion through the woods. I said that would be fine, as I'd never ridden on a motorcycle before. I got on the bike, sitting well back, trying not to touch him, the way I'd seen other men riding on motorcycles together.

But he then revved up the bike and we suddenly set out at top speed along a rough woodland track that sent us bouncing up and down in our seats. I was terrified, convinced we were going to be thrown off. It was a purely instinctive reaction to grab him round the waist and hang on tightly as we hurtled through the forest. It was exhilarating and thrilling but I didn't know what he was going to think about my holding on to him quite so intimately.

At the same time, it had been his idea to bring me on to this dirt track and purposely try to terrify me, and I wasn't going to let go, particularly as I had no headgear or any other protective clothing.

Later that evening I heard Gary and Linda talking in the kitchen. Linda asked how the bike ride had been. "It was like riding with a girl," Gary replied, not without affection.

I think any credence they had placed on my Rita story (and that wasn't much) now evaporated.

When I got home, Linda wrote to me and told me that her estimation of me had gone down. Not because she had realised I was gay but because I hadn't seen fit to be honest with her and Gary about it. I was ashamed and I think I actually blushed when I read the letter. I wrote back immediately coming clean entirely and explaining to her my fear of a bad reaction in such a situation. She forgave me, and our postal friendship resumed. I even went to visit them again when Gary was posted to Cologne in Germany.

As for Carla, the other long-term penfriend who I had never met – it was time to tell her the truth, too. I would be sorry to lose her as a friend if she took the news badly, but at least I was on home territory now in Burns Road and not at anyone's mercy.

I wrote to her the usual breezy letter, but then at the end I said: "I've got something to tell you. Not sure how you'll take it, but I'm gay. I hope that won't affect our friendship, which I value. However, it is important that I am honest with you. Friends should be as honest as they can be."

By return I received a letter which I almost couldn't believe:

Dear Terry,

I feel so close to you now – I always have, but more since your last letter. Do you remember that long space in our correspondence when we didn't exchange a letter for nearly two years? Finally I wrote to you. After such a long time, your letter vaguely said an awful lot. One vibe I picked up was that you were gay. So many times I have wanted to say what I thought I knew but was afraid I might be wrong. I was very moved that you finally said something. I am also gay..."

As well as being gobsmacked, I was delighted. I imagined that we would have a totally different relationship now, more open and more constructive. We could support each other.

But my pleasure was short-lived. A little while later Carla told me that she had been diagnosed with a malignant brain tumour. She said that sometimes her behaviour was erratic and she was finding it harder to write.

I was so very sorry and I had hoped she could recover. But, unfortunately, I never heard from her again and my subsequent enquiries brought no response.

~ *15* ~

My job-hopping continued and amid it all, I still fantasised about finding a gay life of some kind. It had to be one that didn't involve cottages or casual pick-ups. I wanted more urgently than ever a proper love affair with a man (although, in the interim, a bit of debauched casual sex, of a non-threatening nature, wouldn't have gone amiss).

Lodged in my mind was the name of a pub in Sheffield that I had heard being discussed once in the porter's lodge at the hospital all that time ago. It had been described by my crass colleagues as "where them puffs go" and so naturally I had noted it but without any real intention of ever investigating.

Now, though, things had reached such a pitch that I thought I might try my luck at this pub, even though I was terrified at the prospect.

I had never been much of a pub person, they always seem a bit "matey" and male oriented to me, and I had always wondered what it was that people were talking about so intensely over glasses of beer. Drinking ale and discussing football and cars in tedious detail was not appealing. But the upstairs bar of this pub was a place where the elusive homosexuals gathered and where, maybe, my Big Dark Man – the one who was kind and considerate and not a boor - was waiting for me.

It took a while for me to get my courage together, but out of desperation I approached the pub one evening and walked through the door. To my horror I realised that the downstairs bar was straight - and rough. To get to the upstairs bar, and possibly paradise, you had to walk through a billiard room where loutish youths lay in wait.

It seemed no gay person could pass without enduring sniggers and crude comments from the assembled billiardists. Their energy for this ritual never sapped.

If I had known this was the cost of getting upstairs, I would never have considered the idea. And when I did get up there and entered the notorious gay bar, it was even worse. As the door creaked loudly open everyone turned in unison and looked at me. It was as though the creak had been specially installed in the door hinges to ensure that the denizens of this dim and grim place were alerted without fail to any newcomer.

I was being eyed up and assessed by every one of the dozen or so people in there. My face was throbbing red with embarrassment.

In the split second I remained in that dingy room I ascertained that there was no-one fitting the description of the Big Dark Man and immediately decided that I would have to go straight back down the stairs and pass again through the valley of humiliation in order to get out.

Once on the street I felt as though I'd been holding my breath throughout the whole ordeal and now I was gasping for air.

That was it – I had failed again to make any progress. Another avenue had just closed itself off and I returned home feeling dejected and a failure. Another weekend would be spent alone, in front of the television while everyone else, it seemed, was out having a great time.

~ *16* ~

Serendipitously, one Sunday, the newsagent had sold out of the *Sunday Times* and so I bought the last remaining *Observer* instead. Having worked through the editorial sections, I came to the small ads. The smallest possible announcement said: "Homosexual? Interested? send stamped addressed envelope to Campaign for Homosexual Equality, 27A Kennedy Street, Manchester".

I read it again. What could this be? Did they have a branch nearby? I wrote off immediately, full of hope that this held the key that would open the door to paradise.

It seemed like an age before the reply came. No, there wasn't any local branch in Rotherham, they said, but a group had got off the ground in Sheffield. They put me in touch someone who invited me to their next meeting, which was to be at the Anglican chaplaincy at the university in Sheffield.

So off I went, with a mixture of apprehension and excitement. Going into this meeting wasn't anything like going to the pub. I didn't feel that I would be accepted or rejected on the basis of my looks. This was about helping, not about sex. (A small hope still remained, however, that it might eventually be about sex).

It was at this initial meeting that I met Bruce Hugman, a gentle, mild-mannered and reassuring chap who seemed to be one of the leading lights of the group. I later discovered that he was on a very similar emotional trajectory to me. He admitted in his own reminiscences (*Out of Bounds: a thirty year journey to break free* – Kindle Books) that he had been too timid, too afraid of the consequences of opening his closet door. He had put off starting his real adult life until his late twenties but had concluded, at about the same time as I did, that it was now or never. He, too, was hoping that CHE would help open up a new romantic world.

His subsequent life trajectory took a very different course to mine.

There were half a dozen people at this meeting, besides myself and Bruce, there was a young man called Dave Brown and someone else whose name I can't recall, but who was full of fervour.

Bruce seemed very serious and Dave Brown seemed very sensible, practical and determined. We chatted amiably about what we wanted to do – no-one seemed particularly anxious to take on the responsibility of running a formal group, but we decided that we would have regular meetings at the Chaplaincy office and see whether we could attract some more people.

And so this went on with monthly meetings at the university. It was all very slow and earnest, but we were getting to know each other gradually and news about the meetings was spreading on the campus, so a few students began to turn up.

But we were giving each other courage. Naturally, some were bolder than others and people came and went according to whether the group had fulfilled their expectations or had disappointed or frightened them. It was all pretty gentle, no pressure, but even that was too much for some people for whom it had taken all their courage to be in that room.

Eventually we decided that the time was coming to branch out. We had to do something more exciting than simply meet for a cosy chat once a month. It certainly wasn't doing much for me and my ambition to get a romantic life of my own started.

We moved the meetings from the Chaplaincy to the Quaker Meeting House in the centre of town to make them more accessible. The membership was growing. We now had a committee and a social secretary. There were facilities to make tea and coffee.

There were CHE groups all over the country, some of which had been established for a considerable time. They had trail-blazed and provided the template for what other groups could do – we had speakers, quizzes, parties. Over the months the membership continued to expand.

It is difficult to explain the importance of these meetings and events in the lives of the people who came to them. I know many gay couples who met in the early days of CHE and four decades later are still happily together. What might our lives have been like if we had not had the opportunities provided by these early groups?

This, indeed, was the transitional era. We were moving from the days of complete illegality and secrecy when life for the vast majority of gay people had been impossible to a time when all kinds of opportunities were opening up for those with the courage to grab them.

I met so many men at that time who had been raised during, and formed by, the years of silence and persecution. Not all of them were able to shake off the lifetime of indoctrination that had told them that their sexuality was second class or even completely worthless. They peeped out of the closet, but the new world that was opening up out there was too dangerous for them. They didn't know how to cope and were afraid to risk it.

I wanted to do something to help change that, to make sure the next generation would have a different experience. But most attendees at the CHE meetings had no desire to engage in the gay activism that was developing in London and other big cities. Some were even repelled by the idea of speaking out, frightened at the attention it was drawing to the whole hidden gay community. Shining a light on real lives would disturb the safety net they had erected around themselves.

To many in CHE, the activities of the Gay Liberation Front in London, with its confrontational approach to politics, seemed like a trouble causing for the sake of it. They didn't want to do anything that would expose them to their family or employer. They were concerned only with their own personal life and its emotional fulfilment. This was fair enough. That was certainly the way I had seen CHE – as a means of meeting someone with whom I could share my life. Its political ambitions only came to make sense to me a little later.

Nationally CHE was riven by arguments between the activists and the socialisers. It even split at one point to accommodate both groups separately. I joined the national committee briefly, but the meetings in Manchester were dominated by a couple of people whose insecurities resulted in unpleasant and destructive behaviours. It wasn't my style at all, and I quickly resigned.

When I went to the next meeting of the group in Sheffield, the ever-energetic Dave Brown had come up with the idea of having a gay disco, a non-commercial one that would not involve, as the old pub had, being belittled by worthless yobbos with billiard cues. It would be welcoming and cheap and it would be ours.

He had made some enquiries and we could hire a council venue, the unpromising-sounding Cemetery Road Vestry Hall, for a reasonable price on a Saturday evening from 7pm to 10pm. He had a friend who was a DJ and could bring his own equipment. We could buy in our own drinks and run a bar.

This sounded like the ultimate in excitement to me. There was a growing interest in the CHE group as word had spread and so we thought we could get a reasonable number of people to come to the disco. And so it went ahead. The very first dedicated gay disco in Sheffield.

It was a fairly muted evening. The dusty, faintly odorous Cemetery Road Vestry Hall was not entirely conducive to fun and frolics, but there was an unprecedented sense of excitement.

So many other gay people have written about the shock they felt when they first saw couples of the same-sex dancing closely together. My excitement was overwhelming. This is what I wanted, this is what I had been seeking. The possibilities for romance and sexual adventures suddenly seemed to have opened up. What bliss!

Dave Brown was full of ambitious plans after that. We would have more discos and these would help raise funds to support the group's other activities. These dances were held in places more amenable to jollity than Cemetery Road and their popularity began to snowball.

In 1975, National CHE held its annual conference in Sheffield and the Sheffield group was deeply involved in helping organise and run it. It was an incredibly exciting time as 1200 people from all over the country came on to our own turf.

I was given the job of welcoming people and minding events such as a piano recital by the international concert pianist Peter

Katin. Mr Katin was a great supporter of CHE and raised a lot of money for the group over the years.

It was at this conference that one of the first civic receptions ever was given to a gay and lesbian group. At the reception, the more radical lesbians protested after they discovered that the women handing out the snacks were being paid less than the men. One of them, Glenda Goldwag, grabbed the microphone from the hand of the mayor as he was about to speak and started loudly complaining about the inequality.

His Worship, who had looked uncomfortable throughout, took the opportunity and stormed out in an 'I've-never-been-so-insulted'-style huff. That was good for major publicity the following day.

Gay Sweatshop premiered their first show *Mister X* at the conference and Tom Robinson launched a song called *Good to be Gay*, a precursor of *Glad to be gay*. The Paedophile Information Exchange caused a kerfuffle as it sought to persuade CHE to support it.

We were thrilled by all this activity but, by the end, exhausted.

~ 17 ~

It was about this time that I began to think that maybe Rotherham could do with a CHE group of its own. Sheffield was only a twenty five minute bus ride away, but it would be nice if we had something locally.

I had met a few Rotherham people who had found their way to the Sheffield group, so we decided to get together and start the Rotherham group. To get the ball rolling I said I would be the convenor, which was the designation CHE had decided upon for the patsies who volunteered to run the local groups.

We began to meet at the home of one of the new self-nominated committee. His name was Glyn and he had a nice little bungalow in Kimberworth, just a short bus ride from the centre of town.

Also on the committee was Richard Erdley and his partner of a decade Eddie. They were good, solid people but not in any way attracted by agitation or confrontation. They were all for a quiet life with little ambition beyond bringing people together in the hope that they could make a happier life.

Glyn, like the rest of us, was desperate for a boyfriend, and so he tolerated the intrusions into his domestic life, living in hope that Mr Wonderful would turn up at one of his wine and cheese parties. I'm pleased to say that his dream did eventually come true and his new partner – wonderful or not – arrived on the scene before very long.

Sometimes my own anger and desire for activism alarmed my little crew and they occasionally made half-hearted attempts to restrain me if they thought I was going too far or causing too much trouble.

We constantly discussed how we would recruit new members, where we would hold our meetings and so on. My phone rang constantly with people who were interested – we were advertising in the personal columns of the local press now

75

- and the group was getting known around the area. It was a bit cosier than the Sheffield group.

All the same, I thought the time had come for a recruitment drive. The only way to let people know that the group existed in a big way was to get publicity in the local press. *The Advertiser* was the local paper that served all parts of Rotherham, and I had a friend from the British Wagon days, Paul, who was now a reporter on it.

I pitched the idea to him and he was enthusiastic to do a feature about the group. The problem was, he wanted it to take the form of an interview - with me. I would be outed to all and sundry in the town.

It was a big step, but after weighing the pros and cons, the upsides and the downsides, I decided that I would have to do it. The group needed a front man and given that no-one else was prepared to do it, it had to be me. I had absolutely no idea what the reaction would be, but I said I'd do the interview, so long as there was no accompanying photograph. I didn't want to make myself a complete sitting duck for every homophobe on the mean streets of Rotherham

So I met Paul and gave the interview. I told him what the CHE was about, what this group aimed to achieve and what my personal experience had been. I could see him scribbling frantically in his notebooks and I worried what he was going to make of all this. We had been good friends at British Wagon and I was glad that he had gone on to a job that satisfied him. Though Paul wasn't gay, I was sure he wasn't going to stitch me up. *The Advertiser* was not *The News of the World*.

I spent the next few days in a state of high anxiety awaiting the day of publication. It was 17 September 1976 and I still have a copy of the article. It was reasonable, sympathetic and there was nothing in it to frighten the horses. But had there been anything to ruffle feathers at Burns Road?

Like the coward that I am, I had not told my parents in advance about the interview. They had very little idea about my activities away from home, and they didn't ask about them. I would disappear for the occasional weekend or turn up late at night after a disco. But I had not formally come out to them.

All the same, there was no way that Mi Mam could not have known. She above all had watched my development from the beginning, knew my enthusiasms and had caught me out on a few occasions – like the time she found the stash of Athletic Model Guild male pin-up magazines in my wardrobe. But she had preferred to leave it unsaid. That suited me most of the time, but now things were changing.

The interview would ensure that avoiding the issue would no longer be an option. There would be no discreet conversations, no gentle lead-ins, no private discussions. It was all rather brutal and I was ashamed of myself later for being quite so cruel.

I came home from work on that Friday evening not knowing what sort of reception I would get. Mi Mam seemed slightly hurt and angry. "Why didn't you tell us you were going to do this?" she wanted to know. People had been stopping her in the street to tell her about the article, which at that point she hadn't read.

But after the initial anger, she soon calmed down and actually seemed slightly relieved that it was all out in the open. Many had wondered why I wasn't married, wasn't courting, was still living with my parents at this age. Now they knew.

The extended family, too, now had the truth, which I am sure was not a revelation for many of them. If my aunty Rose had worked out that Johnny Ray was gay from just seeing him on the telly all those years before, she had surely worked me out.

So now I could relax and stop worrying that they would "find out". I was free at last from the closet that had brought me so much misery and fear. I was never going back in and wherever I went I vowed to myself that I would be honest. (I was not always able to honour that promise – in some situations, especially late at night on public transport, a sense of survival overwhelmed the desire to wear my "Gay and Proud" t-shirt.)

The first time I went to see Mi Granny after the interview, she was warm and welcoming and made sure I knew that she wasn't going to make a fuss. She wasn't even going to mention it and she produced one of her special Camp Coffees made with boiled milk.

I had grown used to this concoction, sickly sweet as it was, and now if ever I see a bottle of Camp Coffee, I have a Proustian moment and am instantly transported back to Mi Gran's house, which was always warm and cosy and smelled of soap. She had no idea of the joke others would make if they knew she was feeding me Camp Coffee.

I worried most about how my father would take the news (if, indeed, it was news to him). He was notoriously prudish: not only did he not swear, if anything even vaguely sexual or suggestive came on television he became distinctly uncomfortable. If there was a love scene in a play, particularly if it involved nudity or a bed, he would get out of his chair, harrumph loudly, and then poke the fire, rattling the poker in the fireplace as loudly as he could.

This distracted him (and us) long enough for the offending material to disappear from the screen. If it went on for too long he would unceremoniously change the channel. He couldn't even tolerate nature programmes that showed the animals mating.

But, although we didn't discuss what had happened at all, his approach was (according to Mi Mam) "well, if that's how it is, that's how it is."

I had never been particularly close to Mi Dad. I hadn't seen much of him during my childhood because he was always at work, and what I had seen of him I didn't particularly like. But people change and as he got older and retired from the pit, he mellowed considerably.

I never had a moment's criticism or comment about my gayness from my father, who continued to treat me exactly the same as before (when he hadn't been on one of his Sunday lunch time boozing binges, he was a man of few words, anyway). I don't think he would have had the vocabulary or the emotional resources to talk about it directly.

There is a widespread assumption that homophobia is worse outside the big cities and that, in working class communities in particular, life was one long round of persecution and violence for gay people. In such environments you took your life in your hands if you came out of the closet.

This was not my experience – although I accept it may not have been typical. The love that I had received from my many aunties and uncles and cousins and granny did not diminish. The respect I had been shown by them continued unabated. As far as I can tell, it was never an issue. The extended family was so large that statistically there had to be other gay people within it and, indeed, in succeeding generations other members also eventually came out.

The first few meetings of Rotherham CHE were held in people's front rooms. But that had to change. Not everyone liked the idea of inviting total strangers into their home, some of whom might not have had the noblest of intentions for being there.

I tried a few pubs – all of which were hostile. Then I went on to church halls and although there were no outright refusals because we were a gay group, there were repeated excuses as to why they couldn't accommodate us. "Oh, we have regular groups. Housewives Register, Brownies, Luncheon Club mother and baby – so it's always in use. We don't have any vacancies." This was going to be a bit more difficult than I had anticipated.

After countless rebuffs, I was about to give up when we were approached by a clergyman, Rev Michael Grylls who was an Anglican vicar at St Cuthbert's Church in Herringthorpe, just outside Rotherham. He had seen the article in the *Advertiser* and said he would help us in any way he could. He was on the liberal end of Anglicanism, so I explained about our problem in finding a meeting place.

He immediately offered the use of the hall at his own church. It was a modern building on a bus route and relatively easy to get to.

Given the amount of resistance and aggravation that the gay community has had to put up with from the churches over the years, I am struck by how often individual parishes helped groups like ours to get off the ground in the early days.

We could now have our meetings on the third Tuesday of every month. I had expected that we would operate much on the same basis as the Sheffield group. When we grew big enough we might even have a disco at the Assembly Rooms at the town hall on the lines of the Sheffield ones.

But first we had to capitalise on our rising profile and recruit yet more members.

~ *18* ~

In 1972 *Gay News* had been born. This was the first real community newspaper and was pivotal in the development of the gay rights movement in Britain. Now we had a means of communication nationwide. The gay groups that were springing up around the country, promoted by CHE, could report their activities and encourage one another. People could advertise their events and also place personal ads looking for partners.

A famous legend above the *Gay News* contact ads column read "Love Knoweth No Laws" – a reference to the case of *International Times* magazine, which the Law Lords had found guilty of "conspiracy to corrupt public morals" for publishing gay personal ads.

The life of *Gay News* was a melodramatic one and the details have been recorded elsewhere, so I won't repeat them here. But it was vital to the progress of the movement and important to so many gay people personally. It certainly was to me, and its fortnightly appearance was always a treat.

It was regarded by some as an "obscene publication". There was even an attempt to prosecute it for obscenity in 1974 after it published a front page photo of two men kissing, but this failed.

All these controversies made distribution difficult. There was an ongoing battle with WH Smith, which refused to put *Gay News* in its shops or on its distribution network. It was generally only available outside London by subscription or from a few brave independent newsagents and alternative bookshops.

In Rotherham there was one newsagent, the Chocolate Box, that stocked *Gay News* and I always made sure, taking a deep breath before entering, that I bought my copy there to encourage it. *Gay News* was certainly informing my own developing thoughts on gay rights. But most of the interesting stuff seemed to be happening in London.

All the same, CHE nationally was starting to expand and it eventually had about 150 local groups around the nation.

Reading about the treatment that was being meted out to some people made me angry: many were fired from their jobs, kicked out of their homes, rejected by their families. These things were not reported in the mainstream press and so it was important for *Gay News* to bring them to light. It all seemed so unjust.

Now that I had a better understanding with my parents, I decided that I would list the Rotherham group in the *Gay News* listings page, where it might be seen by interested parties. We could also syphon off Rotherham members who found their way to Sheffield.

We needed a contact number so I put my home phone in the listing. There were no mobile phones in those days that would afford anonymity, it had to be a landline (which were expensive and hard to get).

I knew this was a risk because people might ring at any time, and if I wasn't there, my mother would answer. My being honest and open was one thing, but having total strangers ringing up wanting to talk about their sexual problems was something else.

In the listings I specified times when I was certain to be at home, but I knew that such restrictions wouldn't be respected. When people saw it for the first time and decided to ring – as I had rung for information about Sheffield CHE – they would want to do it immediately, whatever time of day it was. Equivocating would create unbearable stress or lead to a complete loss of courage.

And no sooner was the number listed than the calls started. For the most part people rang at the allotted time, and they just wanted more information about the group. But sometimes I found myself listening to dreadful stories of rejection and harassment. One young man told me he had been beaten up by his father and was now homeless.

I was ill-equipped to deal with some of the problems that were coming through the phone line. I had no resources to tackle the sometimes unbelievable difficulties. One man said he was gay but he was married with nine children. I didn't know what to say – I was trying to see it from his point of view, but his wife and kids kept intruding into any sympathy I had for him.

These calls proliferated and I realised that I couldn't possibly cope with it all on my own. I was glad when a dedicated counselling line opened in Sheffield, and I could refer people there. Of course, in the early days such phone lines were run by amateurs with no training and were completely self-financed.

The thinking was that if the authorities won't help us, we'll have to help ourselves. Unfortunately this led to some of the phone lines being manned by people who weren't doing it for entirely altruistic motives.

I certainly remember a confrontation we had inn Sheffield with "counsellors" on our helpline who were using it for dating purposes. Given that some of the people who were calling were in a vulnerable state, we couldn't allow that to continue.

It was a great step forward when gay help services became much more professionalised and groups such as Friend and Gay Switchboard grew stronger and more accessible.

~ *19* ~

CHE was developing nicely. I was now part of the Sheffield committee as well as the Rotherham one. We were very pleased with the success of the discos as well as the meetings at the Friends Meeting House.

Dave Brown was now ready to push us a bit further and he persuaded us that we should organise a spectacular disco at the City Hall Ballroom. This had a capacity of 850 – which seemed rather a large space to fill with the numbers of people we had seen so far.

Still, we now had the cash to take the risk and had made good contacts with Huddersfield CHE, and a few others and so they could help put word about and we would see what happened.

So the hall was booked for a Friday night and we advertised as far and wide as we could manage. Much of it was done through the grapevine. It was to be called CHEckers disco.

The first event exceeded our wildest expectations. People just kept on arriving – more than 500 of them, men and women from all over Yorkshire and beyond. The atmosphere was electric. Nothing like this had been seen in the north ever before, and everyone present seemed to sense that they were part of something very special. Just for a change, this was not a commercial club in a sleazy part of town, under surveillance by the police. We were in the City Hall!

I was allotted the job of selling raffle tickets. I liked this because it meant I could go round the whole hall and had an excuse to talk to everyone.

The room seemed packed with excited men and women of all kinds. Some were rowdy queens – including the legendary Darnall Lil, an elderly transvestite with a fetish for Carmen Miranda - who were loving the opportunity to, as they put it, "scream their tits off". The bar was busy, which would please the management.

The dancing was ecstatic and the level of sheer relief at, for once, being in the majority, was amazing. I could accept a dance when one was offered, I could cling close during the smoochy numbers.

We raised quite a good amount from that disco, but it also showed us that there was an urgent need for more opportunities to socialise. Not everyone was attracted by our regular meetings, some of which might have been mistaken for a gathering of the Mothers' Union with their genteel cups of tea and earnest speakers. Equally the commercial gay scene was not to everyone's liking, either, certainly not to mine.

For instance at the Gemini Club in Huddersfield you had to ring a bell and be approved before you could get in. Of course, running a properly licenced club that just happened to be frequented by homosexuals wasn't illegal. Nevertheless, the Gemini was repeatedly raided by the police. There was a notorious yard out the back where liaisons could and did take place. The problem was that the local constabulary knew all about the hanky-panky and they would quite often burst through the gates and arrest anyone who was thought to be enjoying – or even about to enjoy - carnal activity.

It all seems so prurient now, and indeed at that time the police *were* prurient. Worse than that, they were cruel and vindictive. There was a strong streak of homophobia running through the ranks, which the 1967 law changes had not mitigated. There still seemed a strong desire among some policemen to pursue, harass and humiliate gay people whenever possible. A case of old habits dying hard.

The police activity went well beyond what was required by the law, transforming into a kind of spiteful desire for revenge. But revenge for what? For not being like them? For refusing to fit in and be conventional?

The Gemini Club was somewhere where they could find easy targets. That didn't mean to say they didn't also make easy arrests at other gay rendezvous points – the cottages and cruising grounds that were well known to them.

In 1981 the harassment of the Gemini Club had reached such a pitch that the police were now opposing the renewal of its licence. As a protest, and in solidarity, the London Gay Pride March that year was moved to Huddersfield; as a result, many charges against gay people were dropped and the club kept its licence. Rotherham CHE, of course, had a presence, as it did at all Pride events.

There was also the notorious use of the "pretty police" – good looking officers who were used as *agents provocateurs* to entrap unsuspecting gay men. This all seemed unnecessary and malicious, especially given that they knew that the punishment in terms of social rejection for those they charged would be far more severe than anything a court could impose. Many officers wanted to hurt gay men for no good reason other than crude prejudice. They were, in effect, gay bashers with an institutional sanction.

And the local papers rarely let a court appearance go unreported. These reports from the local magistrates courts never failed to include the full name and address of the "offenders". This was ruinous for some people and felt in some ways like a return of the village stocks. It was a witch hunt that must have given these latter day Matthew Hopkins' a gratifying sense of self-righteousness.

The CHEckers disco had been so successful that we decided that we would make it a regular occurrence. So the City Hall Ballroom was booked each month and we hoped for the best.

There was always the possibility that the novelty of the first event would not carry over into others and the numbers would diminish. But we needn't have worried, subsequent events were even more successful. Word of mouth was spreading fast and at the next disco we had six hundred and then seven hundred and soon we were at capacity. CHEckers discos were a phenomenon and must have generated a huge amount of money over the years. Not quite sure where it all went, but that's another story.

~ 20 ~

It was at one of these CHEckers events that I met Richard.

He wasn't exactly my Big Dark Man – he actually had wispy blonde hair and blue eyes and was shorter than me. But he was good looking, about the same age and seemed to find something in me appealing. We danced and talked and then we went our separate ways.

Then we met again at the CHE meetings and chatted more at the pub after the meeting. (By this time Sheffield had a proper gay pub, the Cossack situated on Howard Street near the Pond Street bus station. It was small and cosy and made a good place to retire to and relax after the meetings. It has since been demolished to make way for luxury flats).

I began to fancy that maybe, just maybe, Richard and I had potential for something more than just the occasional conversation. He was a little earnest, but like everyone else he was at CHE to discover if he could develop his emotional life.

And so when, one day, he asked me to go back to his place, the birdies began singing and the joyous, Hollywood choir – the one that had been silent for so long - arose once more in my head.

He lived with his parents on Psalter Lane, which was in a posher part of town, in a large semi-detached house. There was an enormous cherry tree outside that blossomed magnificently in springtime – a huge blob of pink in an urban road.

Like me, he was still living at home with mum and dad because – well, there didn't seem much point in moving out simply to incur the expense of another abode in which to reside lonely and alone.

This particular weekend his parents were away at their holiday cottage in Anglesey, so we had the house to ourselves. It was an old-fashioned sort of place, one that had not been changed for a long time. Richard's parents must be quite elderly, I thought. However, the good part was that there was no need to be sneaking about or having dangerous liaisons in public places. We could relax and get to know each other at leisure.

What a revelation that weekend was! All that I had dreamed of, all that I had fantasised about was here. We closed the curtains and the carnival began.

What followed would have had my father poking the fire with a vengeance. He would have poked it so hard he would have wrecked the fireplace. But for me this was the beginning of a relationship and, as we all know, those first enraptured weeks tend to be the most passionate, bedwise.

Let us just say that my enforced monkish lifestyle had been discarded in a big way. The virgin state that had been so unwillingly endured for so long was now at a decisive end. The barrier had been breached and hallelujahs rang out.

Richard and I were soon inseparable (except that we lived in different houses in different worlds – me resolutely working class, him upper middle).

He had laid claim to the large front parlour in his parents' house as his own space and so he would often invite me over (and I would invite myself over when I was feeling in need). I met his parents, who were, as I suspected, quite elderly but very pleasant in a middle-class kind of way. His father was a retired property surveyor and his mother had pretensions to be an artist. I think they were suspicious of me at first, but as time went along, they got used to me and we became friends.

When I arrived on their scene, they were pleased that Richard had found a companion that understood him and apparently made him happy.

How much they suspected about what we got up to in that back parlour, with its handy chaise longue and easily drawn curtains, I cannot imagine.

When I visited, there would be preliminary greetings with his parents, then Richard and I would retire to the front room, ostensibly to listen to some of his classical record collection. The door would be locked and the volume of the record player turned up to cover some of the noise (the 1812 Overture was always a good choice on these occasions) – the erotic adventures would resume.

Once or twice his parents tried the door while our clothes were scattered around the room. They did not persist in trying to gain entry or ask why the door was locked on them in their own house.

Richard worked as a gardener in the parks department of Sheffield Council. I thought this was a strange job for someone who had his level of qualification. He had been to university and had a degree in French. He was cultured and knowledgeable about many things, but he chose not to exploit those qualifications and stuck with this rather menial job. He said he didn't want the stress of a high-flying career. I could empathise with that.

But he was truly interested in horticulture and knew the Latin names of all the plants and trees that he dealt with. He liked being outdoors and being close to nature.

We started going about together, to the pictures, the theatre, walking in the beautiful peak district that was just a bus ride away. We went to the Halle Orchestra concerts at the City Hall.

The trips into the Peak District were usually taken on Sunday or a Bank Holiday. I liked the *idea* of hiking through the hills but I wasn't quite sure I liked the reality. It was quite hard work climbing over all those stiles and dodging the sheep dung. My only motivation for doing it was the promise of a tea room at some point, where home-made cake would be available.

One weekend Richard's parents invited the two of us to accompany them to Anglesey. I would have preferred to stay at home and have another unbridled weekend on Psalter Lane. But they insisted and we drove to their cottage in a pleasant little village.

Richard and I were allotted a room with bunk beds, and when the lights were out it was very difficult to carry on as we wished with his parents in the next room.

The following morning, the people living next door popped round to say that they were going out for the day and if "the boys" (us) wanted to watch television (they had one, Richard's parents didn't) we could let ourselves in to their cottage and we could help ourselves.

It simultaneously occurred to Richard and me that this would present the requisite privacy needed for further debauchery. So we accepted the offer and the neighbours left the key and departed for their picnic.

We hurried in to the next door cottage and within seconds our pants were round our ankles. Fortunately, this was as far as we got before the door rattled and the neighbours walked back in, having forgotten their corkscrew.

I ran for the back door, stumbling and tripping ridiculously with trousers binding my ankles, and fled, face throbbing with embarrassment. I'm not sure whether these poor people said anything to Richard's parents about this excruciating incident, but nothing was said to us.

On another weekend on which Richard's parents had thoughtfully made themselves scarce, we had spent a very pleasant evening not watching the television and had then retired to bed. It was such a treat to be able to sleep in the same bed as your beloved and fall asleep in his arms. I was thinking of raising the prospect of us getting a place of our own and living together. Imagine, being able to mank about at will without having to worry about who might burst in on you.

But during the night, the arm that had been so affectionately put around my neck, suddenly tightened. He was making a terrible straining noise as though trying to summon the strength to strangle me. The grip grew firmer and I fought to loosen his arm from round my throat, eventually breaking free. Jumping out of bed, I ran down the stairs ready to flee the house if any further murderous attempt was to be made.

Given that I was naked and my clothes were upstairs, I wasn't anxious to run screaming into the street immediately. This couldn't be Richard, loving affectionate Richard who had been so gentle and patient with my attempts to master the art of gay love-making, could it?

All was quiet from upstairs so I cautiously returned. "Richard, are you all right?" I called out, not wanting to pass the point where I couldn't make a retreat into the street if he suddenly came running from the room like something from *Psycho*. There was no response.

90

I went up a bit further and stood by the door. I could hear heavy, even stentorian, breathing coming from inside. I gingerly entered and saw him apparently sleeping soundly. "Are you OK?" I called again, but it was clear that he was deeply unconscious.

I wasn't quite sure what to do, so I went back downstairs and made myself a cup of tea and waited for a while to see whether he would wake up.

It took some time for the panic to subside and for my mind to clear. Then it seemed obvious. He had suffered a fit. Why hadn't I realised that when it was happening and tried to do something to help? For one thing, Richard had given me no indication that he might be epileptic and secondly I had no idea how you were supposed to deal with a fit.

I spent a long night on the sofa downstairs and the following morning I went up to see whether he had recovered. When I shook him, he awoke. He seemed a little confused, but soon came round and it was as if nothing had happened.

I wasn't sure what to say. He had no memory of anything that had occurred in the night. As far as he was concerned, it had passed peacefully with us wrapped in each other's arms.

That day, which was a Saturday, we went for a walk in the park. It was a beautiful day, the sun was brilliant and we sat on the grass, both happy that we had found each other. But I couldn't keep it from him any longer.

"Did you know you are epileptic?" I said.

"What do you mean? I'm not epileptic."

"Well, you certainly had a fit last night. It scared me half to death."

He was shocked as I told him what had happened. This was news to him and he became quiet and thoughtful. He arranged to see the doctor on the following Monday.

At that stage my knowledge of the nature of epilepsy was non-existent. But as soon as I left Richard, I hurried to the library and clued myself up about it. I also looked at first aid books to find out how to deal with a fit if another one occurred.

I had done all the wrong things. I should have turned him on to his side into the recovery position to stop him choking. I should have waited with him until he recovered – if one fit follows another and another and it goes on for more than thirty minutes, it can be fatal, a condition called *status epilepticus*.

If he had been in status I should have sent for an ambulance. Fortunately he wasn't. The other good thing is that he was in bed. Many people who have this kind of fit fall over either backwards or forwards and because they are unconscious when they fall, they don't put out their arms to save themselves and are likely to hit their head either on furniture or the floor.

He was referred to the hospital for a brain scan. This would give some indication as to whether this had been a one-off – as can happen – or whether he had a lesion on his brain that was likely to mean a diagnosis of epilepsy.

~ *21* ~

It was around this time that I saw another job advertised. It was at the newly-built Rotherham District General Hospital on Moorgate, not far from the now abandoned British Wagon building. It was working with people with learning disabilities or, as it was known at that time, mental handicap.

The job description was for an occupational therapy assistant, which would involve handicrafts, art, simple literacy and numeracy and teaching the skills needed to function in the community - things like how to use money, how to use public transport, how to behave in cafés.

I knew nothing about basket-weaving, origami, rug-making or any other handicraft, but having no knowledge of the requirements of a job had never been an impediment before. Nor had I previously worked in any area of mental health – but, there again, never let a little thing like total lack of experience hold you back.

The other thing that attracted me to this job, I am ashamed to say, was the shortness and regularity of the working day. Monday to Friday 9am to 4.30pm. What bliss – no shifts, no weekends and the pay wasn't bad, either.

So off went the application with a rather attenuated version of my CV. If I had included every job I'd had, the CV would have been the size of a substantial pamphlet and would have revealed just how short-lived many of them had been. The only conclusion that could be gained from it was that I was a flibbertigibbet, which would not have been far from the mark.

Against all the odds I was invited to be interviewed.

The unit I would be working in was called Beechcroft and it was separated from the main hospital building by a short corridor. As is usual, I sailed through the interview and was offered the job. I really must have the gift of the gab or something. I can only remember one or two failures at job

93

interviews. This may be, of course, that the jobs I was applying for weren't exactly high-flying. I think in those few instances where I didn't get employed, the interviewer was a bit wiser than most and saw through my silver-tongued flim-flam.

Anyway, Beechcroft was home to about thirty adults with learning disabilities, some of them very profoundly disabled. There were two wards, Oak and Ash, where the "patients", as we called them then (it would be "clients" or "service-users", now if such units existed any more, which they don't), lived and spent their days. There were also day patients bussed in from around the area.

The consultant psychiatrist at Beechcroft was Mary Myers, a woman of vision and ambition, who had made it her life's work to change attitudes to people with learning disabilities. Mary's approach was not to act the know-all "expert" but to encourage colleagues to learn from others, to bring people together and host conversations and exchanges of ideas and knowledge. She promoted the attitude that people with learning disabilities were citizens with the same rights as everyone else, who were best served living in "ordinary houses in ordinary streets", rather than in hospitals and hostels. This seems taken for granted these days, but in the 1970s many still had to be convinced.

I was always grateful to her for this approach and for her willingness to listen. She was also a lot of fun, and I remember when she heard that I had persuaded the staff to put on a pantomime, she insisted on having a part. She played the fairy godmother in Cinderella and dressed up in a tutu.

She died in 2013 after a lifetime of work trying to improve the lives of those with learning disabilities not only in Britain but around the world. She was a wonderful woman and I wish I had got to know her better.

The occupational therapy department was an innovation in the area of mental handicap. The ultimate aim, of course, was to get these people out of institutions altogether and living as part of the community. Although Beechcroft was an improvement on the other places they had lived, it was still an institution and the ideal would be for proper housing. Part of my job was to make those who were capable ready for such a transition.

After six months I had become established in that community and it suited me down to the ground. What had started out as just another job in the long list, and chosen for the wrong reasons (shortish hours and reasonable pay) was turning out to be a bit of a vocation.

~ *22* ~

Richard had had his brain scan and a lesion had been discovered in the frontal lobe. He was epileptic and the specialist had put him on medication that aimed to control it. From time to time I would see a fit developing. He would begin to swallow convulsively and stare, unseeing, in front of him. Sometimes it never developed beyond this "absence" phase and it would pass after a few minutes. But occasionally it would develop into a full-scale, falling down seizure.

At Beechcroft I had received training in dealing with epilepsy. So many of the patients that we were working with had fits. I was astonished to learn how many different types of epilepsy there are and the way they manifest themselves. Now it was part of my daily working life, I was dealing with fits sometimes three or four times a day.

Richard had not yet had a seizure at work – at least, not one that anybody had noticed. But he was dealing with machinery that might prove dangerous if he became unconscious, so he had to tell his bosses.

They were sympathetic and he continued, but was excused duties that involved hedge trimmers or lawn mowers and other such equipment.

My life now took on a completely new aspect. I had a lovely boyfriend, a job that I actually liked and a social life provided by CHE. But I wanted to earn more money and was constantly thinking about how I might start a little business that would generate that. I was making a bit from writing, but I needed more. Maybe, I thought, I could set up some kind of service to the gay community.

Bookselling seemed like a possibility. Books were an important way of reassuring people or giving them the positive information they needed for a balanced life. In London there was Gay's the Word bookshop, in Edinburgh there was Lavender Menace (later West and Wilde) and nothing in between. *Gay News* had a book service, wherein they would post out the latest books of gay interest.

I decided they could do with some competition, so I did a bit of research into bookselling, found myself a book wholesaler I could deal with and away we went with what I decided to call "Essentially Gay".

It started off very small scale, with a few books that Linda in America sent me. Books that you couldn't find in UK bookshops. I set up a stall at the CHE meetings and then at the CHEckers disco and my stock started to expand.

I would trawl through each week's edition of the *Bookseller* looking for new titles that might interest the gay reader. Then I found myself an "alternative" wholesaler in the United States, one that dealt in the titles that didn't interest mainstream bookshops. They were prepared to deliver discounted books to the UK.

Because the American gay movement was way ahead of the British one, *Bookpeople* of Berkeley, California had a catalogue that was packed with books of gay interest. I made an advance deposit of £1000 - all the money I had - and started to order.

More gay-themed books were also beginning to appear in Britain.

Then I decide to produce a mail order catalogue with the hundred or so titles that I now had in stock.

This was a classic small business enterprise operated on the kitchen table, the sort you read about with the entrepreneur eventually expanding it into a multi-million pound empire.

So where would I find my customers? I would need to advertise.

At that time *The Daily Star* had a relatively cheap small ads column that seemed like a good place to start. But the paper was virulently anti-gay. It carried regular articles defaming, insulting and berating gay people in the grossest terms possible. But that didn't mean that gay people didn't read it.

So I tried to book a small ad for *Essentially Gay*. It just read: "Gay and Lesbian readers send for catalogue of our latest titles" and the PO Box address I had set up.

It was clear that the management of the paper were torn over whether to accept this ad – in one sense they wanted to take it because advertising was their life blood and the *Daily Star* did not have the biggest circulation in Fleet Street. At the same time, they were suspicious that maybe it was a cover for pornography. After all, in their terms, what else could gay books be about?

They wanted to examine the catalogue I was going to be sending out, they wanted to know whether anything else would be for sale, they didn't trust me at all. I tried to satisfy all their demands and eventually after a lot of humming and hawing, designed I think to make me go away, they accepted the ad and it appeared on a Thursday.

I had no idea what to expect, but was gratified when a great wad of enquiries arrived the following day and I duly sent out the catalogues.

Orders then started to trickle in. There were customers out there if you could find them. Some of the enquirers did, indeed, think it was a source of pornography, but there were also lots of gay people who were interested in serious reading. The thirst for information, for positive reinforcement and literature that was relevant to them was out there. All you had to do was let them know you were there.

What, one wonders, were such people doing reading a disgusting rag like *The Daily Star*? Whatever their motivation, I realised that this was going to be a worthwhile enterprise after all.

After that, the advertising department at the *Daily Star* began to call me up and try to sell me a whole series of ads at a discount. Naturally the people working in the advertising department were on commission and so the more they could sell me, the better it would be for their wage packet.

Strangely, the place where I had most trouble advertising was in the *Guardian*. It had taken an initial ad, but then refused to take any more. The paper's liberalism didn't seem to stretch as far as gay businesses. *The Sun* took an ad, but the cost was excessive and didn't justify itself.

Essentially Gay started to grow and the number of titles I was selling was expanding. I was using the spare room at Burns Road to store all these books, and getting my mother to take all the orders, packed and addressed, to the Post Office for despatch each day. She would then pay in all the cheques at the bank (yes, I'd managed to open a bank account with 'gay' in the title). This bit she particularly liked. I think she had always wanted to be her own boss and here was a business that was actually generating real money. She could imagine herself to be an entrepreneur, something that she might well have been if her circumstances had been different.

At that stage it was still only pin money, not enough to live on, so the day job was secure.

~ *23* ~

At Beechcroft I had become emboldened by my coming out at home and was determined that I would now come out at work. I told the women I was working with – with whom I had become really close – and they took it calmly. For most of them it was no surprise.

Jane, the boss, was an evangelical Christian and although she did not receive the news with jubilation, she did not make a fuss about it either.

Now I had coming out fever and felt it was necessary to tell everyone I met. I came out relentlessly and I'm sure those I was working with must have been heartily sick of it. They never said it, but I guess they thought "All right – we know –stop going on about it."

The job was proving just what I had been looking for. Now that I knew all the "patients" and was familiar with their personalities, I was able to make real friendships.

For that was what many of them lacked – friends. They had no independent life of their own. If they lived at home with their parents they were often treated as children. Some of the parents still spoke about their son or daughter's visits to Beechcroft as "going to school" – even though their child was maybe thirty or forty years old.

It was part of my job to make them feel like they were adults who had a respectful friend who cared about what they said and listened to their take on the world.

~ *24* ~

At this point I was writing regularly for a monthly gay glossy called *Q International*. It was a pin-up magazine, featuring handsome young men in suggestive, but not very revealing, poses. It also had quite a bit of editorial content. I figured that if Woody Allen could write for *Playboy*, I could write for *Q International*.

My articles were mainly whimsical pieces seeking to amuse, with the occasional story and sometimes a serious piece.

The publishers didn't pay much, but it was something. But best of all, they presented my pieces very well, with specially commissioned drawings mostly by Tony Reeves who was later to become famous on *Gay News* and *Gay Times*. That made me feel like a real writer, a professional with a big by-line and major two-page features that sometimes even got trailed on the front cover. Even though the circulation of this magazine was small, it boosted my ego and confidence no end.

Q International usually ended up on the top shelf of the newsagents, that's if it ever got in to shops at all. What was needed was a more ambitious gay magazine or paper to get off the ground. Several attempts were made to launch titles, and I usually managed to write a little something in all of them before they inevitably went down the plughole. None of them had yet quite got the formula right.

~ 25 ~

One day my father brought home a copy of *The Miner*, a magazine produced by the National Union of Mineworkers. I looked through it as I looked through just about anything that came into the house.

There was an advertisement in the paper for a travel company called Yorkshire Tours based in Huddersfield. They were organising coach trips to exotic places at prices that were almost unbelievably cheap.

As well as trips to Greece, Spain, Italy and France, you could go to Algeria, China, Russia, Mongolia, Poland, Hungary – and all for a song and on a bus.

This all seemed too good to be true, but I sent off for the brochure. When it came back it was a leaflet produced on a typewriter and a Roneo machine.

Yorkshire Tours was being run by an elderly couple, Laurie and Ida Shaw, from a room in their modest house in Huddersfield. Laurie was an enthusiastic communist and wanted to show the world how marvellous living under communism was. He and Ida had not yet reached the same conclusion as the rest of the world that the Soviet system was repressive and wicked. They were hanging on to the Utopian version which had been shown repeatedly to be untrue. It was another case of people seeing only what they want to see and screening out inconvenient facts to sustain their beliefs. Very much like any other form of religion, really.

So, Laurie and his wife had dedicated their lives to organising the most ambitious trips to places where communism was established, using only a local coach firm and the most rudimentary knowledge of visas, languages, currencies – rules and regulations of any kind.

Nothing seemed to intimidate the pair of them, nothing seemed too ambitious, no destination too exotic.

I showed this leaflet to Richard, who was fascinated by the prospect of going to Poland. Especially as it was only going to cost us £69 for a week. So we booked our places and waited for the coach by the M1 junction at Attercliffe.

The coach eventually arrived from Huddersfield and we boarded. Laurie was to be our courier and sat resplendent in the front seat with a mop of glowing white hair. To entertain us on the way, he gave a lecture over the loudspeaker about the value of canals and how they should be revived for commercial purposes.

All the way to Dover we were stopping to pick people up from different parts of the country. Every time the coach stopped, it had to be persuaded back into life by Laurie pulling up a trapdoor and hitting something with a hammer. It seemed interminable. But that was only the start.

Refreshment stops saw a primus stove and ancient kettle produced from the luggage compartment. Tea was brewed for everyone on the bus, thus avoiding the over-priced drinks in the motorway services. A capitalist scam, said Laurie and Ida, and one wouldn't disagree with them looking at the prices.

When we eventually arrived at our destination, Zakopane in the Tatra Mountains, we had been allocated a room in a small chalet type of hotel. One of the excursions was a trip to the Auschwitz concentration camp, which in those days was not the tourist attraction that it has become now. Then it was a very unkempt and dour museum, looking very much as though it had been only recently abandoned. Visiting it was, as everyone who has been there will tell you, a sobering experience.

The ghastly testimony of the hundreds of suitcases, each individually labelled with the name of its former owner, the piles of hair shaven from the heads of women who would soon be dead, the mountain of shoes stolen from victims, was numbing.

But I found only one mention of the homosexuals that had suffered in this place, along with the Jews and gypsies and disabled. It was on a plaque illustrating the various symbols that were sewn on to the uniforms to identify which category each prisoner belonged to. Pink Triangle was the symbol for gay people. It was only on this small plaque, and nowhere else, that the presence of homosexuals in this carnage was acknowledged.

In one corridor, the walls were covered in photographs of the victims. The Nazis had been thorough in documenting their prey. These photographs were almost impossible to look at, with the faces – one after another, young and old, male and female – staring blankly at the camera. Each individual neatly categorised and recorded prior to extermination.

I was particularly disturbed by the young men in those pictures, the ones who were around my age, staring at us dead-eyed and resigned. But for an accident of place and time it might have been *my* image on that wall. My Pink Triangle would maybe mark me out but not for a quick death in the gas chamber but for being worked to death in a factory or quarry.

Later I was to read a book by Rudolf Hoess, who had been the commandant of Auschwitz, in which he remembered his time running that notorious hell-hole. He wrote it while awaiting trial at Nuremberg and he touched briefly upon the lives of homosexuals in the death camps:

"They (homosexuals) were employed in the claypit of a large brickworks. It was hard work and each of them had to complete a definite amount of work per day. They were exposed to all kinds of weather, since a stipulated number of truckloads of clay had to be filled each day. For this reason they were forced to work in all weathers, summer and winter.... Neither the hardest work nor the strictest supervision was of any help in these cases. Whenever they found an opportunity they would fall into each other's arms."

Homosexuals were classed as "grade three" prisoners which meant they received the harshest punishments, the least food, hardest work and most degrading treatment and were often used as guinea-pigs in experiments which one would have thought the human mind incapable of creating.

But I was glad to see that, quite frequently, they fought back. They occasionally escaped and "refused to give up their vice". Hoess wrote:

"Should one lose his 'friend' through sickness or death, then the end could be at once foreseen. Many would commit suicide. To such natures, in such circumstances, the 'friend' meant everything. There were many instances of the 'friends' committing suicide together."

To the Nazis this was all a matter of light relief. But it isn't difficult to image the poignancy and grief that must have afflicted those gay men who, in such inhuman conditions, lost their lovers – probably the only thing that kept them sane in this nightmare world.

We can see the hypocrisy that surrounded the whole subject. The idea that homosexuals are a threat to society is widespread in many countries throughout the world even now. Gays are still actively persecuted in Africa, Russia, Asia and throughout the Muslim world. And the Catholic Church in Poland is relentless in opposing any progress for gay rights.

The Nazis are estimated to have murdered 500,000 gay people over the years of their dictatorship.

Of course, under the Soviet regime that occupied Poland after the defeat of the Nazis, gays fared little better. The gulags of Russia were still packed with them (us).

Laurie and Ida have now taken that great charabanc tour into eternity, hopefully not, for their sakes, to some post-mortem Soviet Union.

It can't be denied though that their eccentric ideas resulted in some great holidays for a huge number of people, and maybe a few friendships were made across borders and ideologies, which was all that the Shaws wanted.

~ *26* ~

Marlene was coming to London again, this time to do a season at the Wimbledon Theatre.

I decided that we would get a trip together for members of the CHE group. It didn't take long to sign up the full complement, we booked a hotel and minibus and prepared for departure.

A few days before we left for London, I heard Marlene being interviewed on the Pete Murray show on Radio 2. So I suddenly got into my head that if I wrote to her and asked nicely, she might meet the group. I quickly dashed off a letter and sent it to the theatre.

Unusually there were several women on this trip. CHE had always struggled to get women interested in joining the group. Most gay groups at the time were faced with this dilemma, how to include lesbians without driving the men away and vice versa.

Some of the male members of the group didn't want women to be part of it, anyway. There was a strong misogynistic streak among some gay men. They reasoned, I suppose, that the presence of women would somehow dilute their choice of men. But we never satisfactorily solved the problem of how a group like ours could appeal to both sexes. Women usually came to one meeting and were never seen again.

However, on the trip to London to see Marlene we had found some women who really wanted to be part of it. I hadn't realised at this point that Marlene was no stranger herself to lesbianism. It was only later that her affairs with other women came to be generally known about. But obviously for the women on our excursion, the gaydar was sending out signals loud and clear.

One of the women on the trip, Brenda, was married, but after she had realised she was a lesbian and started living as such, she wanted a divorce and to get her husband out of the house they shared. He didn't have anywhere else to go, and given that the house was half his, she couldn't just kick him out. So they decided to divide the place between them. But rather than simply allocating rooms, or saying "I'll have the top floor, you can have the bottom" they built a dividing wall right through the centre of the house. He would occupy one side and she the other.

How long that arrangement lasted, I can't say.

Marlene delivered the same show as I had seen before, every word every gesture identical. Her voice sounded older, her waist was a bit thicker and the orchestra a bit frayed around the edges, but there was still magic, still amazing stage presence, still the unrestrained cheering and clapping at the end, the ceaseless curtain calls, the low bows from the waist.

But there had been no response to my letter. I had entertained fantasies of being invited to her dressing room where we would be served champagne and she would tell us how much she supported the gay cause. Seems it was not to be.

Then, after her final bows and curtain calls she came on to the stage with a hand microphone and said: "Thank you for coming. Sleep well. I know it isn't always so easy to wake up feeling very gay in the morning." There was another burst of wild applause – it was clear we were not the only gay fans in the audience. You can see this moment from some film snatched in the auditorium on Youtube.

Then she wrapped the red velvet curtains around herself and was gone. Was that a signal meant for us? Had she seen my letter? Or was it just a routine message to the gay people who she knew were her most loyal fans?

We rushed round to the stage door to once more witness the tiny goddess disappear into her car and then into the night. As before, there was this shock of seeing the fantasy that strode the stage with such consummate authority turn into this small, fragile and very old lady. It was an object lesson in what extraordinary effects can be achieved by the artful deployment of lights and makeup in the theatre.

I saw Marlene again on several occasions, in Birmingham, Brighton and at the Queen's Theatre in London. There was never any variation in her programme, but I never tired of witnessing the strange alchemy. Her relationship with her audience was a thing of wonder to me. However big the crowd and however many flat notes she sang, she seemed able to control us with a kind of magical power. The wild applause and calls for more seemed pre-ordained. Even if the show had been total rubbish, the extended clapping at the end would still have happened.

Poor old Richard would be dragged around the country with me and made to sit through these shows, even though he had no interest in them whatsoever. While I was mesmerised, he was sitting there thinking about where we were going to be eating afterwards. That's what I call loyalty beyond the call of duty.

~ 27 ~

In 1975, a film of Quentin Crisp's autobiography *The Naked Civil Servant* was broadcast on ITV. It was a big event for gay people because it was one of the very few TV programmes up until then that had addressed the issue of homosexuality head-on. And better still, it was an entertainment film rather than the usual documentary shot in silhouette detailing the supposed tragedy of gay life. Quentin Crisp unapologetically sashayed through his own life and it would never have occurred to him to appear anonymously bemoaning his lot.

He was too busy entertaining sailors and, like me, searching for the Big Dark Man.

Richard and I were all agog that evening, holding on to each other, astonished that this had made it on to our screens. There had been many controversies in the past and many TV and radio programmes banned because they dealt with gay issues, but now something as blatant as this would be shown in prime time.

I was dying to know what other people thought of it – had it been too shocking, would it create a backlash?

The Independent Broadcasting Authority did a survey that showed only 18 per cent of the sample 475 viewers switched off because of the content. And 85 per cent said the production was 'not shocking'. Few felt that Quentin Crisp's story 'encouraged' homosexuality.

Not only was the programme widely appreciated by viewers, it was critically acclaimed and John Hurt, the actor who played Quentin Crisp won just about every award going. Such was its success that it was repeated on ITV soon afterwards and several times more during the coming years.

We were going places.

~ *28* ~

Gay News was now well-established and loved among its readers, but proved a constant source of irritation to those who saw it as the devil's work. I had submitted a few book reviews to the paper and these had been published. As ever, it was gratifying to see one's work in print with a by-line, even if it was all rather modest. I was also advertising Essentially Gay, even though I was competing with *Gay News'* own mail order service.

The paper had raised my consciousness about the amount of hostility there still was towards the concept of gay rights. I was coming more and more to the conclusion that there had to be resistance.

As usual I was late to the party. In other parts of the country gay campaigning had been going on in different forms for decades.

Then in 1976, Mary Whitehouse launched her notorious private prosecution for blasphemy against *Gay News*. It had published a poem by James Kirkup called *The Love that Dares to Speak its Name*.

It was a poem that involved a Roman soldier having sex with Christ's dead body as he is taken from the cross. I doubt that Mrs Whitehouse was a regular reader of *Gay News*, so how she came to be outraged by something it had published is a mystery. Or it is until you remember that, like all moralistic busybodies throughout time, Mrs Whitehouse felt it incumbent to be outraged on our behalf. It is her Christian duty to ban the unsavoury in order to protect us all. We didn't need to be consulted because she had God on her side and so she obviously knew what was best for us.

The case became something of a *cause celebre*. There were protest marches in London (to which the Rotherham CHE organised the traditional mini bus excursion) and questions in parliament.

There was also a fighting fund, established to help the paper oppose Mrs Whitehouse. I wondered what I could do to make my contribution to this and eventually decided that I would donate my signed photograph of Marlene Dietrich for auction. Surely that would raise several hundred pounds.

There are not many causes that would prompt me to let go of any of my fast-accumulating Marlene memorabilia, but I felt this was vital. It was a direct attack on our community, an attempt to destroy its most effective means of communication. Mrs Whitehouse wanted *Gay News* stamped into the ground.

So I put Marlene's photo up for sale and it brought £50. I was reluctant to let it go for such a disappointing amount. It was priceless to me – the divine Dietrich had even written my name on it. But a promise is a promise and the photo went.

I had seen the edition of *Gay News* that had the poem in it, and it had not struck me as anything special, and I'd passed it by without much consideration. In fact, I had thought it rather weird, as though the poet had been on some mind-altering substance when he wrote it.

Now it was notorious and the subject of a court case that would become a classic of British law.

The trial and its aftermath have been well-documented, a travesty of justice brought about by a blatantly biased judge. He was as frighteningly infected with mad-cap religion as Mrs Whitehouse herself.

Because liberal lawyers like John Mortimer and Geoffrey Robertson had seen fit to act pro bono, and the fighting fund had done very well, the paper survived. But it never really recovered. Soon it would be riven with internal arguments that would eventually cause its closure.

But even that would have a silver lining as far as I was concerned, but more of that later.

~ 29 ~

I thought it was time that Rotherham CHE had a big social event of its own, so I made an application to the Town Hall catering department to hire the Assembly Rooms for what was to be the town's very first gay disco. I didn't think it would be a problem. Certainly the initial booking had been accepted by the clerk at the catering department. She balked a little when I said it was to be organised by the CHE group.

"What is CHE?" she asked.

When I told her there was a slight pause, and she said: "Hold the line, please."

A few moments later she returned and said: "Yes, that's all right. We'll pencil in your booking and as soon as you've signed the contract and paid the deposit, we'll confirm."

A couple of days later a rather curt letter arrived from the catering department, signed by the deputy director. "We are unable to accept your booking at the present time," it said mysteriously.

I rushed to the phone and dialled the Town Hall, asking for the director of the catering department. I would have no truck with his deputy, I wanted to speak to Mr Big. A Mr Roland Balmer came on the line. "Why can't you accept the booking at the present time?" I demanded.

"I don't have to give a reason," he responded.

"Yes, but there must be a reason," I said.

"I don't have to justify this to you or to anybody," said he, mighty angry, and slammed the phone down.

I smelled a rat. I detected homophobia. There was more to Mr Balmer's anger than a mere double-booking. I decided immediately that this was a case of discrimination and that we had a genuine grievance. We had to proceed accordingly. It was one thing being turned down by churches, quite another to be turned down by the council, which was supposed to be serving

112

everyone in the community, and to whom most of us were paying rates.

The first thing I did was write to the Mayor of Rotherham, telling him that our booking had been cancelled and how rudely we had been treated. I spelled out the implications for gay people in the town. The chairman of the catering committee, who I discovered was one Sid Bennett, also got a letter of complaint and copies of both letters were released to the local media (*Rotherham Advertiser, Sheffield Star*, BBC Radio Sheffield and Radio Hallam, the commercial station).

To my astonishment the story made big news. All the local papers featured it and I was invited to do interviews for both radio stations. I felt that the coverage was sympathetic. The story was treated seriously, something else I didn't expect.

The council may have thought it didn't have to explain its actions to me, but the press can be pretty nasty if they aren't told the reasons why.

I was surprised by the amount of feeling the press coverage had stirred up. *The Advertiser*'s correspondence column commenced a string of letters about CHE and homosexuality that went on literally for years.

A Methodist minister, the Rev Geoff Reid and his wife Merriel, came out in support of us. "We can see no medical or ethical reason why homosexuals should not be treated in exactly the same way as everyone else."

But another local clergyman took the opposite stand and congratulated the council: "After all, they wouldn't encourage smallpox sufferers to hold a disco in the Town Hall and these people are equally diseased."

The application was now put before the council's Labour Group. It seemed that the ban had been unilaterally imposed by Councillor Sid Bennett, the catering chairman. The Labour Party held something like nine-tenths of the seats in the council, so it was obvious that whatever the Labour group decided would become policy.

At the full council meeting later that month (September 1976) the decision to refuse the booking was confirmed by the full council. CHE would not be permitted to use public rooms in Rotherham.

At the council meeting, an independent councillor, Roy Hunt, of the Ratepayers Association, challenged the council leader on the matter. Why was CHE being treated in this way?

Councillor Jack Layden explained that the council had a duty to "protect staff" who would be required to work at CHE functions and, therefore, the application had been rejected. The staff had made clear to him that they didn't want to work at an event for homosexuals.

The CHE group got together in defiant mood, deciding that "something must be done". The council must not be allowed to turn us into second-class citizens without a challenge. The members were nervous about taking militant action – myself in particular as I knew I was going to be leading from the front.

We discussed what our next move might be. I decided to contact the National Council for Civil Liberties (now just Liberty) and Nettie Pollard, the gay rights officer responded by return. I asked if NCCL would commit to helping us and immediately a press release was issued from their office, pledging full backing to Rotherham CHE and demanding that the ban be rescinded. Not only that, but Nettie Pollard demanded that the council publicly apologise to CHE "for the insulting way the application has been treated."

Now that's what I call aiming high.

The NCCL intervention helped to keep the story fresh in people's minds and so did the continuing correspondence in *The Advertiser*. Now the National Front was involved, with a person describing herself as "a mere woman" wrote to swear that she had seen me outside the local technical college "touting the willing flesh".

The Bible-thumpers were out in force and Sodom and Gomorrah made another come-back. Hellfire and brimstone were summoned to scorch us for our audacity.

Undaunted we made another application on the strength of the support from NCCL and the fact that the local Liberal Association had joined the battle, and written to the council asking them to change their policy.

Pressure on the Council was increasing and we thought it would take this opportunity to deflect further bad publicity. After all, there was little for them to lose and everything to gain from doing a U-turn.

The application was looked at by the Labour Group again. This time they were all sent a letter from CHE pointing out how contradictory their stand was to the principles of socialism. All to no avail – they "re-affirmed" their policy and nothing changed.

~ 30 ~

Given that my home phone number was publicly listed as the contact for Rotherham CHE and because the group had attained a bit of a reputation and a higher profile, I was getting an increasing number of enquiries from people who didn't want to become members, but who had problems that they (and I) imagined I could help with. My number was becoming a sort of Samaritans/marriage guidance council/youth advisory service all rolled into one.

Of course, I was not equipped to do counselling or social work, but all the same I always felt that I had to take some responsibility for the people who came to us. Saying 'no' had not yet become one of my skills.

So, when the letter from HM Prison Wakefield arrived, and a gentleman by the name of Benjamin asked if we could visit him, I felt a bit out of my depth. I wanted to say no, please apply elsewhere, but his letter was so full of pleas for a bit of gay company – just someone who understood what he was talking about – that I felt duty bound to go.

So, defying my doubts and dragging Richard along for support, we went to Wakefield one Sunday afternoon, armed with our visiting order, and met Benjamin.

Wakefield is a maximum security prison and many of the IRA terrorists were imprisoned there. We presented the visiting order at the enormous and imposing gate and then had to pass through a security check in which unsmiling warders patted us down and asked a barrage of questions about what we were carrying. There were notices posted everywhere about the dire penalties for smuggling contraband into prison.

Even knowing that in an hour I would be going out of this place again didn't lessen the sense of dread and the irrational feeling of imminent incarceration and loss of liberty. I was being overcome by a sense of claustrophobia.

Benjamin had not mentioned in his letters why he was in prison, and I was wondering how we could broach the topic sensitively, or whether it was appropriate even to ask.

He was a middle-aged bloke, small of stature and looking very intense and nervous. He had black curly hair and sallow skin – understandable with such a limited exposure to daylight.

After the formalities and introductions, I had no idea what to say. This man was a total stranger who said he was gay and wanted to make some kind of life for himself in the gay world when he came out of prison. Beyond that he was a mystery.

He told us that he had been a tailor in the outside world, had lived in London and Leicester and all over the place. The question that was hanging between us like a curtain was always on the verge of being blurted out. What was he in for?

Naturally Richard and I had discussed it on the train over. "It could be murder," he said, although voicing this thought was irrelevant - it was already at the very front of my mind, and had been since the letter arrived.

But Benjamin was such a slight, unassuming man, he didn't look like a cold-blooded murderer. But then, what do murderers look like? Perhaps it had been a crime of passion, or maybe it wasn't murder at all, perhaps something else equally heinous.

"Yes," said Richard, "but you don't get locked up in a maximum security prison for not paying a parking fine."

We spent the first half hour asking him about life in the prison – was it tolerable? Did he have problems on account of his gayness? Naturally there was a lot of mythology about life in prison for gay men – or any men that weren't able to fend off the rapacious advances of the thugs they had to share space with. Was he victimised because of his sexuality?

The answer to that was no – because no-one in the place knew he was gay. He hadn't come out to anybody. He said he had no family and therefore no-one to visit him and he seemed pathetically grateful that we had made the effort to turn out. This was the first visit he had had from anybody for several years.

117

The allotted hour (and it seemed like several) was almost up and still the question had not been asked. And he was offering up no clues as to what he was doing in this place.

As time was called, Benjamin said: "Will you come again? I'd really appreciate it. It gets very lonely in here when you know there is no-one on the outside to turn to."

I mumbled that, yes, we'd come again, but at the same time feeling like a sprinter on the blocks waiting for the starting gun. I couldn't get out of this horrible, drab but overly-lit Victorian place fast enough. I tried not to show the relief when it was all over, but I could almost hear Richard letting out a long sigh at the first call of "time's up, please".

People at other tables were trying to extend their visit, resisting the warder's order to wrap it up. There were tears as wives and children had to say goodbye again to husbands and boyfriends, but for me, getting back into the street in Wakefield felt like a real liberation.

The sky looked a bit bluer, the air smelled a bit fresher and I almost skipped along the pavement towards the railways station, anxious to be as far away from this dreadful place as possible, as soon as possible.

~ *31* ~

October 1976: Another flurry of letters to the council about our booking for the Assembly Rooms brought no response. Then, out of the blue, a member of the Rotherham Constituency Labour Party telephoned and said that he was considering tabling a motion at the General Management Committee meeting condemning the Council's decision. Could I give him all the details?

There was an element of risk in this. If the motion failed, the council would be able to crow and it would set us back years. We decided to take the risk because we couldn't think of an alternative.

The motion was put down and the debate took place at the local Labour Club. Not being a member, I wasn't allowed to attend and so had to await a telephone call from the man who tabled the motion. He rang about nine in the evening. The motion had been carried overwhelmingly, The Party had condemned its own council for its "ill-considered and discriminatory" action.

We wrote swiftly to the council – surely this must cause a change of heart? Back came a letter from Mr Balmer, the catering director. As far as he was concerned the council minute remained unaltered and, therefore, until such time as it was changed, our booking was unacceptable. What the Labour Party thinks is of no consequence, he said.

The following week the Rotherham Trades Union Council passed a similar motion of censure on the council.

I wrote to the town's MP, Stan Crowther, asking for support. He seemed reluctant to be involved, but ventured to say that the council were taking the wrong course. His colleague, Peter Hardy, MP for the Rother Valley constituency, wasn't so undecided. He told us without any frills that he wasn't interested in the matter and had no intention of intervening. He said he didn't believe that many of his constituents were gay. He thought "the problem lies mainly in London".

Mr Hardy was very much like the councillors, old Labour, socially conservative and very old-fashioned. It would be many years before this old guard could be persuaded to change its approach.

~ *32* ~

I had read a review of Quentin Crisp's one-man show which he had presented at the Edinburgh Festival. After the fantastic success of the *Naked Civil Servant* on TV, he had put together this entertainment, in which he told a few reminiscences and anecdotes and then answered questions from the audience. Understandably, he wanted to cash in on the interest in him like everyone else was doing.

I decided to ask if he would bring the show to Rotherham. I knew he wasn't interested in gay rights, in fact he was quite hostile to the concept, but he was becoming increasingly famous and might bring a bit more interest to the CHE group.

So I wrote and asked him if he would come. There was no problem tracking him down: he insisted on having his name, address and phone number in the public directory. He didn't discourage anyone from contacting him. He lived in London, so it was a long shot that he would be prepared to travel all the way to Rotherham for a £50 fee.

But he wrote back a few days later, in his flowery, over the top style, saying that he would be delighted to come, and I should let him know full particulars.

My plan had been to try to hire the council's newly-opened Arts Centre, which was governed by the Library and Arts Committee. I put in an application fully expecting to get another brush off, but to my astonishment there was no resistance. They had considered the show to be of artistic merit and the Arts Centre was available on 17 December 1976.

So it was booked, but presenting this show would make a big hole in the group's funds, so in order to keep costs down I wrote back to Mr Crisp and gave him the details and cheekily asked if he would mind travelling up to Rotherham by National Coach, the cheapest method I could find. He didn't bat an eyelid at this. Now we had to find somewhere for him to stay.

A member of the Sheffield CHE group was particularly excited about Mr Crisp's visit. Alfie was a transvestite with an alter ego called Shirley.

In Alfie's mind, Shirley was a glamorous sex-pot. Unfortunately, the cheap wig and British Home Stores frocks that transformed Alfie into Shirley didn't quite do the trick. This was not helped by the fact that Alfie was a portly, middle-aged railway guard with rather large, hairy arms and a voice that wouldn't disgrace Paul Robeson.

But he was a proud transvestite and was actually campaigning with the railway authorities for the right to go to work in a skirt. I'm not sure whether he ever attained that ambition, but he was certainly tenacious about it. I worried what sort of reception he would get from the uncomprehending public, but he was utterly unselfconscious once dragged up.

I liked Alfie a lot, and enjoyed the parties he threw at his house with his partner, Johnny. These parties always gave Shirley the opportunity to emerge and sparkle in sympathetic company. After the initial shock of encountering the rather large and butch woman in the flowered alter neck and sling backs, you soon got used to it.

Anyway, Alfie and Johnny wanted to help out, so I asked if Mr Crisp could stay over with them in their spare room after the show. They were delighted. Alfie was fascinated with Crisp's cross-over sexuality, the wearing of make-up, painted fingernails and flamboyant clothes, the unabashed public flaunting of these feminine traits.

I reminded Alfie that Mr Crisp had suffered at the hands of thugs and homophobes in his time. (It seemed appropriate always to call him Mr Crisp, not Quentin. He insisted on addressing everyone else as Mr this or Mrs that or Miss the other. Actually Quentin's real name was Denis Pratt).

I had arranged to meet Mr Crisp at Pond Street bus station where the coach from London would arrive. I had no problems spotting him on the platform and neither did anyone else. The mascara may have been a give-away or the blue rinsed hair or the artfully fluttering chiffon scarf. He was wearing a pin striped suit, sandals and a fedora.

122

We took a taxi to Alfie's place. Alfie was at work, sending the trains on their way, but Johnny was at home and made us tea.

It was a good five hours before the show, which was going to be easy to stage – Mr Crisp just wanted a chair from which to hold forth. So I sat with our star in Alfie's living room and attempted to chat. It was all a bit forced. I was star struck and desperately trying to think of things I might talk to him about.

But it was like talking to a robot. You asked a question and he would respond in a manner that suggested that he had pre-prepared and heavily rehearsed the answer. Every sentence he uttered was beautifully formed, exquisitely polished and not an 'um' or 'er' anywhere to be heard.

Whether asking about the journey up from London or how long the show would last, the response came in the same nasal monotone, complete with commas and full stops.

Johnny was even more over-awed than I was at having a genuine celebrity in the front room, and served the tea as though we were at the Ritz. Then he sat down and stared unwaveringly at Quentin as I tried to make this nonsensical conversation.

Tony was going to drive us over to the Arts Centre in Rotherham and there our little band of volunteers would run the show. Richard in the Box Office, Annie as usherette and Michael on refreshments.

I had wanted to present the show like a major West End production, with introductory music and lights fading up and down, all kinds of razzamatazz, but Mr Crisp wanted to keep it simple. He wanted to just sit on a chair on the stage as the audience arrived and then, when the allotted time came, start to speak.

We compromised, in that he would enter from the wings to applause after I had introduced him.

He gave his usual hour-long introductory spiel, again rehearsed to the point where it sounded as though it was being delivered by an I-speak-your-weight machine. He got the laughs where he wanted them and then asked the audience for questions.

This is where I feared we might fall down – would a Rotherham audience have questions for Quentin Crisp? I had planted the first one to ensure that when the request came there wasn't an embarrassing silence.

As it turned out, there were plenty of questions and he answered them with the same exactitude of language, always having something appropriate to say and not thrown off course by anything.

One thing I didn't ask, and should have done, was why he ever agreed to come to Rotherham in the first place. I think perhaps he wanted to practice his show before he went big-time with it, touring the country and eventually moving to New York, where he used the same material endlessly and to great acclaim.

Alfie got a few moments with him the next morning before Mr Crisp left for the bus station in order to take his coach back to the metropolis.

Quentin Crisp was an extraordinary person, quite unlike anyone else I'd come across. He seemed a little bit detached from the human race, although he was polite, charming and uncomplaining.

He said that he wanted whatever we wanted and always did as he was told. How he had come to this point I don't know. I'd read his autobiography and admired his style and courage, but you can imagine that nobody ever really got very close to Quentin Crisp.

~ 33 ~

At Beechcroft the staff team had become like a second family. Although they were all women, I felt very much at home in their company. This was good for the "patients" too, because they picked up the friendly atmosphere and enjoyed it.

A particular friend among the team was April. We had hit it off from the start. She was in her late thirties and had two teenage children, having married very young. Now, as her children were looking to strike out on their own, she had become disillusioned with her life with Kevin, her husband.

She began to tell me about how she had grown weary of Kevin's macho nature, his vulgarity and lack of ambition. She didn't hate him, but she didn't love him anymore, either.

On a girls' night out, she had met another man, Mark. He was promising to provide her with all the things that Kevin couldn't. One day he came in to Beechcroft to pick her up from work to take her out on a date.

I was stunned by how handsome he was, how well-dressed and charming. Good grief, April, I said, you've won the first prize there. Mark was truly swoon-worthy, and I was trying not to stare. He would have qualified as my Big, Dark Man if only his pesky heterosexuality hadn't got in the way.

But she felt terribly guilty about betraying Kevin. Even though she was fed up to the back teeth with him, she still felt a loyalty after all those years together. Nevertheless, she had been given a new sparkle by this affair. Not that it didn't occasionally get her into tricky situations.

One morning she walked into work wearing Mark's overcoat, the one he had been wearing when he collected her. It came right down to her ankles. She was carrying a plastic bag stuffed with clothes.

"What's happened?" I asked.

She told me that she and Mark had driven out into the countryside to find a bit of privacy, so that they could enjoy hanky-panky away from prying eyes. They had parked in a field miles from anywhere and after all passion was spent, they realised that the car had sunk into the mud and no urging of the engine could persuade it to move. April would have to get out and push.

Of course, she was all dolled up in her best clothes, but out she got and immediately fell over into the mud. Dragging herself out of it, she went to the back of the car and pushed as Mark tried to persuade the car to free itself. It did - suddenly lurching forward, sending up another shower of mud all over April, who promptly fell again face forward into the mire.

Her clothes were absolutely caked in murk, her shoes were ruined and her hair was now a tangle of earth-matted rats' tails. Her face was dirt-spattered and she put me in mind of my father after he'd done a shift down the pit.

Naturally she couldn't go home in that state, so she had called Kevin and made some excuse about staying over with her girl friend who was too sozzled after their night out to get home on her own.

I laughed so much at this tale which sounded just like the sort of thing that would happen to me that I was merry for the rest of the day.

Although it had been a funny incident, it actually triggered for April another bout of guilt about betraying her husband. She kept asking me "What shall I do? Mark is prepared to take me in if I leave Kevin, but I just can't bring myself to do it."

I didn't have an answer for her. I would face the same dilemma myself before long.

~ *34* ~

November 1976: The CHE group was angry and frustrated. What could we do now to harass the council into letting us use the Assembly Rooms? It looked like some kind of more militant action was necessary.

Someone at the committee meeting suggested that we book the Rooms in the name of an individual member who has no apparent connection with CHE, and then invite as many gay people as possible to come along.

We considered the myriad things that could go wrong with such a plan. With so many people involved could we really keep it secret until the day? What would happen if the council got wind of our scheme – would they lock us out, send for the police or something even more unpleasant?

After a lot of discussion, with many doubts and a lot of fears expressed, we decided that we must go ahead regardless. It took three weeks to organise the event, which was scheduled for 20 November and was ostensibly a birthday party for one of our members, Richard Edley.

As the date approached, the tension mounted. The day before the event, with about 250 people in the know, I became convinced that the council must be aware of what was going on. Perhaps, I remember thinking, they've got secret plans of their own for some kind of humiliating counter-offensive.

Then a reporter from the *Sheffield Morning Telegraph* rang. Was it true that we were going to hijack the Assembly Rooms for a gay disco?

I asked how he had found out about it, which, of course, he wouldn't tell, and implored him not to publish anything until after the event. He agreed to keep it quiet, but I feared he might think that by telling the council he'd get a better story. In the end, he kept his word.

On the evening of the 20th, I was somewhat reassured to arrive at the Assembly Rooms to find the disco set up and the

127

bar staff preparing for a busy evening. These women were the very people who were supposed to have objected to serving us. These were the very staff that the council were using as justification for their continued ban. If it was true, and if they realised what was going on, would they down tools and cover the pumps, leaving me to apologise to the punters, some of whom had come a considerable distance to be present?

The first guests sauntered in and the disco got off to an uneventful start.

I was tense throughout the evening, convinced that at any moment the doors would burst open and the police would arrive to arrest us all. I had visions of us being carted off in a fleet of black marias, in the manner of a prohibition-times raid on a speakeasy.

In fact, it was all passing off smoothly, so I took the opportunity to talk to the staff. It hadn't taken them long to realise it was a gay event – the men dancing cheek to cheek and the lesbians snogging in the corner might have given them a clue. I bought the manageress a drink and asked why she and her staff had objected to serving homosexuals.

"Objected?" she said. "We've never been asked! Look, love, I'm here to do a job and I'll do it. I'll serve anybody so long as they aren't violent or offensive." And that, she said, went for the rest of the staff.

I was a bit taken aback by this but it didn't take long to register: Yes! We'd caught Councillor Jack Layden out in a lie. He said the staff had objected to working at a gay event, but now we know they'd never been asked.

The rest of the evening went without an incident and everyone went home happy and greatly relieved. I slept soundly for the first time in weeks.

On Monday morning I bought the *Morning Telegraph* and there, on the front page, was: "Gays lead council a lively dance." It quoted Councillor Sid Bennett of the catering committee as reacting "bitterly". He fumed: "I think it's a despicable thing to do. We take private bookings but the council minute is that we don't allow these people to use the rooms as an organisation. You can't expect us to be a gestapo and check every booking. Councillors searched their minds and made their mind up. It doesn't matter why they banned it. Let them accuse me of what they like, but I would personally object to them using the rooms because of the experiences I had around the world as an ex-serviceman seeing what happens to young people."

The story spread. *The Advertiser*'s version of it quoted Sid Bennett's deputy, Councillor George Gleadhall, who thought the incident was "absolutely deplorable". He said: "If they want to be recognised as a responsible group then they have got to act responsibly... I shall be asking for the booking procedure to be looked into to see if we can stop this happening again."

The story was also picked up nationally by the *Sunday Mirror*, whose headline was "The Cheeky Gays Hijack a Dance". Predictably they made it sound sleazy or ludicrous. "What a strange dance it turned out to be," the story began, "with men dancing cheek to cheek at the town hall."

It quoted council leader Jack Layden as saying: "This was deplorable. There is no doubt we were conned. We shall take steps to ensure it doesn't happen again. These people did have some sympathy among council members but I am afraid that will have diminished due to their action."

Radio Hallam, the local commercial station serving Sheffield and Rotherham thought the whole thing a hoot. I gave an interview to Roger Brooks, the reporter who covered Rotherham news for the station. He had covered the whole saga from the beginning. It was a gift to him – a bit of drama and novelty in what was generally mundane reporting. We counted him as a friend and sympathiser.

Roger Moffatt, one of the presenters on Radio Hallam, asked Roger Brooks on air whether he was worried about being mistaken for "one of them". Quick as a flash Roger Brooks retorted "No, all I'm worried about is being mistaken for *you*."

Pressure on the council started all over again.

Gaycon, the Conservative gay group, wrote to the five Tory councillors in Rotherham. "I appreciate that as a minority party in a socialist area, the influence of the Conservative group is limited: this does not mean you cannot uphold the good name of the Conservative Party in matters of individual liberty. I would ask you to invite the Conservative group to support the application by CHE", wrote the-then treasurer of Gaycon, Christian Elliot.

He never got a reply. The Tories never spoke a word on the subject.

Using the fact that we were not convinced that the council had, in fact, asked the staff their opinions, we made another application for the use of the Assembly Rooms. This time things were slightly different.

The Labour Group was in foment. Many of the councillors had now changed their minds and wanted the ban lifted. Although the meeting was in private, I was told later that some of the members had wanted a free vote on the issue but this had been refused. In the end it was the chairman's casting vote that decided that the council's policy would remain unchanged.

~ *35* ~

A couple of weeks after the visit to Wakefield Prison, my heart sank to see another letter with the familiar HMP logo from Benjamin. And inside was another visiting order. His letter contained pathetic pleas for us to go over to the jail again. It would mean so much to him, he was so isolated etc. etc.

Reluctantly I agreed, and once more Richard was hauled in as my very necessary support. This time I was determined to find out who this man really was and what he had done that would land him in a place like Wakefield, with its gruesome collection of serial killers and terrorists.

We arrived as before, went through the same intimidating security procedures and then into the waiting area. There we were seated with a dispiriting array of misery. Although there were toddlers happily playing with toys, their mothers were ranged from soberly dressed middle-aged women to vulgar, loud-mouthed girls with extremely short skirts and tons of make-up.

I tried not to be judgmental, but I couldn't help wondering why I was in their company. What the hell was I doing here when I would rather be anywhere else in the world?

In the visiting area, Benjamin was waiting at the table. After the formalities I decided that we should not delay further.

"Why are you in here, Ben?" I asked.

He seemed slightly fazed by my directness. He had obviously planned another hour of obfuscation. But I needed to know what exactly I had let myself in for, and whether I wanted to continue with it.

"I'm in for fraud," he said.

"Would you like to tell me about it?"

Out then came an extraordinary story. It seems our Benjamin was a con-man extraordinaire. Using his tailoring skills, he had made for himself a very convincing replica uniform of a high-

131

ranking army officer. It was complete in every detail, with all the pips and epaulettes and the hat. He obviously knew something about military life, although he was saying nothing on that topic.

He had then turned up at an army base, conned them into thinking he really was a Major and persuaded them that he needed urgently to take a helicopter to a top secret meeting in London.

The base had laid on the helicopter and flown him to central London, where he was decanted into some Ministry of Defence building. He had then simply walked out into the street, no questions asked.

This seemed like a likely tale, but then he said that he'd pulled it off more than once, before someone had become suspicious and he'd been rumbled. I can't imagine anyone looking less like a Major General than the guy sitting across the table from me. A pipsqueak with a slight lisp. But this did seem to indicate the power of suggestion that uniforms can have. I've heard of criminals walking away from the scene of their crimes unchallenged because they were wearing a high visibility vest. People simply assumed they were some sort of official.

Presumably none of the army personnel who were duped by these cons wanted to question someone who appeared to be of such a high rank - just in case they get on his wrong side and ended up in big trouble. They were probably thinking if this little squirt can become a Major, so can I.

As he told this tale, it was difficult to read him. He didn't relate it as though he was talking about some funny prank that had gone wrong, and he didn't look in the least bit sorry about it, either. I had a feeling that finding out his motivation for doing such a bizarre thing would be difficult. There were a lot of holes in his story that would need to be filled in before we could get to the truth about this man. It was as much about what he didn't tell as what he did.

But given that he hadn't been violent and nobody had been hurt by this, how come he was in one of the toughest prisons in the country, usually reserved for serial rapists and bomb-planters?

132

He told me that he'd requested the move to Wakefield from what had been a less demanding, open prison elsewhere. He had been reading about Rotherham CHE, following our story, and he wanted to be as near as possible so that he could make contact.

Oh my God, was that a compliment or something we should worry about? His prison sentence had two more years to run, although good behaviour could reduce that substantially. I gulped at the prospect of where all this was leading.

After he had told us his story (or as much as he was prepared to tell at that stage) we reverted to chit-chat.

Returning home on the train, Richard and I discussed the implications. What was he expecting from us (or, more specifically, from me)? It was scary that he had such high expectations of what we could do for him, and besides which – how much of it was true? Was his con-man activity restricted to just these incidents with the military and its helicopters?

And given that he was such an ace deceiver, how much of what he told us could we verify? With the internet we could have done some checking, but there was no internet. There was no way we could find out what was true and what was an old lag's tale.

I was now losing sleep over whether some awful sting was being planned for when he came out of the nick.

And once that idea was in my head, I couldn't get it out.

~ *36* ~

April 1977: The council in Rotherham had made a mistake. They'd claimed to have asked their staff's opinion about working at a CHE event at the Assembly Rooms when all the time they hadn't. Now we could consider making a complaint to the Local Government Ombudsman, who oversees the functioning of local authorities. He can investigate claims of "maladministration", which this surely was..

Maladmistration means that if the council have, at some point, made an error in their procedures that has led to discrimination, they have to say why and put the matter right.

Once again, it was a risk. The Ombudsman investigated only a small percentage of the complaints made to him. In an even smaller proportion did he find that maladministration had occurred. If he was to find in the council's favour then we would really be in the cart. Such a decision would give them all the ammunition they needed to defend themselves against our attacks.

But as there seemed little alternative, and our case appeared – to us at least – to be strong, we decided to go ahead.

We needed a member of the council being complained about to forward the complaint on our behalf to the Ombudsman in the north of England, Mr Pat Cook. This favour was carried out by Councillor Roy Hunt of the Ratepayers Party – the only councillor we could identify who had publicly supported us, and who seemed happy to have the opportunity to cause more trouble for his colleagues.

Mr Cook received the complaint and told us that he would have to make some "preliminary enquiries" before he could decide if it fell within his remit and whether a full investigation was justified.

~ 37 ~

I was constantly trying to come up with new ways of embarrassing and pressurising the council and I took inspiration for my next move from Sheffield CHE, which had been trying to get *Gay News* into the city library. Unusually there had been resistance and a campaign had started to try to make the council change its mind.

So, I then put in an application to the Library and Arts Committee to have *Gay News* displayed in Rotherham Library. After all, the Communists have their journal on display, as do the Labour Party, the Tories and the Liberals and the society of pig-breeders, the anglers and the amateur photographers.

Nobody denies them the right to have their journals read by all and sundry in the library, although it did seem that *Eurostat News* and *The Aquarist and Pondkeeper* were hardly ever opened, let alone read.

True to form, our application was turned down unanimously by the 44 member Labour Group. In a way, this was a good thing because out flew the press releases and lots of lovely publicity followed, leaving the council looking even more bigoted.

I wrote to our MPs telling them how strongly incensed we were that a local council could just write off a whole section of its constituency with an explanation like: "We do not want to be responsible for making material of this sort available to adolescents during their formative years."

(I was even more insulted by this comment because by this time I was contributing regularly to *Gay News* myself).

The MP for Rother Valley, Peter Hardy, wrote back: "Yes, I support fair treatment for homosexuals as I support the rights of any minority group. But I agree with the decision of the council wholeheartedly, and have no intention of intervening."

Stan Crowther was less equivocal: "I consider *Gay News* to be an obscene publication," he wrote.

The local councillor who was the chairman of the Libraries, Museums and Arts Committee, Ron Hughes, wrote back following our letter of complaint about the decision:

"You speak in your letter of a 'homophobic person' and adjective with which neither I nor the Oxford English Dictionary is familiar... I am shocked that a debate of such importance should lead you to use such terms as 'waffle' and 'ignorant committee' and 'blatant prejudice'... Many heterosexuals are sympathetic to the problems of homosexuals and at no time would I seek to use abusive terms about them... The contents of Gay News *could be offensive to some, but particularly I didn't like Captain Jockstrap's Diary [a satirical gossip column in the paper] which in my opinion was titillation...*

Some of the personal advertisements were, I felt, veiled offers for procurement and these, too, I felt could corrupt. There are, as I pointed out to the Labour Group, some real heart cries in these advertisements and for these I have real sympathy... I do deplore the flaunting of sexuality in any of its forms and feel homosexuals like anyone else, are capable of forming their relationships in their way...

I am alarmed at some of the more aggressive undertones of your letter which can only lead to alienating of those who are basically sympathetic. I reiterate our decision not to allow Gay News *on display."*

That was like the proverbial red rag, especially when Councillor Hughes put out a press statement saying: "We think some of the areas covered could be upsetting and I was not happy with some of the personal advertising. Adolescents should not be exposed to such material."

I wasn't going to let it go at that, and there followed a long and acrimonious correspondence between Councillor Hughes and myself. This correspondence helped clarify in my own mind what the best approach was to campaigning. And it was becoming more militant by the day.

I had wanted to know: what if this hypothetical adolescent that the council was so anxious to protect happened to be gay? Suppose he or she didn't know that *Gay News* or CHE existed and would be greatly relieved to read of the nearby presence of other gays who are capable of loving one another and living happily with no attendant shame or guilt.

I'm sure that Councillor Hughes would be quick to point out that keeping gay information out of public view was not an attempt to discriminate against gay adolescents but to 'protect' straight ones. I doubted that Councillor Hughes could be convinced that such a thing as a gay adolescent even existed. He would probably see it as a 'phase' that would pass if it was left alone.

Councillor Hughes' crocodile tears about his sympathy for the 'heart cries' in the personal ads didn't extend to him wanting to do anything about the misery and loneliness they indicated.

It was perfectly OK for the local papers in his library to carry column after column of 'heart cries' from lovely straight adolescents and adults. No veiled procurement there, right?

He deplored the 'flaunting of sexuality in any form' forgetting that his own prominently displayed wedding ring might just say something about his own sexuality. By wearing it, he had declared for all to see that he had obtained legal and religious sanction to have sex with his wife. But that's not flaunting sexuality, is it?

He said *Gay News* could 'corrupt'. I looked it up in his precious Oxford Dictionary: "Rotten, depraved, wicked" it said. Yes, he was saying that, indirectly, about me. Any wonder that I was angry? Yet he objected to his committee being called "ignorant" ("lacking knowledge, uninformed" – OED).

He was alarmed at our 'aggressiveness' but could not grasp what we had to be angry about. We are only alienating him and his colleagues, he said. But in the end what does that matter? The result would be the same however we had approached this. Indeed, the result would have been the same whether the Labour Party or the National Front ran the council. We would receive no quarter from either.

137

There was one difference, though. With direct opposition (which we were, indeed, getting in spades from the local National Front) you know where you stand. But with 'sympathetic' opposition the result is a weakening of the will to resist.

So now we had two campaigns running against the Council and despite the anger they were generating (on both sides) they were doing nothing but good to our membership figures.

Every time we got int the paper or on to the radio, the enquiries would spike and we were seeing more and more people at our meetings.

In many ways, I hoped the council would continue with its intransigence – it was turning public opinion increasingly in our favour.

~ *38* ~

June 1977: In the meantime we had complained bitterly to the leader of the council, Jack Layden, about the developments in relation to our hiring the Assembly Rooms. As a result he invited a deputation from CHE to meet a deputation from the council.

The four of us, Glyn, Eddie, Lisa and me, went to the Town Hall in preparation for the confrontation. We had also asked along the current convenor of Sheffield CHE, a guy called Chris Reed, so that he could testify to the success of the discos at the City Hall in Sheffield.

The manageress of the bars at the City Hall had, all the while, been following this case with a sense of outrage and had sent a letter of support for CHE to the council, telling them that their fears for the safety of their staff were groundless. Her staff loved working at the gay events and would compete for shifts on these evenings. That's because there was never any trouble – no fights, no abuse, no inappropriate comments to the barmaids. Everything was always so jolly and yes, gay.

Our small deputation faced the councillors across the council chamber. Among them was our nemesis, Sid Bennett. He had a bull neck and a bitter expression on his face, as though he had a mouthful of wasps. He was now face-to-face with his worst enemies, you could almost imagine him having convinced himself that there'd been nothing so threatening to the British way of life since Hitler had been defeated. He was clearly the moving force within the council to keep the policy unchanged.

He opened the council's remarks by saying that he had had experiences in the navy which had convinced him that homosexuals were intrinsically corrupt. He feared that no-one else would want to use the Assembly Rooms if they realised that homosexuals had been in there before them.

139

He informed me in passing that I was "unchristian and immoral". The former was certainly true (and becoming more so), the latter was a purely subjective opinion. I could have levelled the same charge against Mr Bennett for his bigotry.

Then he accused us of sending him "disgusting" anonymous letters.

"How do you know they were from us if they were anonymous?" I asked, puzzled.

"I've shown them to the council, these letters are despicable and sick," he replied evasively.

"Where is the evidence that they came from CHE?" I persisted.

"Councillors have seen them and I have thrown them away. They were disgusting."

I asked the chairman of the meeting how long we were going to have to put up with these unproved and unfounded allegations – it was clear that Councillor Bennett was trying to smear us.

The meeting, which lasted about 75 minutes, seemed to have a more positive effect on some of the other councillors. They looked thoughtful and had asked sympathetic questions. But the whole thing served to make Councillor Bennett even more determined to keep us out. "You'll never get the Assembly Rooms while I have a say in the matter," was his parting shot.

I was angry that we had been subjected to such a tirade. It seemed to me that an attempt had been made to undermine our dignity in the eyes of the other councillors present. Bennett's intolerance might well have worked against him that day, but it was still an extremely unpleasant experience.

But it was also a wake-up call. The depth of homophobia in Britain was profound. I had somehow managed to shelter myself from its worst effects personally, but it was clear that there were a lot of people, sometimes in powerful positions, who clung to the mythology that still surrounded homosexuality. Councillor Bennett's opinions were not uncommon, even among well-educated and experienced people.

The press were not long in picking up this anger and next day there were headlines in the papers to the effect: "Insult claim after meeting clash." The chairman of the Labour Group, Councillor Terry Sharman, said that the meeting had been well received and there had not been the "mud-slinging" that I had alleged. He admitted that some comments by councillors had been "misunderstood".

Regrettably they had not been misunderstood. Their intent was as clear as day. That Councillor Sharman was unable to accept that calling gay people "immoral" and suggesting that they are so unclean that decent people wouldn't want to use the same premises as them, didn't leave much room for misunderstanding. There was no awareness how hurtful such comments were.

I didn't mind the press picking up the story and challenging the councillors with it. It ensured that the next time we met we were treated with more respect and courtesy.

The culmination of the meeting was that the councillors asked if we wanted to make another application. We said that we did. Perhaps they thought we would withdraw our complaint to the Ombudsman if they granted the application and save the council from further embarrassment.

In fact, the Ombudsman decided that the council did have a case to answer and announced that he was launching a full inquiry. We were asked to meet his representative, Mr Frank Pedley, and present our case. This we did.

Mr Pedley was a retired civil servant, and a pleasant bloke to talk to. I felt immediately that he had sympathy with what we were trying to do. I told him our side of the story and presented the correspondence that we had accumulated.

The inquiry took several weeks and involved Mr Pedley travelling around the country, as far as Torquay to find Mr Balmer, who had retired there.

He went into the case minutely and interviewed everyone involved. He told us to expect a long delay before a decision was reached. The Ombudsman must take account of his actions before setting a precedent.

~ *39* ~

After the ban on *Gay News*, we decided that we would hold a demonstration outside the recently opened library and arts centre. We would take copies of *Gay News* and ask library users to sign a petition if they thought the decision to ban it was wrong.

Poor old Richard was hauled in as usual, although he wasn't particularly keen on the idea. He could have found a thousand more congenial things to do with his Saturday morning. Bolder members of the CHE group and some supporters from Sheffield were in attendance, so it did look a little less like a one-man band.

We stood outside the library entrance with our little banner reading: "If you think banning *Gay News* is wrong, sign our petition" fully expecting the police to be sent for by the chief librarian to move us on. But actually, one by one the staff from the library came out and signed the petition.

Reactions from the public were generally supportive and gradually, over the space of three hours, we collected 570 names on the petition. Only a few people had refused, and their disapproval was expressed not by abusive tirades, but by the tutting and glaring that was the usual form of dissent from old age pensioners in the north. And even then, it was more likely they were objecting to our making a show of ourselves than to *Gay News*.

The only thing that was likely to arouse pensioners to loud objections in Rotherham was if you pushed in front of them in the bus queue. That was one of the few mortal sins that Rotherhamites would not tolerate.

Our petition seemed an impressive achievement to us and would provide grounds for an appeal to the Council. So, in went the petition with a request that the Library, Museums and Arts Committee reconsider their ban on *Gay News*.

The *Rotherham Advertiser* reported our campaign to get *Gay News* into the reading room (25 May 1976) as follows:

"Following demonstrations outside the library in Rotherham, the Campaign for Homosexual Equality have submitted to the Borough Council a petition signed by 570 people saying they have no objection to 'Gay News' being displayed in the new library.

Earlier this year the magazine was banned from display on the grounds that it was offensive and that it might be a bad influence on young people.

In a letter to the Council, CHE point out that under the Libraries and Museums Act 1964, libraries are for the use of all people and that Section 7 (1) states: "It shall be the duty of every library authority to provide a comprehensive and efficient library service for all persons requiring to make use thereof and for that purpose... to provide and maintain... such books and other materials... as may be required."

Mr Terry Sanderson, convenor of the local group of CHE said: "The Library Association have already laid down in a statement that magazines and other materials must not be excluded from libraries on any moral, religious, political, racial or other grounds, except if they are illegal.

"The Rotherham Labour Group on the Borough Council have flown straight in the face of this directive.

"Our petition has proved that the decision made by the council does not reflect the opinions of the citizens of Rotherham.

"Out of 600 library users who were approached, 570 were prepared to sign the petition saying that they would not object to Gay News being available in the reading room.

"In view of the statutory legislation and the directive from the Library Association, the council have no further grounds for continuing this piece of token discrimination.

"Our letters to the Town Hall are ignored. It seems that the politicians who make these decisions don't feel the need to justify them."

Councillor Ron Hughes, chairman of Rotherham' Libraries, Museums and Arts Committee, said he took the decision with his

*vice-chairman, Councillor George Milburn, after advice from
the controlling Labour Group.*

*"It was taken after members had seen a copy of 'Gay News,'
and he agreed with the ban.*

*Councillor Hughes said that the petition would be referred
to the Labour Group for further consideration.*

The Labour Group were all given copies of *Gay News* to
read so that they couldn't accused of being 'ignorant' the next
time they turned down our application. We had anticipated any
attempt to justify the ban on financial grounds (as had happened
in Sheffield) by saying that CHE was willing to pay for the
subscription.

Then something extraordinary happened. One of the
councillors had taken his copy of *Gay News* home to study at
leisure. There his 20-year old son had seen it lying around the
house and been thrilled to bits to find it. He had discovered my
telephone number in the listings as contact-person for CHE.

When he rang and told me how he had found the number, I
didn't know whether to believe him, it seemed so incredibly
ironic. But he wanted to come to the group, so I invited him to
the next meeting.

He duly turned up and told his tale. He hadn't been
following the story of CHE in the papers (like most young
people, he didn't bother with *The Advertiser*) and the *Gay News*
saga was a complete eye-opener for him.

"I'm going to go home and confront my dad about it," he
said, full of outrage.

I was a little bit worried for him, but I wasn't going to stand
in his way.

The following day I received a call from the irate councillor
and newly revealed parent of a gay son, asking what the hell
was going on. I could only say that his son had found his own
way to CHE, we had not recruited him and nor had we
encouraged him to challenge his father.

It would be up to father and son to decide what direction
their relationship took next.

After he calmed down he started to ask sensible questions about how he should handle the situation. I resisted the temptation to say: "Put *Gay News* in the library so other people in the same situation might make some progress."

No, this was a personal matter and I wished him and his son well.

The young man never came to the CHE group again, but that may have been because he felt it was a bit boring for someone of his age. I doubt whether his father would have been able to stop him.

It was frustrating not to be able to make this story public, but that wouldn't have been fair and it probably wouldn't have done CHE's reputation any good either.

~ *40* ~

While all this was going on, I came up with what I thought was the perfect wheeze to step up the pressure on the council even more.

The theatre company Gay Sweatshop, which I had seen at the Sheffield Gayfest, was putting on plays of gay relevance in London to much critical acclaim. It was all part of the effort to let people know that gay lives were not all as portrayed in the straight media. To some critics Gay Sweatshop's efforts were pure propaganda but to fans they were a much-needed corrective.

One of the actors in Gay Sweatshop's first production was Simon Callow. Many years later, he wrote in *The Guardian* about the effect his experiences in teh troupe had on him in the 1970s.

"I had no inkling of what performing that play in front of a gay audience would be like. The sense of their truth being told, of them in their ordinary lives suddenly existing, was overwhelming. I don't believe I've done anything more rewarding or more emotionally overpowering on any stage or in any medium."

Now my plan was to bring Gay Sweatshop to Rotherham and present one of their shows at the Arts Centre, which was fully equipped for theatrical productions. So in went a request to put on a single performance on 2 November 1977 and I booked Gay Sweatshop's play *As Time Goes By*.

This time the booking would be considered by the Libraries and Arts Committee. Given that there had been no problem with the Quentin Crisp show, I did not anticipate any resistance and, indeed, there was none.

This was too easy. So I thought I would up the ante a bit more and put in for a grant from the council. After all, they had a budget for promoting the arts, why shouldn't we have a share of it?

Our application was referred to the Rotherham and District Arts Council. Whatever they recommended would then be considered by an arts sub-committee of the Libraries, Museum and Arts Committee. All this kerfuffle over a measly request for £90.

This time round, Councillor Ron Hughes, who had been so insulting about *Gay News* and with whom I'd had such a long and sometimes bad-tempered correspondence, seemed a little more conciliatory. Maybe he was being persuaded by my arguments.

Quoted in *The Advertiser*, he said:

"The play is a serious attempt at trying to explain the difficulties facing the homosexual throughout his life. I think it would be unfair to compare it to pornographic movies. Gay Sweatshop are a serious drama workshop who are not trying to propagate people into homosexuality but are trying to explain what it is about."

It wasn't clear who had likened Gay Sweatshop's plays to pornographic movies, but his statement was a move forward.

A grant of £166 had been given to us by the drama panel of the Yorkshire Arts Association, of which councillor Hughes was a member. All of a sudden he was on our side!

His deputy, Councillor George Milburn also supported the application, saying that he hoped prejudice would not stop the grant and the play should go ahead "so long as it did not affront public decency".

Ooer – were we having an impact at last? Was the wall of resistance crumbling?

At the debate of the Libraries and Arts Committee there was an element of dissent. Some of the councillors were smarting about our protracted battle over the hire of the Assembly Rooms and in no mood to be nice to us.

The Mayor, Councillor Roland Benton, said: "They use the word 'campaign' and that means people who are campaigning their particular opinion. I do not favour this grant unless the play is of the highest artistic value."

Despite this, the application was approved, but it was not for the £90 requested, it was just to waive the cost of hiring the theatre, which would be about £25.

In an attempt to ruffle other feathers, I had also put in an application for financial support to South Yorkshire County Council's Culture, Recreation and Health Committee. They were to consider it at their monthly meeting, so I turned up to listen and was faced with a bewildering barrage of insults.

The request was introduced by a councillor saying: "Here's an item there's something queer about", causing schoolboy sniggers around the table. There followed a discussion that I can only describe as a cross between vulgar bar room banter and a religious-tinged tirade worthy of Mary Whitehouse.

I had been told earlier by a council official that although a report to the councillors had wholeheartedly recommended the grant, the committee members had considered it a "political hot potato" that they were anxious to be rid of.

The grant was rejected on the grounds that CHE had enough money to finance the show itself. But I noticed at the same meeting a grant of £500 was made to Doncaster Rugby Club which had, on its own reckoning, a cash surplus of £3,000. I was not shy of making the press aware of all this.

In the end, it was no tragedy that the council had behaved in this way; it brought even more publicity for the show and another opportunity to draw attention to the raw homophobia that still pervaded public life at that time.

The show would go ahead with or without public money, and as a publicity stunt I invited some of the councillors who had been most vociferous in opposing CHE's use of public rooms to attend.

None of them did.

Gay Sweatshop arrived to present *As Time Goes By* and we managed a full house in the admittedly small performance space. The play covered three periods of history – the first section was set in a male brothel in 1896, a year after the Oscar Wilde trials. The next part was set in Berlin just before the rise of fascism. The final section is set in a gay bar on Christopher Street in New York in 1969.

The audience was responsive and not all of them were gay. We counted the evening a success, and certainly the publicity we had generated from it was bringing an ever-higher profile for the CHE group.

~ 41 ~

Richard and I went on a romantic trip to Italy, via Yorkshire Tours. Laurie and Ida had brought us to a beautiful place, blessed with glorious weather and lovely food. It was like a honeymoon and we had a wonderful relaxed time, cuddling and making love for a whole week.

On our return, I had joined a drama group in Sheffield and we were producing a Noel Coward play, *Hay Fever*, to be presented at the Lantern Theatre. My acting confidence was growing, and I now felt that I could live with the stage fright, that had thwarted my ambitions so far, and not have a nervous breakdown over it.

The play went well, and we were asked by a local women's organisation to put on a special performance for them on Saturday afternoon. We were flattered to do this.

But then the girl who was playing the maid was taken ill. She sent word that she wouldn't be able to come for the Saturday performances. This was a blow, but after a little thought I came up with a solution. I would ask Richard if he would play the part in drag. We could equip him with a tea tray on which his lines would be Sellotaped. He only had to make a couple of entrances and say a few lines.

He was understandably reluctant, but after much persuasion and cajoling, he agreed to do it.

We found him a maid's outfit that he could get into and ran through the scenes a couple of times with him. Acting was not his forte. Despite encouragement from the director, his reading of the lines was just that, reading. There was no attempt to give character. Still, we had little option, and we went ahead with the substitution.

The play was going well until he made his first entrance. He walked up to me and read the lines very ostentatiously and obviously from the tray. He was about as convincing as a maid as Alfie had been when going into Shirley mode.

Such were my nerves that I couldn't contain them and the actor's worst nightmare came upon me – I corpsed. I started laughing uncontrollably and nothing I tried would get me back into character. I simply couldn't stop giggling and every attempt to speak my next line resulted in more hysteria. It was mortifying and although I generally like laughing, this was a most unpleasant experience. I had no control over myself, and it was beginning to spread to other cast members.

In the end, I had to exit stage left and the whole production ground to a halt. It took me a good ten minutes to recover my composure, but I knew that if I went on the stage again it was all likely to repeat as soon as Richard came on to the scene.

Much to Richard's relief, the play had to be abandoned and I felt so guilty about spoiling it for everyone that I stepped down from the group immediately.

Richard was also no longer prepared to accompany me on the monthly visits to Wakefield to see Benjamin, and was encouraging me to wind them down. Benjamin, meanwhile, had used his time in the prison workshop to make an overcoat which he presented to me on one of these visits. It was an expertly made garment and I accepted it with gratitude, although I had no intention of ever wearing it. I gave it to my brother who thought it was marvellous to have a handmade coat for the winter. I somehow just wanted it off my hands.

I felt the time had come to share the burden of Benjamin and I asked around in the Rotherham and Sheffield groups until I had guilt-tripped someone into taking him on. I felt immensely relieved when these other people consented to visit him on a rota basis. I would ensure that I was not on the rota, and gradually I stopped going altogether.

I felt slightly guilty, because I think Benjamin probably was genuine and wasn't planning to relieve the group of its funds (all £230 of it) when he came out of the clink. All the same, the guilt was tempered by sheer relief and I don't know what happened to him after his sentence finished. He did not, as I had feared, turn up at the CHE group.

~ *42* ~

October 1977: Still the issue of the Assembly Rooms was not settled. But then a registered letter arrived from the Ombudsman. This was it. This was the long-awaited report. It could settle the matter one way or the other.

I opened it gingerly full of hope but ready for disappointment.

To our intense delight, the council was found "guilty of maladministration leading to injustice to CHE".

The Ombudsman found that the council had been wrong to declare that staff had objected to the discos without actually asking them.

And even more satisfactorily, he criticised Councillors Bennett and Gledhall in no uncertain terms for cancelling the disco in the first place and, in doing so, formulating council policy without bothering to consult the council.

He demanded that the council consider the report and let him know what they intended to do about it.

Once again, there was a furore in the press. This time we were being presented as the victors rather than the downtrodden minority, which made a pleasant change. The *Daily Mail* headed its story "Victory for the gay dancers".

Of course, it was nothing of the sort – the ban was still in place - and the *Mail*'s report ended with a telling comment from the mayor of Rotherham, Councillor Benton, who said that it was unlikely that the report would change his council's mind. Indeed, the Ombudsman had no power to enforce anything in his report. If a council decided to ignore it, they could.

~ *43* ~

As the years passed, Richard's condition seemed to be getting worse. His fits were more frequent and sometimes dangerous. I walked into the kitchen of his parents' home one day, where he was heating some soup, to find him in the midst of an "absence", standing at the cooker with his hand on a lighted gas burner, completely unaware.

I managed to get his hand out of the flame before too much damage was done, but it had to be bandaged for a few weeks afterwards. His parents were shocked, Richard was horrified, not just about his injuries but about the fact that this could have happened. And if this could happen, what else might?

This was shock enough for him, but then he lost his job, ostensibly because the council was cost-cutting, but he suspected, and I agreed, that it was because of his medical condition. His personality had changed to an extent, and he was often short tempered.

The sacking sent him even deeper into a depression that was very difficult to cope with. His whole personality seemed to be disintegrating.

When I spoke to his mother about this, she said that she was increasingly worried - he had become very morose around the house and his moods were unpredictable. Sometimes she thought he was on the edge of violence. "I love him," she said, "but I'm beginning not to like him."

By this time I had become friends with his parents (his mother painted the placard that features on the front cover of this book), but they were elderly and suddenly they had this problem on their hands.

The religious feelings that Richard had suppressed during the time we had been together began to surface again. He started going to the Quaker meetings on Sunday morning and from there he progressed to the Unitarian Church. I know neither of these two religious bodies is particularly anti-gay, but I was still extremely dubious about religion of any kind.

Eventually I persuaded him to go to the doctor, who referred him to a psychologist at the hospital.

The specialist put him on anti-depressants and for a while they worked, but soon he began to sink once more into a black hole.

I sometimes wondered whether it was the medication that was partly responsible for this – he was now on pills for the epilepsy and for depression.

His appearance changed, too. He went from being fresh-faced to being sallow and his hair – which wasn't the thickest at the best of times – began to thin out in patches.

He did manage to get another job, this time gardening in the grounds of a bottle manufacturing company. This perked him up and gave him a bit of a new lease.

We continued our relationship, but it felt different.

~ *44* ~

January 1978: After a long, long delay at last the council considered the Ombudsman's report. Its reaction was to set up a new committee, "the special lettings sub-committee". It would give consideration to all applications to use council rooms that came from "doubtful" organisations (as CHE was now branded – along with the National Front and Socialist Revolutionary Party).

We put an immediate application in to this special sub-committee to test it. Its members were the chairmen and vice-chairmen of each of the council committees with public rooms under their control.

We were invited to meet the committee and put our case. The usual little band from CHE went along to see what would happen.

At this meeting we made an impassioned plea for the lifting of the ban. Councillor Bennett who was, of course, serving on the committee, sat stony-faced throughout. Then he went into smear mode again, bringing up the anonymous letters. This time he was admonished from the chair for being irrelevant.

The committee gave consideration to our application, as we sat nail-chewing in a corridor outside. They said they could not come to a decision immediately. They must have time to consult the staff and their unions. Once more, anti-climax had left us with a surfeit of adrenalin that served no purpose.

As I walked out of the Town Hall, a large, black car with Rotherham's insignia on the front drew up beside me. It was the civic Rolls. The back door opened and a stocky man with white hair said: "Terry?"

"Yes," I replied tentatively, wondering what the hell was going on now. Were they going to kidnap me and dump me in the canal?

"Gerrin, lad," said the man. I climbed into the car and the chauffeur began to drive.

The conversation went something like this:

"Does tha' know who I am?"

"No." I said.

"I'm Jack Layden, leader of t'council. I know y'dad. We used to work together at t'pit. How is Sandy, is he all right?"

"He's fine", I said.

"Now look, lad, about this campaign you're running against t'council. You're not going to get nowhere with it. You know that, don't you? You don't get nowhere by rubbing folk up the wrong road."

"I've tried being polite," I said. "That didn't get me anywhere, either. The council doesn't take notice of anybody. This is a matter of justice."

"Nay lad, don't be so daft. You want to calm down and stop dramatising. You want to do things right."

"Have you got any suggestions?" I asked.

"I want you to give over with this nonsense to start with. Stop making a show of yourself with all this trouble making. It'll get you nowhere. Are you going to pack it in?"

"Are you going to let us hire the Assembly Rooms?"

"That's not up to me. All I want is for you to stop causing trouble for t'council."

"I'm afraid I've only just started. This is a matter of principle."

He turned his attention to the chauffeur: "Harry – pull over." The car stopped.

"All right, lad, if that's the way you want it. Gerrout."

The door swung open again and I was decanted, actually feeling a bit shaky. It hadn't exactly been threatening, but there was something manipulative about it.

Jack Layden subsequently went on to be knighted for services to local government. He was a good egg underneath it all, who gave 43 years of his life to public service, but he was also a man of his time with all the consequent prejudices. He had wanted to protect his beloved Rotherham Borough Council from my attacks, but there was no way I was going to ease up until justice was done.

There's a pub named after Sir Jack in Maltby and a racehorse bore his name, too.

156

The newly-formulated policy was that staff should be consulted and if they objected to working at a gay event on the grounds of conscience, they would be permitted to say no with no disciplinary action being taken.

It took two months for the sub-committee to carry out the consultation. Not only were the staff asked for *their* reactions but the unions involved (NUPE and NALGO) were also consulted.

When it reported, the sub-committee said that each of the staff had been asked independently and each of them had said a definite no to the idea of working at a CHE disco.

The message was clear, there would be no gay disco in the Assembly Rooms.

Sid Bennett was delighted. We were disconsolate. It seemed the Ombudsman's report had achieved nothing. The council had succeeded in closing all the loopholes.

~ *45* ~

Mr Cook, the Ombudsman, had asked me to keep him informed of developments. I wrote to him telling him what had happened and admitting that we had run out of ideas.

By return, a friendly letter arrived inviting me over – expenses paid – to his office in York to talk about what could be done. I went to York and had a good, solid chat with Mr Cook. I told him all about the setbacks we'd encountered as well as the few successes.

He was a tall, cool, affable chap and had a keen interest in what CHE was trying to do. He struck me as being almost like a benign family doctor with his cultured voice and careful attention to detail. He obviously had a concern for the people with whom he came in touch. After the formal business, he asked if I would like a guided tour of York.

This took me a little bit by surprise, but we spent a very pleasant afternoon looking at the Minster and the Mumbles and other historical places in the city. Mr Cook was very knowledgeable about it all and then bought me lunch. It was all very congenial. I wondered if every complainant got this treatment.

"Leave it to me," he said, as I set out for the station. "I'll see what can be done behind the scenes".

I felt reassured by this. He had seemed so confident that he had an answer, even though he didn't say what it was.

A few weeks later a letter arrived from Laurie Frost, chief executive officer at the council. He was Rotherham's top civil servant and wielded a great deal of power, in a *Yes, Minister* sort of way. He wanted to see me.

I arrived at Mr Frost's office to find another kindly sympathiser. He explained that he wasn't gay himself (this is a testimony many people I dealt with seemed compelled to make), but he could see the injustice of what we had endured. He didn't like the idea of 'his Authority' being seen as prejudiced and practising unjust discrimination. He had been in close touch with Mr Cook, and together they had, he said, come up with a possible solution.

It seemed that the main opposition to our application came from within the catering department. (I think we'd worked that one out for ourselves). Would we, asked Mr Frost, be interested in hiring a school hall for our events?

He had been inquiring at the education department and it was feasible that we could have the main hall at the Technical College. We'd have to provide our own bar facilities but the advantage would be that only one member of staff would need to be on duty, the caretaker.

It meant compromise. The Technical College was very much second best and I worried that by accepting it we would also be accepting our status as second class citizens. The proposed new venue was only a few hundred yards from the Assembly Rooms in distance, but a million miles in principles

After giving it some consideration, the CHE committee decided to accept, and Mr Frost said he would make the arrangements. An application form for the hire of the college arrived and we completed it full of hope. It seemed we were closer than ever to actually having a council-owned venue for our disco, albeit not an entirely satisfactory one.

But then came a problem. Mr Frost said that although there was no objection to the dance from within the education department, the application will have to go before the college's Board of Governors. "It's just a formality," Mr Frost assured us. Good natured Mr Frost had not seen the depth of opposition or felt the hot breath of prejudice on his neck as we had.

The Board of Governors was not entirely happy. They decided that they must consult their staff, and so they did – they asked for the opinions of the college lecturers, technicians and even the tea-ladies.

With a characteristic desire to please, the staff gave a unanimous thumbs-down to the plan. The Governors were therefore absolved of responsibility, just like the council. The application was refused.

I was furious and objected strongly. What is the relevance of the opinions of staff who won't be anywhere near the place when the proposed event takes place? Perhaps they, too, think there will be residual uncleanness left by the dancing nancies.

Mr Frost agreed with my objections and said he would take the matter up with the governors. But he was now up against the same brick wall we'd been trying to dismantle for the preceding three years. I could see his enthusiasm for the battle was evaporating rather quickly. Eventually his efforts fizzled out.

At Christmas that year I couldn't resist sending a card to Sid Bennett at the council. The legend on the front of the card was "Peace on earth and good will towards all men". Inside, I had written "With good wishes and thanks for all the free publicity you have provided for us throughout the year – our membership is booming."

Mr Bennett told the *Sheffield Morning Telegraph*: "It is in very bad taste and shows just what kind of people they are."

January 1979: Throughout the battling years we had made many allies inside and outside the council. I was asked to speak at the local Trades Council and to my amazement they were very well-informed about gay rights. They told me that they intended to actively take up the banner on our behalf.

Rumours reached us of behind-the-scenes scenes. Large-scale rows were reported. There were meetings and further meetings. Fallings-out had taken place.

We waited until we thought the time was right and then started collecting names for a letter of support that we intended to submit with our next application.

The Vicar of Rotherham, the Rev Ian Harland, headed the letter followed by the president of the Trades Council. We added women's groups' representatives, students' union president, psychiatrists, doctors – anyone with status who would put their name to it. They all signed willingly except MP Stan Crowther who said he intended to make his own private representations to the council for a change of heart.

We applied again and our letter was put before the "special lettings sub-committee". We must wait until the necessary staff consultations had been completed.

We hoped that the council would eventually realise how unfair it was to let the whims of the staff dictate who could and could not use council property. We were all paying taxes. It was the council's business to decide policy, not leave it to bar staff.

An application form arrived from the new catering director, Mr Brian Brown, in anticipation of the success of the appeal.

On 20 June, Mr Brown telephoned me to say that he could confirm our booking for the Assembly Rooms. Enough staff had changed their minds to make it possible.

Why had they changed their minds? I like to think we had managed to persuade them through our persistence and our arguments. I hoped that they had realised it was a matter of human rights. Perhaps they were just sick of being asked the same questions over and over. We'll never know.

We'd made it. The disco was set for July 6 1979. I breathed a long, loud sigh of relief.

~ 46 ~

Now that we'd overcome the resistance to the Assembly Rooms, I had thought that we would be able to put on events quite freely.

I had heard of a small theatre group - an off-shoot of Gay Sweatshop - and their revue called *Double Exposure*. Written by Noel Grieg, it was basically a two-man show starring Alan Pope with musical accompaniment by Alex Harding.

They were willing to come and so I thought it was just a matter of form to book the Arts Centre again. After all, the show had been well reviewed and had an important message.

Unfortunately, I came up against the "special lettings subcommittee" again. Although we had a date pencilled in, this was subject to the staff being consulted. And so they were.

It was at this point that the eraser was got out of the desk drawer and our pencilled-in booking was rubbed out. A caretaker had objected to working at the event and so it was cancelled.

Mr Ken Raynor, secretary of the local branch of the union NUPE – which represented employees - told the *Yorkshire Post*: "It has been our policy to stop the CHE group from using council property. They have used the Arts Centre before and caused problems."

Eh? We had used the Arts Centre to host Gay Sweatshop and Quentin Crisp. This was in the days before a single prejudiced member of staff could simply say "no" to the "special lettings subcommittee". Both events had been well-received and had gone off without problem. What was Ken Raynor talking about? (And to make things worse, I was a member of NUPE and paying subscriptions, only to be treated like this!)

I was disappointed, but the well-practised routine of sending out press notices about the bigotry of the council led to another round of condemnation in the papers and on the radio.

Now the trick would be to keep the story going.

162

What would embarrass the council most? Well, what about transferring the show to a municipal venue in Sheffield – a mere five miles down the road, and where there was no such convoluted problems about bookings, and never had been. Surely Rotherham councillors would see the foolishness of their policies when the show was given an airing by a neighbouring – and demonstrably more enlightened – authority. Surely that would illustrate to them the idiotic pickle they had got themselves into?

So, *Double Exposure* was transferred to the City Hall in Sheffield, which had a small theatre attached called the Memorial Hall. It held about 500, which was ambitious in our terms, but the purpose was not only to get the show on but, at the same time, give the finger to Rotherham Council.

The performance was fixed for 19 January 1979. Richard's parents would be away, so I had commandeered their house on Psalter Lane as accommodation for the two performers.

Alan Pope and Alex Harding arrived in Sheffield that morning, and we went to the venue so that they could see what the facilities were like. They had a little run-through, tested the acoustics and the quality of the piano.

All was ready but then, in the early afternoon, the weather closed in. It had been a very bad winter altogether that year, the ground had been frozen for weeks and there had been a lot of blizzards. It began to snow heavily, with strong winds piling up huge drifts. By late afternoon the buses had stopped running, roads were impassable and the outside temperature was freezing. And still it was snowing.

As the time for the show approached it became clear that the city, and indeed, just about the whole of northern England, had been brought to a standstill by what was one of the biggest blizzards on record.

By the time the show got underway, there were about half a dozen people in the audience, including April from work and her boyfriend Mark who had heroically somehow managed to get through. The show went ahead but it was a severe disappointment that the weather had ruined it.

The evening held one compensation. In the main hall there was a military tattoo – one of those demonstrations of the soldiers' marching routines, with bands playing martial tunes and where guns are assembled and disassembled. The City Hall had been transformed into a miniature Edinburgh Castle for the evening. Their audience was only slightly bigger than ours – and they had 2000 seats to fill. Indeed, there were far more people in the show than there were in the audience.

But the backstage corridors, which were shared between the halls, were awash with young men in various stages of undress, preparing for their big performance. The air was thick with testosterone and that was almost worth turning out for alone.

I told Alex and Alan about my plan to pressurise Rotherham Council and to use this performance as leverage. They said they would be willing to come again if we could book the Arts Centre.

They were as determined as I was that we would overcome the council's discriminatory policy and ready to do their bit.

~ 47 ~

Naturally, when I reported the show to local journalists and media, I omitted to mention the absence of an audience. I edited out the snowstorm and hyped it as a great success, adored by the gathered multitude. Of course, I always managed to tack on the end a comment about how stupid and disgraceful it was that we had not been able to present it in Rotherham as planned.

Using this reported success as an excuse, I applied once more to present the show at the Arts Centre.

I think maybe the message had got through because I received a call from the new director of libraries, museums and arts, Mr Chris Williams, who was pleased to inform me that the Arts Centre was at our disposal if we wanted to present the show. There would be no last minute cancellations this time. I'm not sure what had changed, but it was clear the council didn't want another furore.

But the decision did not please everyone. *The Advertiser* carried a story about a man they called "a leading pastor" who launched an all-out attack against the gay community. *The Advertiser*'s story was headed "Gays are Not Welcome in My Church".

Pastor David Powell said he "very much regretted" Rotherham Council's recent decision to allow the local Campaign for Homosexual Equality to stage their gay review *Double Exposure* at the Arts Centre. "I was just about to express my appreciation to the council for taking a stand against them," he said. "Now they have given in. It is very disappointing."

David Powell was the leader of Rotherham Pentecostal Church which had the biggest congregation of any church in the town. He let rip with a fire and brimstone sermon on the "sickness that is threatening society". I suppose by keeping such a high profile, CHE was inviting this kind of thing (the attacks by the National Front in the letters column of *The Advertiser* were continuous).

165

Pastor Powell was organising a lecture entitled "The Gays – sickness or sin?" He said that he was prepared to answer questions from gay people, but not in his church. They weren't welcome there. He told *The Advertiser*: "I will welcome homosexuals – but only if they come seeking help. I will not welcome anyone who practices it and refuses to give it up."

He said he wasn't aware of any homosexuals among the 500 members of his congregation, but if he found any he would ask them to leave. "This does not mean they would not be welcome to listen to our preaching and they could attend Communion services," he said. "But they would not be acceptable as church members unless they altered their ways. I believe some of these people need and deserve help. I would like to get through to parents to help prevent their children from being influenced by these degrading practices. I want to get to people on the fringe and help them to give it up. I want to warn the gullible."

The pastor went on: "I see homosexuality as a threat to the whole of human society – Sodom and Gomorrah were destroyed because of it."

But another clergyman, the Rev Geoff Reid, who was already familiar to us from previous skirmishes with the council, came to our defence. "I am glad to see that the council have finally allowed the local Gay community to put on their musical," he told the *Sheffield Star*.

This caused the *Star* to editorialise about this new development on 8 August, 1979:

"Rotherham Council has had a long-running problem with its attitude to events staged by homosexuals and only recently – after declarations by the Ombudsman – has it relented and let the gay movement use its premises.

It banned the staging of a musical show then changed its mind and the show is going on. That is not the end of the matter – now a pastor at a local Pentecostal church is objecting, while on the other side a local Methodist Minister welcomes the decision.

Does the virtue of tolerance extend only to one part of the Christian religion?"

All this fuss did no harm to ticket sales, and we had a full house for *Double Exposure*, which was performed in August 1979, the day before the lads were taking it to the Edinburgh Festival.

It's just as well Pastor Powell did not attend, as the show represented a scathing attack on religious bigotry of all kinds, most of it mouthed through a Mary Whitehouse-style figure, played by Alan Pope in a skirt and voluminous (and oft-glimpsed) bloomers.

Now that we had free access to the Arts Centre we made full use of it, and in October that year we were presenting a screening of the US film *Word is Out*. It was basically a series of talking heads telling their coming out stories, but it was so well edited and the stories were so compelling that it made a gripping documentary for anyone who is interested in human happiness.

Naturally, Pastor Powell was on the invitation list, so was Sid Bennett and everyone else in the council who had expressed negative opinions about gay people. We also took the opportunity to invite social workers and Samaritans.

Again, it was a full house, although none of those with a bee in their bonnet about gay people turned up.

The continuing brouhaha next attracted the ire of the vicar of Brinsworth, the Rev Gordon Harper. Writing in his parish magazine, Mr Harper said:

"In the Bible God makes it clear that homosexual acts are forbidden and are, therefore, sinful.

"Those who practise these acts are just as normal biologically as anyone else and have no irresistible urge to commit them. Just like any other sinner they are responsible for what they do" He likened gay people to thieves, adulterers and malicious gossips. *"Persons who practice such acts stand in need before God of repentance and faith in Christ for forgiveness as are the thief, adulterer and malicious gossip.*

"And I believe if there are practising homosexuals in the Church they should be asked to leave until they have found guidance and regained normal heterosexual tendencies."

167

Mr Harper told *The Star*:

"More often than not, the practising homosexual is a miserable, unhappy and insecure person, frightened and in desperate need of care and help. Like all sins, homosexual acts are destructive."

Mr Harper did not seem to grasp that it was attitudes such as his that added to the hostility that in turn made life for gay people so difficult. Nor did he grasp that if, as he recommended, all gay people were asked to leave the church, it would collapse overnight.

All this was not doing anything to revise my increasingly negative opinion of religion. Instead, I was becoming rather militantly opposed to it.

~ *48* ~

One evening, after I had come home from work and was enjoying one of Mi Mam's baked bean confections, someone knocked on the door

I went to answer and found two plain clothes policemen standing there, making enquiries into a murder of a gay man. They produced a photograph of the man, asked if I knew him, and when I said "no", they then asked if I had information to give them about a murder that had occurred in the area. I gave them an emphatic no, they seemed satisfied and went away.

I was shaken, but pleased that they hadn't insisted on coming inside – Mi Mam and Dad would have been horrified at the prospect of such a thing. They were terrified of most authority figures, but particularly the Bobbies. I just told them it had been the Jehovah's Witnesses who I'd sent off with a flea in their ear.

I don't suppose I should have been surprised. I had kept such a high profile that it would not have been difficult for them to track down my address.

But a couple of hours later, Tony from Barnsley, who was a Rotherham CHE member, called. The police had been to his house, too, wanting to know the same information. Within the hour four other members rang to say the police had been to see them and what the hell was I doing handing out their names and addresses?

In one instance the police officers had called on someone who hadn't come out to his parents. They had insisted on entering the house, where his parents were watching TV. He was distraught that he had been forcibly outed like this in such sordid circumstances.

I was mystified. Where on earth had they got these names and addresses? Our membership list was secure. It was on paper and I had the only copy outside of CHE head office in Manchester. Besides, some of the people who had been visited

169

hadn't actually signed up for membership, so we didn't have their personal details.

It took me ages to figure it out, but eventually it came to me. At a previous meeting of the group at St Cuthbert's Church Hall there had been a man tending the garden, apparently tidying up the flowers around the building. I had never seen anyone there before and it was clear that this man was an undercover police officer collecting the registration numbers of the cars parked outside the church hall.

This was confirmed in my mind when one of the people who had been visited told me that when the police arrived, they had asked for his father by name, insisting that he was a member of CHE. In fact, the real member had used his father's car to come to the meeting on the night of the surveillance.

As this realisation dawned on me I felt sick. What on earth had we done that could justify being treated like potential criminals who had to be kept under surveillance? It had been more than ten years since the 1967 Sexual Offences Act had legalised gay sex for those over 21. Why were we still being treated like outlaws simply for gathering together to talk?

I went into action straight away. The police would have to be held to account for this and the list they had compiled destroyed. This must not happen again. It had proved disastrous for one member and acutely embarrassing for others.

I wrote to the Chief Constable of South Yorkshire, Mr Stanley Barratt and enlisted the help of the National Council for Civil Liberties. I also wrote to MP Stan Crowther.

But most of all I made as much of a stink in the media as I could. What I had learned from my dealings with those in authority is that if they think they can get away with it, they will fob you off or ignore you. But the one thing that public officials are afraid of is questions from, and negative exposure in, the media.

The local police were also approached, but silence reigned in that department.

At first the South Yorkshire Police denied compiling a "dossier" of names and addresses. The deputy chief constable of South Yorkshire, Frank Gutsell, had ignored my letter, but when

The Guardian approached him he had to break the silence: "There is no campaign by the police against homosexuals in Rotherham," he told the paper, "and we are certainly not compiling dossiers on homosexuals."

This was self-evidently not true and I asked Stan Crowther if he would ask the Home Secretary to launch an inquiry into these happenings. He subsequently did this, telling *The Guardian*:

"The police are known to keep dossiers on almost everyone" but the accusation that the group had been harassed during inquiries into a recent crime was serious enough to justify a Home Office enquiry. The group alleges that at least six members of the CHE, who had no connection with this murder at all, were visited by the police; and it is also alleged that these visits took place solely on the fact that they are members of the group. If they were visited only because their cars were seen outside their meeting place, it would not seem a particularly good reason for the police to be interviewing them."

The pressure on the police was growing, and they are as sensitive as politicians to bad publicity.

Eventually I got a phone call from a police officer in the Complaints and Discipline Division of South Yorkshire Police, asking if it would be possible to attend our next meeting and talk about events. I said, yes indeed. We would welcome it.

At the meeting, two senior officers turned up, the epitome of politeness and accommodation. They talked to the gathered membership about how difficult their enquiries into the murder had been. They had to look at all sorts of leads to make progress.

I told them that I realised how important their investigation was and we wouldn't want to do anything to obstruct it, but why had they been spying on us and collecting our personal details?

"Nobody has been spying on you," said cop one, all reassurance. "There is no dossier."

"So how come only people who attend these meetings in their cars were visited? How come you asked for Tony's father when it was Tony who was at the meeting, using his dad's car?"

171

"I can assure you that we've got more to do than gather this kind of information."

"But you did gather it, and you used it. All we want to know is – why?"

"When you're involved in a murder enquiry, you have to follow all kinds of leads," says cop one.

"Yes, but you had our details on your files before the murder even took place. I saw your plain clothes guy in the garden outside. It was weeks ago – why were you collecting our details then?"

"Well, it's very difficult in some cases," said cop two.

"But why were you collecting information about us?"

"You see, when you're investigating a murder, all kinds of avenues have to be explored."

I was obviously not going to get anywhere with these two. All direct questions about the motives for gathering information about CHE members were deflected.

It was a while later that I discovered that in 1966 a similar list had been compiled in Sheffield by police officers noting down the numbers of cars parked outside a pub frequented by gay people. When they had been caught out that time, they had promised that a new policy would prevent such a thing in future. Now they were at it again.

Stan Crowther's request to the Home Office for an inquiry into the incident was rejected, but such was the level of publicity, local and national, that eventually South Yorkshire police admitted that the dossier did exist. Frank Godsell, deputy chief constable called it an "unofficial list" that had been made during inquiries into a serious crime.

"What was done was done with good intentions, but it was contrary to a decision taken in 1966. The list was unofficial and has now been destroyed."

But given that the list had been compiled before the crime was committed, Mr Godsell's explanation didn't quite add up. But there was to be no explanation as to why the list was compiled or what its real purpose was.

~ *49* ~

Richard was now regularly attending hospital appointments not only for his worsening epilepsy but also to see a psychiatrist who was trying to help him with the depression that was dragging him down.

One day I went over to Psalter Lane to spend some time with him, only to find him beaten black and blue. His eyes were swollen and black, his lips were cut and bruised and one of his ears was sticking out. He was almost unrecognisable, like one of those pictures you see in the papers of elderly mugging victims who are just one mass of bruises.

He had been beaten up by one of the other patients while awaiting his appointment at the hospital. Apparently he had been sitting in the waiting area minding his own business when this disturbed man had simply set about him. Poor Richard was in no state to defend himself, nor was he equipped for fisticuffs. He was a sitting duck for someone with violence on their mind. It must have been quite a sustained beating to leave him in this state. My stomach was in knots as I tried not to think about it.

I didn't want to cry in front of him, but it was such a shocking and somehow pathetic sight that I really was having to bite my lip. I could have thrown myself on the floor and sobbed, but it would have been with pity and that didn't seem right.

I knew it was my job to reassure and support him, but all I could do was feel intensely sorry for him. Seeing a loved one violated like that, especially someone so gentle who had become vulnerable, was almost unbearably sad.

He appeared not to be too badly traumatised by it and said he wasn't in pain, asking everyone to stop fussing. But despite the attempt to shrug it off, the incident sent him spiralling downwards, the depression intensifying.

The consequence of this was that he lost his job at the factory. It had been a rather menial job, but one that permitted him to feel he had a purpose. His deteriorating mental health meant he had taken more and more time off and at last his employer had asked him to leave.

His parents were distraught, unable to cope with this adult child who was disintegrating in front of their eyes.

Richard's mother, Lisbeth, seemed completely out of her depth, she asked what they could do – how could they help him, how could they help themselves? Their old age was suddenly blighted by this terrible burden.

I told them I would do whatever I could to try to get Richard on his feet again. We had shared so much together, so many happy times. He had been a companion to me at all the moments I needed support most. I knew that whatever scrape I got myself into, he would be there to come through it with me. And if I needed to go somewhere outlandish, he would always be by my side.

Now the hard times were here, and it was up to me to hold his hand just as he had held mine.

~ *50* ~

My hostility to religion was increased even further the following year when a young man came to Sheffield CHE asking for help after he was sacked from his job at a "Christian nursing home".

Simon Daniels was employed at the Hetherleigh Nursing Home in Grindleford, Derbyshire as a chef. When his employers discovered he was gay they sacked him because their Christian principles wouldn't permit them to have "a gay" on the premises.

Simon, who was 19 at the time, said: "I explained to them that I am a Christian who just happens also to be a homosexual and they told me I couldn't have the job." Not only was his employment terminated, but he was kicked out of his lodgings, too. Since then he had been sleeping on the floor of friends' houses and had been denied unemployment benefit until an inquiry could be conducted into the events.

With Simon's permission, I took his case to the press. There was no legal recourse at that time.

Ian Marshall, a spokesman for the Home, told the *Daily Telegraph*:

"This is a Christian nursing home run on principles laid down by God. This young man professes to be a Christian and then admitted that he was a homosexual. We told him this was against Christian principles. We said if he was willing to renounce his way of life and repent, we would give him the job and pray for him through this difficult time. He decided he wanted to continue this practice and we were unable to offer him the job. Many of our patients are elderly and from another generation and we had to consider their feelings too."

Gay people were regularly fired from jobs, kicked out of accommodation and refused services in the 1970s. It would be some considerable time before that was put right. A couple of years earlier, there had been the very high profile case of Tony Whitehead, who had been a trainee with British Home Stores.

He had appeared in an early TV documentary about gay people and was shown kissing his boyfriend. The following day he had been sent for by his manager and asked, McCarthy style: "Are you a practising member of CHE?"

Tony said yes, but it wasn't a problem as all his colleagues already knew about his sexuality. Nevertheless, he was suspended and eventually "let go". This sparked a big show of support among activists who picketed BHS stores around the country.

Tony Whitehead went on to become one of the founders of the Terrence Higgins Trust.

Of course, it would not have been appropriate for the CHE group to picket a nursing home full of vulnerable and fragile elderly people.

But in the meantime, I questioned why any self-respecting gay person would want to have anything to do with religion which seemed to hate them so much.

And we were able to express a little bit of that hostility when Mary Whitehouse came to Sheffield to give a lecture at the big Methodist Hall. Whitehouse represented everything that was wrong with religion – a desire to censor, a terrible certainty that God was personally telling her what to do and most of all her aggressive attitudes to homosexuality.

A group of about twenty of us turned up at the hall and sat in the balcony. When she started to speak we began to applaud and shout and whistle. She waited until we stopped and began her speech again. We started the racket again. Every time she tried to restart we drowned her out. This went on for some considerable time before the heavies arrived to escort us from the premises.

It had been satisfying to demonstrate to the blue rinse brigade in that hall that Mary Whitehouse was not a hero to everyone.

~ *51* ~

August 31 1981: Richard had lost enthusiasm in CHE along with just about everything else. He was turning increasingly to the Unitarian Church for comfort, an interest which I could not share. He would ask if I'd like to go along one Sunday morning, telling me that the church was fully accepting of gay people. But I couldn't get past my suspicion of all religion – and the fact that none of it made any sense to me. It didn't matter how friendly the church that promulgated it, the message was still nonsensical to my mind. In fact, if you stepped back and analysed it even briefly, the whole thing just crumbled. I couldn't bring myself to waste time on such drivel.

But I made no criticism or objection to his going, and I didn't say what I really thought about that church or any church, because it was something that was obviously important to him and a focus that took his mind off the depression.

At one point he had told me that he wanted to end our relationship, which had hurt me deeply and which I was reluctant to accept. I suspected that despite his claims that the Unitarian church was gay-friendly, there was still a conflict in his mind between his growing religious beliefs and his sexuality.

So, we went our separate ways, temporarily. However, our paths crossed a couple of times and eventually, without really discussing it, we resumed our friendship (which is what it had become by then).

I wanted to help him, I wanted to get him back to a place where he could resume a life that would make him (and me) happy. But trying to lift a cloud of depression from someone's mind is a difficult job. It's not just a matter of trying to cheer them up, sometimes that only makes things worse.

I tried to see what he wanted, what might make him happy and to penetrate the black mood at least for a few minutes. But it was as much about recognising what he didn't want as what he did. Pressure and stress were not good for him, so I tried not to create any. I still encouraged him to come with me to the concerts that he liked and to walk in Derbyshire on Sunday afternoon. These things we could still enjoy together.

Over the August Bank Holiday, CHE was holding its annual Gayfest conference in Durham. I wondered if he might like to go but it was too much for him to even contemplate. A couple of friends from the Sheffield group were driving up to the conference and they invited me to tag along with them.

The conference was being held at the University for three days and I had reserved a small room on the campus in the student accommodation.

The business of the conference was, as was usual, rather self-important and consequently a bit dull and boring. But there was to be a disco that evening.

It felt strange without Richard or any of the other gang of supporters that usually attended events like this with me. There were so many people milling around that I found it a bit overwhelming, even though by this time I was quite well-known in gay circles and people would approach me to say how much they liked what I was doing. I hadn't lost the shyness and sense of inferiority that had been with me all my life and I still found it difficult to simply insinuate myself into conversations as other seemed able to do.

I felt out on a limb and on my own, the classic 'lonely in a crowd' syndrome.

I decided that I would not stay for the whole of the conference. I would take a train home the following day.

As a last ditch effort to rescue something from the weekend, I went along to the disco in the Students Union bar. I did it with trepidation. It was packed to the rafters with people – mainly men – all apparently having a fabulous time.

With so many people and so many possibilities, it should have been thrilling, but I was finding it daunting, going solo and not feeling very confident. Everyone seemed to be with someone. Conversations were somehow being held even though the music was deafening.

I sat on a step looking, I guess, rather disconsolate, thinking that maybe it was time for me just to retire to my room and then leave for the station first thing.

It was then that a young man approached, smiling. He introduced himself as Keith and wondered if I'd like to have a dance. Suddenly I perked up. He was quite a looker. Not the Big Dark Man, admittedly, but rather a smaller version with light coloured hair.

We got on the dancefloor and had a half-hearted boogie. I think neither of us were natural dancers, certainly we weren't very good at the free-form writhing that was the style of the time. We were relieved when the song came to an end and Keith asked if I'd like a drink.

The bar was seething, with a crowd about five deep all trying to get the bartender's attention. After a while he came back without the drinks. "I can't get anywhere near the bar," he said. "But I've got some wine in my room. Would you like to have a drink there?"

My heart gave a little flip, I wasn't going to see his etchings, but the wine was probably the equivalent. He led me from the bar (for which I was very grateful) and down the corridors to the accommodation block, where he had a room very similar to mine.

From his bag he produced a large bottle of cheap Italian wine. The fact that it tasted like vinegar was of no consequence. The circumstances made it seem like champagne. This felt like something special, a celebratory moment.

At previous CHE conferences I'd been sharing a room with other people. You didn't know who it would be until you got there.

On one occasion – I think it was in Coventry – I'd been bunked up with a man who was into spanking. He was quite a nice guy, so I gave him access to my buttocks so he could slap them gently for a while, which pleased him no end, but left me completely cold (except the buttocks, of course, which were red and burning by the time he'd had enough).

This was different. Keith was a gentle man, properly rounded and mature, who seemed perfectly normal. He didn't have any alarming requirements.

He may not have borne a physical resemblance to the Big Dark Man of my fantasies, but he did have the right character.

He was a real, proper grown-up to start with. There was none of the silly frivolity that I tried to pass off as a personality. He was practical, sensible and everything I wasn't. I was deeply attracted to that.

We had our wine and the conversation flowed freely. We sat on his bed, then lay on his bed. He was from London and had been in CHE for almost as long as I had. He was a businessman by profession, quite high-flying it seemed.

Soon the wine began to have its relaxant effects and we got down to the real business. The Big Dark Man couldn't have fulfilled the role better.

I wondered if this was going to be just another one-night stand (listen at me! There weren't many of those in my sexual CV) or something else. It just felt different.

I had returned to my room in the early hours as the exceedingly narrow single bed wasn't really conducive to sleeping two adults.

The next day I woke with a song in my heart. What a wonderful evening it had turned out to be. And no, I wasn't going back on the train. There was another night to be enjoyed.

The problem was I hadn't made any arrangements to meet Keith – and now he was gone from his room. I went to the dining hall for breakfast and he wasn't there. I searched the conference rooms and he wasn't there, either.

It seemed I'd let him slip through my fingers, so I sat in the on the conference, listened to the speeches and debates and hoped upon hope that he would be in the dining room for lunch. He wasn't.

But as I sat forlornly eating my indifferent vegetarian meal, another young guy asked if he could join me. I can't remember his name now, but we chatted easily and got along very well. The lunch break passed a little more congenially than I thought it would. Maybe, given the disappearance of Keith, I could spend some time with this friendly chap.

But as I was leaving the dining hall to return to the conference, I spotted Keith. We greeted each other with big smiles, and he said he had been searching for me everywhere. Seems we had been looking in different places at different times

180

and constantly missing each other. Never mind, we had coincided now.

We agreed that we'd skip the afternoon session of the conference and instead explore Durham a little. The weather was lovely and the city looked glorious (maybe I was looking at it through rose coloured specs). Even the cathedral, which is world class according to those who care about such things, looked spectacular.

We found a path by the river and strolled along for a few miles, comfortably chatting and getting to know a little more about each other.

Keith soon discovered that I wasn't enamoured of religion and he responded that he felt exactly the same way. In fact, he was a life member of the British Humanist Association. This sounded like the sort of group I had been looking for.

He lived alone in a small flat in north London, he said, and was working for a grocery company as a senior accountant. He was expecting to be made a director fairly soon. This was coming from a world that was a mystery to me, but it sounded very important.

He had been born in Edinburgh – an only child - but raised in north Yorkshire, in Ripon. We smiled at the memory of both having had school dinners provided by the West Riding County Council.

His father was an artist and, at the time, Ripon had been the ideal location for him. Keith regarded himself as partly Scottish and partly Yorkshireman, but ironically, he had spent most of his life in London, where his father had taken a job as a designer at Aspreys, the posh jewellers on Bond Street.

Now that his parents were retired, they had built themselves a house back in Scotland, on the west coast in the small village of Arisaig.

I told him about my efforts for gay rights and he was equally impressed.

It had been a lovely afternoon, and we still had another night in the accommodation before we had to part – he for his high-flying life in London and me back to Beechcroft.

The next day, after another extremely delightful night of passion, Keith offered to drive me back. He was going down the M1 anyway, so he could drop me at the exit nearest home. I didn't want him to come all the way to Burns Road, and see the smoke-blackened houses in Maltby.

My life was so different to his, and I didn't want to break the magic we had created over the weekend.

It was quite an emotional parting, because I didn't want to let him go. There was something special here, and I felt that he thought so, too.

But I hadn't got my hopes up too high. Long-distance relationships are hard to sustain and he would probably get back to his home and resume his regular life, just as I must. Eventually our lives would continue in whatever way they must.

We would have to think of this as an enchanted interlude.

~ *52* ~

The girls at work could tell that there was something different about me, and as we usually shared everything, I was quick to tell them about the romantic weekend.

"When are you going to see him again?" they wanted to know, but I had no answer to that. We had exchanged contact details, but I had no idea whether Keith would want to try to make something of this. I didn't have the confidence to chase him myself.

Several days passed and I heard nothing from him, so I eventually gave up and accepted that it had just been a brief encounter, albeit a special one.

A few weeks later I had a call from Richard's mother. Richard was in hospital, desperately ill. He had experienced some kind of brain seizure and was now unconscious and in a coma. If I wanted to see him, I should go to the hospital quickly.

I had felt guilty about apparently being disloyal to Richard on my sojourn to Durham, but at the same time it was clear that he was dubious about the future of our relationship anyway. Now I felt terrible and hurried to the hospital to find that he was in the intensive care unit.

When I arrived at the unit, the nurse told me that only immediate family were allowed to visit. I explained that I was Richard's partner, but the nurse was adamant, that was not good enough. You needed to be a close relative, not 'just a friend', before you could visit anyone in the intensive care.

She could see that I was distressed and said: "You could get the permission of his next of kin and if they say it is OK, then you can visit."

I had to wait until evening for his parents to arrive before I could gain access to the unit. Richard was hooked up to all the usual tubes and wires and drips. He was deathly pale but peaceful. I asked the nurse how aware he was, and she said it was difficult to tell, although she thought he was unconscious.

"How bad is it?" I asked.

183

"Being unconscious for two days is not a good sign," she said, but could tell me no more.

He was in intensive care for another twenty four hours, when he regained consciousness and was transferred into another ward. I planned to visit him there after work.

When I arrived he was sitting in a chair. He was totally confused and didn't recognise me. He was speaking gibberish, as though a telephone exchange had got all its wires crossed and random bits of conversation were coming out of his mouth.

He didn't seem unhappy, but this wasn't Richard, it wasn't anybody, he was just mouthing this stream of nonsense.

The nurse asked me to talk to him normally, to try to help him get his garbled mind into some kind of order. This I tried to do, chattering away about things that I knew interested him and that we had shared. It was difficult to get his attention – he had no idea who I was and although I was trying hard to present a cheery front to him, I was constantly on the verge of tears.

I went each evening for a week, and each day he seemed a little more in control. After a fortnight or so he was back to normal. Somehow his brain had re-programmed itself and Richard returned.

But he was subdued, frightened and the depression deepened further. My self-imposed task of rescuing him from it was proving more and more difficult. I would take him out for a meal or encourage him to socialise with our gay friends, but his world seemed to be getting smaller and smaller.

Although my efforts sometimes made life seem a little more bearable they also sometimes seemed to drive him even further into the despair that was overtaking him.

For my own sanity I was turning to other people to provide the social outlets that I had once shared with Richard. And spending more time on my own, reverting to the years of isolation I had endured as an adolescent.

At Christmas, a card arrived from Keith. In it was an invitation visit him in London.

This was the best Christmas present of all and I was on the phone to him straight away, making the arrangements.

A few weeks later, I was on the train from Sheffield to London and Keith was at the other end to meet me. It was so exciting to see him and we went at once to his flat in north London. It was a two storey maisonette on top of a branch of the supermarket chain that he worked for.

On the mantel shelf were cards of congratulation. "I've been made finance director of the company," Keith said, "so let's go and celebrate."

He took me to Hampstead for a visit to the King William IV, an old established gay pub. It was pleasant enough, but I'm not a pub person and I was glad when we went back to the flat and resumed our intimate relationship.

It was a heavenly weekend, and when I got back to work at Beechcroft, the girls were anxious to know what sort of time I'd had.

"What was the weather like?" April asked

I hadn't a clue. We had hardly been outside the flat for the whole time – and the curtains hadn't even been drawn back. It had been a sort of erotic holiday.

This gave me a whole new fillip and my spirits rose. And after that I would take at least one trip a month to London to visit Keith and have a wonderful time. He began to introduce me to his friends and show me parts of London that I'd never seen before.

I had fallen for him in a big way and returning to Rotherham on Sunday evening became ever harder. I wanted to stay with him, I wanted to make a life with him.

In the end, after so many tearful partings, he said: "Why don't you come and live with me?"

It was the question I had wanted to hear, but it was also the one that terrified me most. To simply give up everything I knew and loved for a leap into the unknown was an intimidating prospect.

The girls at work were urging me to go. "You might never get another chance like this."

My parents had met Keith on one of his visits to Rotherham and they liked him.

But to move to London knowing only one person – someone who spent long, long hours at work – was daunting. I would only do it if I could find a job that would give me an independent toe-hold.

Almost directly across the road from Keith's flat was a large psychiatric hospital, Friern Hospital. It had once been a Victorian asylum and it was certainly a forbidding-looking building with a wide frontage and huge grounds. Keith said his mother had worked there as a volunteer when she and his father lived nearby.

I wrote to the head of the occupational therapy department asking if there were any vacancies and eventually a letter arrived inviting me to come in for an interview.

Suddenly the prospect of the big move was a reality. I went to Friern Hospital for the interview. Its 19th century origins were still very much in evidence, not only in the architecture but in some of the patients who had obviously been there for a very long time. Many of them drifted aimlessly along this immensely long corridor (at nearly a quarter of a mile you could hardly see one end from the other), searching endlessly for cigarettes.

Despite the fact that I had not done a job interview for almost eleven years, the old silver tongue started wagging and, of course, I was offered the post.

This was crunch time; I could no longer prevaricate. The job would not be available for ever, so I accepted and said that it would take me a couple of weeks to move into the flat across the road.

Now it was time to break the news to my parents, who were worried that I was jumping into the unknown. As far as they were concerned, London was on another planet. And nowadays, I can almost agree with them. But they saw that I had made up my mind and they were happy,

Then came the awful prospect of telling Richard. It was a horrible thing to do to someone who was in such a vulnerable state, but he had been very unsure about the value of our relationship to his own mental health. He had often questioned whether continuing to see me was the right thing to do. I think there was a whole stew of reasons. In some ways, I think, he blamed his illness on his homosexuality and, by extension, me. His increasing dependence on the Church had only reinforced that, although I know the Unitarians were not encouraging or agreeing with it.

Yet he also seemed to appreciate my company. When we went out on Sundays for our walk in the countryside he seemed happiest, and we chatted in much the same way as we had done in the better days. He had found himself a small job tending the flowers around a church. It was only part time, but it was unpressured and allowed him to do what he loved doing.

But I couldn't help feeling that my own life had been swallowed up by his illness. It seemed there was no real prospect that it would improve, and although I was willing to support him, his constantly shifting attitude to our friendship made me slightly resentful.

He took the news of my intended move relatively well. His mother was less happy. We had grown fond of each other and she occasionally rang me to have a chat about the home situation. It was now clear that Richard would be with them for the rest of their lives, and his condition would slowly deteriorate.

I felt deeply sorry and guilty for leaving them. But my own life was reaching a point where it would become meaningless unless I made a move to revive it. Although I loved Beechcroft, my colleagues and the "patients", it was becoming routine and repetitive. I fear I had given all I could give.

So, now it was time to say goodbye to them. I had watched many of the patients grow from school leavers into young adults and they did not understand when I said goodbye to them. They lived from day to day and if I was not there, they would soon adjust. They had spent their whole lives seeing people come and go, making friends that disappeared overnight.

On my final day, Keith drove up to Rotherham to collect me. There was to be a farewell dinner at a local restaurant. About thirty of us gathered - all the people I had worked with, including the cleaner and the consultant and those who had them brought along their own partners, girlfriends, boyfriends and husbands and wives. They toasted Keith and me and bought us a slow cooker for our new home.

I wept buckets, but it wasn't until later that I realised what had happened. These people – ordinary working-class folk like me – had come together to celebrate a gay relationship and wish it success and happiness.

What I had been fighting for all these years, the right for gay people to live their lives openly with dignity and respect, was actually happening, and in the most unlikely of places.

I could not have had a better send-off, and I realised that the public battles had played only a marginal part in it. The slogan 'the personal is political' made perfect sense to me. I could see that only by changing our own personal worlds will we change the world at large.

The happiness we are all seeking isn't granted by politicians, although I accept they can create the circumstances that make the achievement of happiness very difficult.

At that time, of course, unemployment was not the issue that it is today, neither had we the experience of AIDS, but I still maintain that the most important changes we can make are the ones inside our own heads.

I had handed over the running of CHE to members of the committee, but didn't have much confidence that it would survive very long. Most of them had now achieved their ambition of finding a partner, and most of them didn't share my impetus to campaign to make things better.

But in many ways it had served its purpose. The council had now removed all restrictions on gay people having access to their services (except for *Gay News* in the library), so I would call it a day in Rotherham with a clear conscience. Who knows what opportunities there might be to continue to fight the good fight in London?

~ *53* ~

I moved to London on 14 February 1983 – very appropriately on Valentine's Day. This I now regard as the start of my second shot at life. Since that day, Keith and I have celebrated two anniversaries – 31 August, when we met at Durham and 14 February, when our life together began. (Later still, it increased to three – when we got our civil partnership).

It was all rather stressful. I felt like a stranger in a strange land, having to get used to a whole new culture.

London was far more cosmopolitan than Rotherham was at that time. I was astonished at the number of different languages that were being spoken in the streets and the sheer variety of races. This influx from all over the world showed me that I was not the only individual trying to adjust to being in a completely new environment. I was surrounded by people who had come from somewhere else.

I had brought Essentially Gay with me – with all the stock now being stored in the spare room of the flat. I had arranged a new Post Office Box, so that I could collect the mail and the orders from the local sorting office. That was one bit of continuity.

I had also been keeping up with the developments in gay media since the demise of the original *Gay News*.

Several magazines had started and folded. Indeed, the title *Gay News* itself had been bought by a millionaire businessman Nigel Ostrer and re-launched as *The New Gay News*. Unfortunately this new version did nothing to enhance the reputation of the much-missed original. It was poorly-written, badly proof-read (if it was proof-read at all) amateurish in design and cheaply printed. In short, it was like a third-rate school magazine. It was a doomed enterprise and soon came crashing down. Nigel Ostrer sold the title on to Millivres.

Millivres was a thriving gay publisher (still is, in fact). I was contributing to its early magazines like *Mister*. Millivres had built its empire on pin-up magazines *Zipper*, *Vulcan* and *Him* which sought to push the boundaries of erotic photography

There was now a gap in the market for a more general interest magazine, and Millivres began to turn *Him* into *Him International* and include editorial content and news (as well as the occasional priapic youth).

I had started contributing to it while I was in Rotherham and was always trying to come up with new ideas for features.

In issue 62 (December 1983) of *Him International* I wrote an article titled "Glad to be Gay – How to be a Happy Homosexual". It was meant as a few tips for coming out which had been gleaned from my own experience and those of the hundreds of others I had talked to over the years.

It proved to be very popular and there were several letters of appreciation in the next issue. Frances from Chesterfield wrote:

"Telling my mother was difficult, but it didn't get the shocked reaction I thought it would. Life is too short, as Terry says, to stay in the closet. Too many people put it off to right time that, of course, never comes."

In the same issue I had written an analysis of recent coverage in the straight press of gay matters. It was headed "Mediawatch". The editor thought this might make a good regular feature, so he asked me to produce a column analysing newspaper coverage each month. I imagined that this would run for a few issues and then peter out.

Another article idea I pitched to them was to invent a young gay man with a problem and send it round to all the agony aunts on newspapers and women's magazines to see what response it would bring. We could then do a rating of the quality and relevance of their answers. This was published in issue 64 of *Him* (January 1984).

Roger Benson was the name of this imaginary 18 year old, and this was his problem:

"To stop myself getting bored, I joined an angling club and there met Jim, who is 24. We have so much in common and

190

eventually we fell in love. But Jim tells me that it is illegal for us to make love as I am under 21. Is this true? All I want is for us to make love and be happy. Please don't let my parents know as I couldn't stand it if they found out."

I sent the "problem" out to the Agony Aunts, enclosing the mandatory stamped, addressed envelope, and awaited their replies.

It was a mixed bag of advice, from discouragement to a simple referral to a counselling agency. Out of the ten of them, only one received full marks, and that was Julia Kamlish on the *Woman's Own* Confidential Counselling Team. Whereas all the others had been reluctant to give any solid advice about whether or not "Roger" should get rogered, Julia had replied:

"Yes, the age of consent for male homosexuals is 21. However, apparently it is very rare for legal action to be taken against two men of your age, since really the law is there to prosecute, for example, a man under 21 who is having a sexual relationship with a younger boy say of about 15 or sixteen. If you and your boyfriend would like to have a sexual relationship, as long as you don't have sex in public places, but in the privacy of your own home, it is unlikely that any action would be taken against you both, and you needn't worry about the law too much in this case.

"It might interest you to know that if any prosecution were to be taken, it would have to be referred to the Director of Public Prosecutions, which is a very lengthy and complicated process and it is very unlikely that anything would happen anyway. It would need to be proved that you and your friend were having sex, which is a very difficult thing to do."

She ended by saying that "Roger" was doing OK and that "everything will work out fine for you."

I awarded her the Golden Gay Agony Aunt of the Year Award (which I'd just invented for the occasion), saying she was "realistic, well-informed, positive and not afraid to stick her neck out." I suggested that if Gay Switchboard was recruiting, they might consider offering her a job.

I didn't give it much more thought and moved on to the next project, but that particular article would come back to haunt me later.

The Mediawatch column was going down well and soon became a fixture in the magazine. I didn't know at that time that it would end up running for twenty-five years without a break. I was becoming a real journalist with a recognised by-line.

~ *54* ~

My day job would be at Friern Hospital, and I started with some trepidation. It was a very sinister-looking place, out of synch with the modern world, a throwback to a time when people were incarcerated in the "Lunatic Asylum" for a variety of reasons, not all of them related to madness.

As part of the hospital's archive, there was an admissions book going back to the end of the 19th century. As I leafed through this catalogue of misery, I spotted the names of several women who had been admitted accompanied by a servant, or sometimes two servants.

I was told that these were well-to-do young women from prominent families who had become pregnant outside of marriage. One way to deal with such 'scandals' in those days was to simply declare the girl insane and admit her – with a suitable dowry - to Friern Hospital (which had previously been called Colney Hatch Lunatic Asylum). That got her out of sight and out of mind.

Friern's long history had included a catastrophic fire in which 52 people had perished and numerous suicides on the railway line that ran alongside the hospital (it had had its own station at the beginning so that relatives could get easily from London for visiting).

And it wasn't just the patients who topped themselves - the previous head occupational therapist of the department I was working for had hanged himself from a tree in the grounds not long before I started.

Even so, Colney Hatch had been regarded as progressive at the time of its inauguration, and was opened with great pomp by Prince Albert in 1853.

In its early days it had been home to two and half thousand people, it had its own farm, water supply, orchard, dairy and even a brewery and an artesian well.

By the time I arrived there, it was coming to the end of its life as a hospital.

There were plans to place the remaining thousand or so inmates 'in the community', which I worried about. The local MP was Margaret Thatcher and she was on an austerity drive. I worried that the people who had called Friern their home for decades would be cast out to fend for themselves. The policy was called "care in the community" which was fine on paper, so long as the resources would be provided to operate it properly. I felt strongly that they wouldn't be.

In the capable and humane hands of Mary Myers in Rotherham, care in the community had seemed like a passionate and achievable ambition, but in Margaret Thatcher's grasp, I wondered whether care in the community would eventually end up as care in the shop doorway – simply a means of saving money.

There were a lot of elderly people who had lived in Friern Hospital for most of their lives. They were thoroughly institutionalised and I saw no evidence of them being prepared for a life away from what they had come to regard as a safe haven – an asylum, indeed. The wards were dark and many of them smelly.

Friern Hospital was as far away as you could get from the warmth and openness of Beechcroft.

~ 55 ~

Keith was working incredibly hard in his new job as finance director. He left early in the morning and returned late at night. We were only seeing each other for a couple of hours a day.

At weekends it was different. We would go off on expeditions around the London and because he had lived here since he was a child, he knew a lot of the city intimately. I was glad to do the tourist circuit and then see some other things besides.

One of the shocks as we passed through the posher areas was the amount of wealth that was concentrated here. London was awash with big, fancy cars, and big palatial houses and VIPs galore.

It seemed so unfair that the Rotherham that I had left was so poverty-stricken by comparison. The steelworks and the pits were creating the wealth that was then being spent in London on these ostentatious lifestyles.

This left me feeling distinctly out of place. I didn't belong here: the noise and bustle I could cope with, but the unfairness of it all struck me every day.

At work I was getting to know some of my colleagues in the OT department, but it was difficult because of having to move around from one department to another. I was working with someone different just about every day.

As I moved around I realised that there were many tragic and extraordinary stories in Friern Hospital. Some of the older people had been in Nazi concentration camps during the war and although they had survived the physical horrors, they had not entirely survived emotionally from the experience.

I also saw what stress can do to the human mind; it can even cause it to shut down entirely.

And I was coming to realise that I was not immune to the physical manifestations of mental stress. I had developed a bad case of eczema on my hands which itched and bled. Nothing seemed to cool it.

I knew that I was not making this transition into a completely new life without consequence. The skin condition was a message from my subconscious telling me that I was emotionally all at sea.

Although the work at Friern was interesting, I was not anxious to stay there. It was grim and unhappy. I needed to get away from the place.

~ *56* ~

One day I received a letter from HM Customs and Excise. They had intercepted and confiscated a consignment of books that was to be delivered to me from Bookpeople in California. Among them had been copies of *The Joy of Gay Sex*, a very popular manual which the customs had decided was obscene. But instead of just removing the few copies of that book and delivering the rest, they had seized the whole lot.

The letter said that I could appeal against this seizure, but this would be an expensive procedure costing far more than the thousand pounds that the books had been worth.

But this was not the only consignment that was seized. After the second one was destroyed, I knew that I could not sustain the losses. I had to close Essentially Gay and sold on my spare stock to Gay's the Word for a song.

Of course, Gay's the Word later had its own confrontation – a far more serious one - with the customs in 1984.

On 10th April, as part of what they called 'Operation Tiger', Customs and Excise officers raided the GTW shop on Marchmont Street in Bloomsbury and seized all their imported books – about a third of its total stock.

The homes of the shop's directors were also raided and thousands of pounds worth of other imported books were impounded at their ports of entry.

The customs were using the Customs Consolidation Act of 1876, an obscure law that had been revived almost specifically for the purpose of destroying Gay's the Word.

But the customs were not simply intercepting "pornography", they were also taking charge of all imported books, even those by writers such as Oscar Wilde, Armistead Maupin and John Paul Sartre. If they did release any of them, they had invariably been damaged and were not sellable at the retail price.

This all created a huge controversy with many straight people and more liberal newspapers coming to the defence of

Gay's the Word. There was a strong suspicion that this persecution had originated in government from someone of a Mary Whitehouse frame of mind who was determined to put the shop out of business.

Undeterred by the public outrage, the customs charged the shop's eight volunteer Directors and one member of staff with "conspiracy to import indecent or obscene material".

Support for GTW came from a wide range of sources. Obviously the LGBT community got behind the shop and there were fund-raising events and protest marches. But strangely it was a blow-up sex doll that helped save them.

A company called Conegate had tried to import the sex dolls from West Germany but these had been seized by the customs, saying they were "indecent or obscene". Conegate fought back and took their case right up to the European Court of Human Rights, arguing that there was no restriction on manufacturing these items in the UK, therefore a ban on importing them was a restriction on trade.

This helped the Gay's the Word case, but in fact it was a change of government that ended the persecution. Sir Patrick Mayhew – reputedly a book lover himself - intervened, looked at the seized stock and immediately ordered it to be released. This gave credence to the theory that someone in Westminster had taken it upon themselves to launch the attack.

All this came too late for Essentially Gay, and I had wound it up by then.

Writing the Mediawatch column in *Him* magazine (which had now morphed into *Him/Gay Times* and eventually just *Gay Times* after the *Gay News* title had been incorporated) meant I had to constantly search newspapers and magazines for material. This took me to the library reading room, where I could browse through the newspapers without having to buy them (I was only being paid for the article at that point, not the expenses). There was no internet then, so access to newspapers was on paper only. It was a laborious business leafing through them all every day and then photocopying the relevant articles.

The press were publishing an increasing amount of comment and news on gay issues and it wasn't difficult to find enough to turn it into a column. It wasn't pleasant and the tabloid newspapers were particularly aggressive. The language being used to describe gay people – 'poofs', 'poofters', 'queers', 'benders' was the language of the gay-bashers. The supposedly intelligent papers, like the *Daily Telegraph* and the *Times* were still putting the word gay in inverted commas, as though it wasn't real. There were frequent letters to the editor complaining of the "hijacking of that lovely little word gay, by people who are anything but gay."

Writing a monthly opinion piece about these crude attacks was easy, but a sinister pattern was developing. The onslaughts were getting more and more ferocious and extreme. The language was getting increasingly virulent. This was something that needed to be watched closely if it was not to result in some kind of violent backlash.

The appearance and spread of HIV was also fuelling a growing hostility towards gay people. We were being blamed for the virus and for its spread. The tabloid papers were increasingly hysterical about it.

We were also becoming a political football. The Conservative-leaning papers had discovered one or two minor grants to gay groups that had been made by the Greater London Council, and thus was born the concept of the "loony left". The battles between the Conservatives and the Labour Party would increasingly involve the gay issue, and the newspapers would make full use of the propaganda opportunities it offered.

The Conservatives had decided that the gay community was unpopular enough and small enough to be used as a scapegoat and also a distraction when there was bad news to be covered up. If there had been some political catastrophe or the polls were looking bad for them, the Tory press could be relied on to find some negative gay angle to a story and use it to keep the bad news off the front pages.

It was on one of my sojourns to the library, while leafing through more abuse, that I found, in the jobs column of the *New Statesman*, an advertisement for a counsellor to work on the agony column of a woman's magazine in the IPC stable. This seemed interesting – it could combine my experience in the mental health field with my ambitions in journalism. I realised that my chances of landing such a job were remote – to start with, I wasn't a woman and I didn't know of any male agony aunts at the time. Secondly, I was a gay man – what would I know about women's problems? I hadn't been married, didn't know what straight relationships were like (except as an outside observer) and had never had children – in fact, I was several steps removed from the issues that concerned women at that time.

All the same, Friern hospital's gloomy atmosphere was not something I wanted to endure for much longer. I could see how people who stayed there might be driven to desperate measures – it was the last place you would want to be if you were depressed.

So, off went my application, with much hope but little expectation.

200

~ 58 ~

I was keeping in touch with Richard by phone, and eventually asked if he would like to come down to London and spend a day. We had done this often when we had been together, just taken the train or bus and wandered around the city for a few hours, looking at its wonders.

I took a day off work to entertain him, but when he arrived it was a bit awkward. How were we to regard each other now? Were we friends, ex-lovers or lovers in abeyance?

He had changed, appearing slightly unco-ordinated and clumsy and sometimes a little strange and distant. It was clear to me that the episode with the brain seizure had done more damage than we realised.

He still entertained a faint hope that this emigration was a temporary arrangement and that I would soon return north. What could I say that wouldn't hurt him more? His fragility was very obvious, so I tried to keep the day gentle, with a walk in the park and a meal. It was a steamy summer afternoon and in the restaurant he took off his shirt, which drew a few disapproving glances.

When we paused in our walk or sat on the grass and I looked at him, I felt tears welling up, though I knew I must act the optimistic friend. I felt so sorry for him, but didn't know what I could say that would reassure him. The truth was, I wasn't coming back to Rotherham. London was my new home. Difficult though adjustment was proving, I was going to see it through.

I saw him off on the bus back and said that he should come again, often, and we'd really get to know London together.

~ *59* ~

Keith's parents sometimes came from Scotland to London to visit and renew their acquaintances with people they had known when they lived here. They regarded Keith's flat as their *pied-a-terre* and were obviously used to simply moving in and setting up camp there. Keith wasn't around most of the time, so they could regard it as home from home.

When I had entered the picture, however, there was a bit of initial resentment. Keith was an only-child and both his parents were only-children, which meant, of course, that he was the end of the line. There was no other family to speak of, so this little triumvirate had grown very close.

Keith had come out to them some time before I arrived on the scene, so his gayness was no great surprise to them. Until then, though, it had all been theoretical. My presence moved it into the realms of reality.

My initial meeting with them was tense and not without drama, but over the months and years we gradually got to know each other. With Keith, I visited them several times at their home in Arisaig, a beautiful place right on the edge of the sea on a wild and rocky headland. They had designed and built this house themselves, making it exactly as they wanted it. They were now well-established in the community and knew just about everyone in the area.

Keith's mother, Margaret, was a small woman but feisty. She had done important work in the diplomatic services during the war, but had then devoted herself to supporting her husband's artistic endeavours.

Keith's father, James (or Jim as he was known in the family) was an artist with a long career in the design and manufacture of very expensive *objets d'art* in silver and with precious stones. In Arisaig he had a studio attached to the house and in his later years returned to his first love of landscape painting and produced many wonderful seascapes and landscapes, reflecting the local area, which he had loved since cycling there as a teenager.

Keith and his parents were a trio who had shared so much and it was natural that there would be some resistance, especially from his father to this apparent interloper.

Later on, a childhood friend of Keith's, who had known the family for decades, said she thought that his parents' initial reaction to me wasn't anything to do with me being gay. They would have reacted in exactly the same way if I had been a man or a woman. In fact, there would probably have been even more resistance if I'd been female.

It took some time to resolve, but we got there in the end. Keith was adamant that it was their choice whether or not to adjust and accept me because I was now part of his life - and that wasn't going to change whether they liked it or not.

In the end, they did adjust and they did accept and we became good friends.

~ *60* ~

To my astonishment, I received a letter from IPC inviting me for an interview for the agony aunt job. Who, me? What on earth were they thinking of? Even I wouldn't have gone that far!

It would be as part of the Confidential Counselling Team on *Woman's Own* magazine. The letter was signed by Anna Oliver, who was head of the team. I was sure that once I presented myself at the office, Ms Oliver would snort derisively and ask me to be sure and close the door behind me as I left.

When I arrived at King's Reach Tower, the skyscraper on Stamford Street that housed IPC and its many magazine titles, I couldn't help but think about the dozens of short stories I had despatched to this legendary address from Rotherham. None of them had been published, and now here I was, about to ask them for a proper job.

The Confidential Counselling Team was accommodated in an open-plan office on the 6th floor. There were about ten people working in there, mostly women of course, but with one man sitting at a desk. Anna Oliver's office was separate, but overlooking this clattering workforce.

I performed as I usually did in interviews, trying to convince Ms Oliver that I was just what she had been looking for. I was asked to demonstrate my typing skills, which were satisfactory (thank you British Wagon) – there were no computers or word processors at that stage so hulking great typewriters were the technology of the time which, in my case, required the accompaniment of gallons of Tippex.

She told me to disabuse myself of any idea that this was a journalistic job. The official agony aunt was a woman called Angela Willans and it was the Confidential Counselling Team's job to be her back-up and deal with the 200 or so letters that were received each week. The magazine prided itself on offering a reply to everyone who wrote to the agony column.

Ms Oliver showed no sign that she had been dazzled by my usual flow of inflated claims and promises of innovative thinking. We parted on a non-committal basis with her assurance that she had at least half a dozen others to see before she could reach a decision.

Still, it had been interesting to see inside the factory that produced so many periodicals and with whose rejection slips I was so intimately familiar. I went home imagining I would receive a similar communication sometime in the immediate future.

But the following day I received a call from Anna Oliver. She was offering me the job at *Woman's Own*.

I was excited beyond belief, not only because I would be moving into something fascinating and new but also because I could get away from Friern Hospital. I just couldn't wait to hand in my notice.

(Friern Hospital later carried to fruition its policy of integrating its patients into the community. Now that awful building has been converted into a block of luxury flats. Who knows what happened to all the people who were resident there towards the end of Friern's life as an asylum? Hopefully they went on to better things.)

I had to commute each morning into London on the tube when I started at *Woman's Own*. It was a bit of a culture shock. The trains were incredibly crowded. It was OK going in, we were at the end of the District Line so I could usually get a seat to Blackfriars. But on the journey home, by the time the train reached the station it was already packed and that meant standing all the way back.

At first it was a novelty, but that soon wore off and the sheer discomfort of the journey, particularly in the summer, began to feel oppressive.

Now, as I settled into this job, I started to feel that I had a real reason to be here in this grand and exciting city. The sense of alienation was diminishing. I felt less as though I was a perpetual tourist and more like I had a legitimate reason to be here.

The thrill of walking over Waterloo Bridge each morning and evening never diminished. The views in both directions were staggeringly glorious, with the Houses of Parliament in one direction and St Paul's Cathedral in the other.

The job itself consisted of ploughing through some of the 200 readers' letters that were received each week and trying to answer the many questions that were posed.

The Confidential Counselling Team consisted of four of us dealing with general queries – me, another guy, Peter, Sue, who also assisted Claire Rayner, and .... Julia Kamlish, the woman to whom I had awarded the Golden Gay prize in my article in *Him* about agony aunts.

I wasn't sure whether she had seen it and, if so, how she had taken it and didn't know whether I should tell her it was me. I waited a few months until I had got to know her better before I revealed the truth. When I did, she exploded.

"You? You did that?" she was not at all pleased. I was glad that quite a bit of time had elapsed or she might have been a little less accommodating.

"Did you know I was thinking of calling the police about it? I was tricked and defrauded."

I tried to reassure her that the purpose had not been to humiliate her and, after all, she had won first prize. She was not happy about it and I wondered whether perhaps I had got her into trouble with the boss, given that she had been so cavalier about the law. But by this time we had become quite good friends, so it didn't take her long to calm down and grudgingly forgive me. Later Keith and I socialised often with Julia and her girlfriend.

Also on the team was Alison, a woman who specialised in divorce matters and could give information about the law, then there was a nurse who dealt with the medical problems a couple of "health and beauty advisors" who were as ill-suited to their jobs as I was to mine. The health advisor was vastly overweight and the beauty advisor was a gor-blimey cockney girl with flaky skin and ratty hair.

As part of my three month induction, I was sent off to Rugby to attend a course on counselling provided by The Marriage Guidance Council (or Relate as it's called now). I was getting myself all prepared to be let loose on the letters that were flooding in to *Woman's Own* from all over the country and on all kinds of topics.

Angela Willans, the official agony aunt, had been on the magazine for twenty-five years and for many of those had been published under the pseudonym Mary Grant. Now, using her own name, she worked from her home and one of our tasks was to pick out letters that might be suitable for her to answer on the problem page of the magazine.

She occasionally came into the office for round table meetings with the team, and we would ask her opinions about issues that had cropped up in the letters that left us scratching our heads. Of course, having been in the game for so long, there wasn't much in the way of human misery that she hadn't already encountered.

We also had at our disposal a large collection of letters that Claire Rayner had written to people over the years, all categorised by subject – abortion to haemorrhoids, loss of sex drive to out-of-control teenagers. If we were stuck for an answer, we'd probably find it in the Claire Rayner file.

It seems incredible now, when information of all kinds is instantly available on the internet that people still needed at that time to write to magazines for support. But they did and we had a whole battery of leaflets, book recommendations, support group contacts and so on to satisfy the demand.

Soon I was officially approved as capable of replying to the letters under my own steam and I buckled down to get on with it.

~ *61* ~

It was on a Sunday morning when we were having one of our lazy bed days that the phone rang. It was Richard's mother.

"I've got some bad news for you, Terry," she said. "I'm sorry to tell you, but Richard died on Thursday. It was very peaceful and he didn't have any pain."

I was so shocked that I couldn't speak. It was as though I had a brick in my throat, no words could pass the obstruction. She sensed this and said: "Cry for yourself, dear, not Richard. He's at peace now."

After what seemed like an age of trying to say something – anything – I still couldn't speak and put the phone down. But then the tears came and they were bitter and long.

The following weeks were possibly the most painful days of my life. Each hour that passed was like a dream. Everything I did was muted, as though someone had turned my senses down to a low level. I trapped my hand in a car door and hardly felt it. I was unaware of the time and hours would slip by unnoticed as I hovered in a strange state, suspended outside myself.

His parents had arranged the funeral and all I had to do was attend.

Over the eleven years our relationship lasted we had been lovers, friends, supporters, defenders and cohorts. How could I explain to people that perhaps the most important third of my life up until then had been shared with Richard, that we had gone through simultaneous periods of growth together: coming out, discovering sex, fighting for our rights and finding out what love really feels like. It was an experience that belonged to just to two of us, its intensity was personal and impossible to communicate to a third party.

The funeral was the way Richard would have wanted it, at the Unitarian Church. But no mention was made of his gayness, not even an oblique reference was made to our relationship. It was as though it had never existed. Our joy in each other did not figure in the life that was described by the minister in the pulpit.

I blame no-one for that. It seemed almost inevitable that it would not be mentioned. It would have jarred and seemed out of place. And yet somewhere not very far below the surface there was a resentment that our love – the most important and transforming thing in both our lives – was brushed aside as at best irrelevant and at worst shameful.

Why didn't I protest at this airbrushing of our partnership? I was in such a fragile emotional state at the funeral that I was unable to control the crying. The idea of speaking a eulogy or even speaking at all was out of the question. Mi Mam had come along as a supporter and she helped me through, but I wouldn't have wanted to cause a fuss for Richard's elderly and grieving parents.

They invited me back to Psalter Lane afterwards, but I couldn't go. I couldn't stop crying while everyone else there was simply being polite. The thought of being in the house where we had shared so much and him not being there was unbearable.

There was also the issue of guilt. I had abandoned him at his lowest point. I had not been around when the crisis came. I rationalised that the relationship – important as it had been for all those years – was over, anyway. Richard had wanted it to be over, although he had wanted us to remain friends.

What was I to do, when the opportunity to rescue myself came in the form of Keith? My being around in Sheffield would not have saved Richard. I knew from the few times I had seen him in the days since I came to London, he was fading. It was the epilepsy that had finally claimed him.

But that guilt haunted me for many years, and even as I recall that time now, the old feelings well up again.

After the funeral I never saw his mother again, she died soon afterwards. His father, though, moved to France to live with his daughter in Paris. *En route* he turned up one Sunday morning at our house in London and had a cup of tea. It was excruciating, the hour he sat in the dining room trying to tell me about what had happened since his wife died. I didn't know what to say to

209

him – he was now setting out at his advanced age on a journey even more daunting than my own had been.

I grieved for years for Richard, but it was a strange sort of grieving because no-one in my new circle had known him at all. I couldn't share it with anyone.

I was rapidly embarking on a second life that would become detached from the first. In many ways it would be completely different, but there would also be many similarities.

~ *62* ~

The headquarters of Keith's firm had been moved all the way across to west London and his commute was adding an hour or more a day to his working time. Not only was he working endless hours in the office, there were now extra hours travelling. It was unsustainable, and so we decided that the time was right to get our own house nearer to his job.

Keith had never felt the need for a house before. Living on his own, he had treated his flat, rented from his employer, as simply a place to sleep between days at the office. Now there were two of us it seemed more worthwhile to invest in our own place and create a home.

After a reasonably brief search, we ended up in a leafy west London suburb, living in a house that I could never have dreamed of in the Maltby days.

A three-storey modern town house, with a huge cedar tree in the garden, it had been built in parkland that was once part of a now-demolished stately home. At night I could hear an owl hooting, in the evening hedgehogs could be found snuffling around the garden and foxes were sometimes glimpsed, silently vanishing from view at the approach of humans.

That led to the usual furnishing frenzy and choosing things to go in the new love nest.

This was all new to me, I had never had a space of my own, so I was a little bit overawed by the idea of making decisions that we would have to live with for years.

All this happiness was overlaid by the sadness of grieving. They say it takes two years to even start to recover from the death of a loved one, and my experience as a counsellor over the years told me that no two people grieve in the same way. I would just have to endure the pain and bewilderment, in the same way that the majority of people have to at some time in their life.

~ *63* ~

The work at *Woman's Own* was proving a revelation. Reading all these letters from women around the country was giving me a real insight into life behind the net curtains of suburbia.

We had to keep a record of the topics that cropped up in the letters that we answered. This gave the editor of the magazine an idea of what was of particular concern to the readers at that time. They could then commission articles on those topics.

For instance, if we had a large crop of letters asking for information about domestic violence and how to escape it, there would be an article about it in a subsequent issue.

One of the things that struck me most was the low self-esteem of so many women, and the way they seemed totally in hock to their husband/boyfriends. Even when their men were violent or abusive many women seemed to see it as somehow being their fault.

I remember one letter that summed this up. A woman had written about her husband constantly beating her, putting a plastic bag over her head to frighten her, once throwing her down the stairs and constantly abusing her verbally. Her question was: "Do you think I should leave him?"

Another woman told of how her husband had forbidden her to continue with her beloved horse riding because he feared she was getting sexual thrill from being in the saddle. This brought to mind the oppression of women I had seen all over the Muslim world and concluded that it isn't just with religion that men can keep women enslaved.

We would also sometimes get letters from people who were obviously mentally ill. One woman complained that there were people in the television watching her and another thought that a small alien had entered her ear and was whispering obscenities to her.

In these cases all we could do was encourage them to visit their GP and hope that he or she would spot the problem.

One woman wrote in convinced that her husband was poisoning her. She thought he was putting something in her tea. Once again, I suggested that she visit her doctor and explain the problem to him. But a few weeks later, the police came to the office wanting to see the letter she had written to us. They had found my reply in her drawer after she had died from poisoning, and now they wanted to see what she had said. I didn't find out the outcome of that case but it seemed almost Victorian in its melodrama.

At one end of our office was a small library of books on relevant topics that we used for reference and to recommend to people. A very useful series was published by The Sheldon Press, an off-shoot of the SPCK, the Society for Promoting Christian Knowledge. The series, with its uniform black and white covers, was called "Overcoming Common Problems" and consisted of self-help books usually with the words "coping with" in the title. "Coping with Depression", "Coping with Bereavement", that sort of thing. The nurse on the Confidential Counselling Team had been commissioned to write a book called "Coping with Irritable Bowel Syndrome".

I got to thinking that maybe the Sheldon Press would be interested in a book about "coping with" homosexuality. I remembered the article I had written in *Him* about being a happy homosexual, and so I decided that I would pitch the idea to them.

They were interested and asked me to send a detailed proposal. This was very exciting and I set about planning what the book would contain. What were the issues that troubled gay people?

Coming out was obviously the big issue of the day – and still is - and that took up most of the book. But practical information that was not readily available in one place (no internet at that time) and would also be included.

I submitted the proposal and Sheldon Press accepted it. I had given it the title *How to be a Happy Homosexual – a guide for gay men* but they didn't like that and wanted to call it simply *So, you're homosexual.* I wasn't enamoured of that, I thought my title was better, but if it made the difference between being published and not being published, I'd go along with it.

So I signed the contract and received the advance payment. Now all I had to do was write it.

~ *64* ~

Trying to make a new circle of friends in Ealing was not proving easy. There was The Ealing Gay Group, which Keith and I joined, but it was mainly elderly gentlemen who just wanted to socialise. That was OK, but not very exciting.

One of the more interesting members of the group was called Peter Knight. The flat he shared with his partner Neil Henderson was just a short walk from our new house. They were a long-established couple and both had been married before they set out on their gay life together. Peter had two grown-up children and Neil had a daughter and a son with whom he kept in contact.

It seemed that both had kept good relations with their wives and families and it all seemed very civilised. It illustrated again to me – and I had seen it many times in the correspondence at *Woman's Own* – just how versatile and flexible people can be when the survival of their happiness demands it. Divorce had created so many complicated family situations with children finding themselves with two sets of parents, step-parents and surrogate parents.

Love, it seems, can conquer all, and I'd seen many instances of families overcoming seemingly intractable fall-outs and splits and then reassembling in some new way. When we need to – and when we want to - we can get through crises and adjust to new circumstances that will preserve previous relationships in an altered form. It is only the people who are emotionally inflexible and incapable of accepting change that never find happiness. And this was true of parents who discovered they had gay children. Often it was religious people or extremely conservative people who found that their reaction was fixed and unshakeable, and who were unable to adapt to the news that their child did not have a conventional sexuality. I felt sorry for those who allowed their religion to destroy their love for their child.

Peter, like me, was concerned to do a bit of campaigning and so between us we formed the Ealing Gay Association, which would concentrate on raising awareness of gay issues in the borough.

At the time Ealing was ruled by one of the notorious "loony left" councils and we would be coming to their defence every time the Tories launched another attack on them. I had a good platform for this in my Mediawatch column.

We got the EGA group off to a start by giving a joint interview to the local *Gazette*. This interview was not as traumatic as the one to the *Advertiser* had been all that time ago, but it was our first public foray and meant we were in business as part of the Ealing scene.

Perhaps the most high profile of EGA's campaigns was a protest at the murder of a local gay man. Michael Boothe who was beaten to death outside the public lavatories in Elthorne Park in Ealing on 29 April 1990. Mr Boothe was a small-time actor whose claim to fame was a bit part in *Dr Who* and touring with Derek Nimmo.

The police said he had received "an extraordinarily severe beating of a merciless and savage nature." His injuries "ranged from the tip of his toe to the top of his head." One of Mr Boothe's feet was half severed from his leg. The pathologist was unable to count the number of times he had been kicked and punched.

Michael Boothe had almost certainly been cottaging that night, but his death was only one of a series that had happened over the previous year in west London. In September 1989 a gay barrister, Christopher Schliach, was murdered in his west London home. He was stabbed more than 40 times.

Three months later, in another part of west London, a gay hotelier, Henry Bright was stabbed to death at home. The following month gay hotel porter William Dalziel was found unconscious on a roadside in Acton. He died soon after from severe head injuries.

The murder of Michael Boothe was the last straw for many people who felt that the police were not taking these crimes

216

seriously because, perhaps, somewhere deep down they thought the victims deserved it.

Ealing Gay Association marched with hundreds of other lesbians and gay men from Elthorne Park to Ealing Town Hall, where we held a candlelit vigil. It was a powerful and emotional demonstration and out of it sprang the activist group OutRage! which began campaigning for the police to stop arresting gay men and instead start protecting them.

But it was only by confronting the police's apparent indifference to this series of murders that we made them stop and think about their approach. That demo may have been the start of a sea change in attitudes in policing for gay people. Instead of being afraid of the police, we gradually came to trust them and saw them as allies. But that was a long time coming and there were many more confrontations to be had before then. It was a conservative institution and attracted people with deep-seated antipathy to anything gay. The macho "canteen culture" would prove hard to change.

However, in 2002 the police re-opened the Michael Boothe case with a £15,000 reward for information that would lead to convicting his murderers. Unfortunately, the case remains unsolved.

Outrage! – the driving force of which was the indefatigable Peter Tatchell – went on to challenge many aspects of injustice directed at gay people. Their confrontational tactics didn't suit everyone, but I thought they were very effective. I had come to realise that unless you disturb people's complacency, they will not make any effort to change. Why should they? If the status quo is in their favour, why would they want to upset it?

So, when Peter Tatchell called me up one day and asked if I would join a protest march in Westminster aimed at challenging the rule that there should be no political demonstrations within a mile of Parliament, I had to say yes. The idea was that we would cross the mile boundary and then sit down in the street.

When I arrived at the assembly point there were a hundred or so people ready to go.

The police knew all about these plans and had come equipped for the moment that the demonstration – which was

217

attended by such luminaries as film director Derek Jarman and singer Jimmy Somerville – reached the line that must not be crossed, and then crossed it. I had no idea what the Bobbies were going to do about this defiance – would they charge at us with batons and shields, as I had seen them do during the miner's strike? Would they turn water canon on us, fire tear gas, rubber bullets, trample us with horses?

No, my overactive imagination and my inherited fear of the police were dampened when an Inspector lifted a loud hailer to his lips and demanded that we walk back over the line. If we did not do so, we would be arrested.

Arrested! If Mi Mam had been there she'd have been having the vapours. Getting on the wrong side of the Bobbies, or having any contact whatsoever with the police for that matter, was her ultimate phobia. I don't know why she was so afraid, she'd never done a thing in her life that would interest the constabulary. Our Albert and Roy once got into trouble for trespassing on the railway, and maybe that's what set it off. She wasn't generally a frightened woman, but the police and thunderstorms would both set her trembling. Her – and my father's – greatest fear was "getting summonsed". If you stepped even slightly out of line, in any area of life, my mother would say: "don't do that, you'll get summonsed."

Of course, once we had crossed the line in Westminster and sat down, we ignored the inspector's imprecations to cease and desist and go back across the boundary. He knew his part in this pre-ordained drama and he played it. He was well aware that we weren't going to follow his instructions as there wouldn't have been much point in the demo if we had. But then I saw the row of police vans parked down a side street. They had come equipped all right, equipped to cart us off to the nick.

One by one we were lifted bodily from the road and placed into the vans, which had bars on the windows and caging to separate us from the constables. It was at this point, as they slammed the door on us, that I was suddenly overcome with slight panic. No, it's a mistake, officer – let me out. I'll get the tube home, thank you.

But this wasn't a taxi and we weren't going to be let out. We were now under arrest and *in custody*. I was a *prisoner* – me, a prisoner! - and felt a bit sick. We drove through London as I observed the passing landscape through the bars on the window and wondering what the hell I had got myself into. Memories of Wakefield Prison danced before my eyes.

At the police station we were processed by the duty sergeant and put into cells. I was billeted with Derek Jarman who could see that I was petrified. "Don't worry, Terry," he said. "They'll just give us a caution and we'll be out of here shortly." And, indeed, that is what they did. I gladly signed the paper accepting the caution and just about sprinted through the door of the police station, heading home with enormous relief.

I suppose if you are going to join the roll-call of great dissenters you have to spend at least some time in prison for your beliefs. But I was no Nelson Mandela and those two hours in the police cell were long enough for me. I've never been so pleased to get back to Keith and safety.

~ 65 ~

Marlene had retired from public life in 1975 after falling from a stage in Sydney, Australia and breaking her leg. She was now living in grand seclusion in an apartment on the Avenue Montaigne in Paris.

Whenever Keith and I went to Paris – which we did often, as fortunately we shared a love of the city – I would make the pilgrimage to the Avenue Montaigne, locate Number 12, and stand for a little while gazing at the window, hoping that the goddess might pull back the curtain and reveal herself one more time. She had retired to this place in order to preserve her image as the ageless beauty. She did not want anyone to remember her as anything but the perfect artefact she had been in her glory days.

Of course, she never did appear at the window. By this time she was bedridden. But in 1982 Maximillian Schell, an actor who had starred with her in the film *Judgment at Nuremberg*, had persuaded Dietrich to let him make a documentary about her. She agreed to give a sound interview, but refused to be filmed, so Schell had to assemble a montage of images and clips from her career and played the sound interview over the top.

The movie was having its first showing in London at the Royal Festival Hall, so naturally I was on the front line for tickets. This would be the first that had been heard from Marlene since she had ill-advisedly taken part in a film called *Just a Gigolo* with David Bowie. She had sung the title song – her swan-song – and it had been released as a single. I had bought it and found it to be intensely sad. A real farewell to the world, ending with the words "When the end comes I know, they'll say just a gigolo, and life goes on without me."

Now we were to get a final word from the great diva in the form of this documentary called simply *Marlene*.

It was quite a roller coaster ride, with Dietrich, sounding very old and occasionally inebriated. She was in turn charming, crotchety, bad-tempered, rude, challenging, insulting and in the end heart-breaking. From very unpromising material, Maximillian Schell had crafted a wonderfully revealing portrait of a defiant legend who was in her eighties now, and not ageing well.

Dietrich was reportedly unhappy with the movie, but she was unhappy with everything. She had savaged the commercial recording of her famous show in London in 1972. It had been broadcast on the BBC and released on video, but she bad-mouthed it so severely that the producers ended up suing her.

However, when the Schell film received an Academy Award nomination and several prestigious European prizes, she changed her mind and softened a little towards it.

I thought that this was surely Dietrich's final curtain, her last word. I was sad that we would never see that magical concert again on stage and I had failed in my ambition of knowing her personally. But hang on a minute, it wasn't quite over yet....

~ *66* ~

The new version of *Gay Times* was going from strength to strength under the editorship of John Marshall. The editorial content was stronger with each issue and, fortunately, John liked my style and was commissioning extra articles from me besides the regular Mediawatch.

At the same time I was working on the Sheldon Press book, the dismally titled *So, you're homosexual,* doing the research and writing the text.

It wasn't so difficult, most of it I'd already written many times over in articles and in letters to readers of *Woman's Own.* It was only to be a small handbook, not exactly *War and Peace,* but I wanted to ensure that I'd included all the essentials that would be important to the emerging young gay man. I'd tried to pitch it in language that was reassuring and wouldn't frighten the horses – or the Christians at Sheldon Press.

When the text was finished, off went the package to the commissioning editor and now all I had to do was wait for it to be printed as a book and then the cash would start rolling in.

Except the text *did* frighten the horses, it did upset the Christians – somewhere along the line someone at SPCK had panicked and forbidden Sheldon Press from publishing it. It had been intercepted literally on the way to the printers.

I was called by the commissioning editor, who said that he was terribly sorry to disappoint me, and maybe he could help me get another publisher interested. But I was so upset and angry that I just told him to sod off. I think he may have been living in hopes that I would refund the advance payment. No chance. I had kept my part of the contract, the book had been written and delivered in a publishable form. It wasn't my fault that they didn't have the guts to go with it, apparently because it was "anti-establishment" and they didn't like what I'd said about pretty police activity.

I tried it with a few other publishers who equivocated and delayed and eventually I thought – bugger the lot of you, I'll publish the book myself.

I knew a little bit about publishing from my days of selling books through Essentially Gay. I knew that I would have to have the book printed myself, would have to somehow get it into the shops and would have to promote it myself.

It was at this point that I found a woman called Lydia who hired out her skills as a self-publisher to those who wanted to see their work in print but couldn't get a look in with "straight" publishers. She would explain how to go about it, for a small fee, of course. Given that I had the £2,000 advance from Sheldon, I thought it would be money well spent and indeed it was.

Lydia had a huge amount of red hair that stuck out in all directions in the style of a pre-Raphaelite painting or maybe the Lady of Shallott in the famous picture by John William Waterhouse.

She advised me to set up my own publishing house, which sounded very grand but was really just a label under which I could publish my book and make it look less like a vanity opus. Keith and I brainstormed and eventually came up with the name 'The Otherway Press' (based on the old euphemism "he's a bit the other way"). Then I would have to get someone to design a cover, then I would have to have the text typeset and the books printed. Then they would have to be distributed to bookshops, unless I was prepared to go around the shops myself doing my own trade deals. That didn't appeal.

What would be a realistic number of sales I could expect? Don't order too many, Lydia said, most self-publishers end up with mountains of unsold books under their beds and in their garages. But also remember, the fewer you order the more expensive they are to print. She accepted that this was an almost impossible estimation to make – who knows what will take the public's fancy? It might be a bestseller, it might bomb – there was no previous form on which to base a decision.

However, Lydia thought there was more hope for my book than the usual first novels and autobiographies that were the stock-in trade of most self-publishers. It had a defined market that could be targeted, whereas most general interest books had to compete for exposure in the media with tens of thousands of others. I also already had a following among the target readers, so an ideal ready-made platform to launch it from.

Although there was a never-ending supply of self-help books (some of which were chart topping successes) there was nothing specifically for gay people. Not in the British market, anyway.

In those days there was little in the way of digital printing, it was the old fashioned linotype that had to be set on traditional presses. But this technology was for the specialist and I was happy for the experts to do the job for me.

As for the cover, I didn't know any artists but I had been working voluntarily in the London Lesbian and Gay Centre which had been funded by the Greater London Council under Ken Livingstone, accompanied by endless controversy and "loony left" media abuse. There I had met a young guy who was a student of graphic art. I asked if he would like to do a cover for the book. He was thrilled, being a student he was desperate to accumulate a portfolio, so he drew me a cover for little more than a few quid. It was a simple cartoon of a young man with a quiff-style haircut, a cut that was all the rage at that time among gay men.

Lydia helped me assemble the package for the printer and at the same time she introduced me to a newly established book distributing outfit in north London called Turnaround. This company was going to specialise in distributing books and magazines for the "alternative" market. Their titles would range over the whole left-wing political spectrum, including anarchy and socialism, as well as religious topics like shamanism, Buddhism, Wicca – the lot. These were the kinds of books that had trouble finding their way onto the shelves of conventional bookstores. Turnaround would sell them to the alternative book shops which were much more numerous then, a plethora of specialist booksellers of all kinds could flourish before the iron boot of Amazon came to crush them.

Turnaround was happy to take on the Otherway Press, mainly because it was anxious to get itself up and running with a reasonable catalogue. And best of all, they would be doing the selling.

The book reverted to its original title *How to be a Happy Homosexual*. Now it was at the printers. This title was much better and more eye-catching than the dreary thing Sheldon Press had wanted, although thinking about it over the years, I suppose a more accurate title would have been *How Not to be an Unhappy Homosexual*. Nobody can tell you how to be happy, there is no formula. But there are certainly measures you can take to make an unhappy outcome less likely.

You needed to know about the law which, at the time of the publication of the first edition, still had restrictions – namely, the age of consent being 21. Young gay men needed to know about the health risks of gay sex (or any sex, come to that), they needed to know what their rights were if they fell victim to discrimination (very few at that stage), and where to find other gay people and specialist support.

The main message of the book was to be honest, not only with other people but also with yourself. Living in the closet is not healthy and although I was careful not to try laying down any hard and fast rules, I did opine that living the life you want - and not the one other people want for you - is best.

It was a positive message and one that wasn't widely promulgated among young people at that stage. There were very few reassuring messages, but plenty of negative ones. All I needed to do now was to let people know that the book was there. In other words, I had to market it.

I had been brave and ordered 3,000 copies. This, to Lydia, seemed like a rather optimistic number, but what the hell, if nobody wanted to buy it, so what? There was always the dump.

Then, the books arrived. My very first book! My little darling.

Like a doting parent, I couldn't stop looking at it. Although it wasn't much more than an extended pamphlet, it had my name on it and a glossy cover and a spine. I kept holding it and caressing it and flicking through the pages. It was just as exciting as the day, a couple of decades earlier, that I had first

225

seen my name as a by-line over an article in the *Sheffield Morning Telegraph*.

I had agreed an official publication date. I sent out copies to all the gay magazines for review, I also sent it to all the agony aunts. And anywhere else where I thought I might get publicity. As an added bonus, I had collared Claire Rayner in the *Woman's Own* office and badgered her to say a few words about it, which she kindly did and which I was able to quote from on the first page (and in later editions, on the cover).

"This is a splendid book, honestly felt, honestly written and honestly presented. It's jam-packed with common-sense advice and should leave all it readers feeling much more relaxed about themselves and their lives. I've only one regret about it – it's unlikely to be read by enough heterosexual people. It should be. They have as much to learn from it as homosexual people."

So now not only was I a writer but also a publisher. It was great because I would get profits from both activities. It would all be mine - on the proviso, of course, that I could sell 3,000 books.

The Confidential Counselling Team was proving a bit too expensive for IPC to support. The circulations of magazines and newspapers were dwindling generally, and the IPC titles were no exception.

We had been given several warning signals that the service was unsustainable and so it didn't come as much of a surprise when we were called to a meeting and told that the department was to be closed. There would no longer be an 'everyone-gets-a-reply' service for *Woman's Own* readers. The problem page would no longer solicit a stamped addressed envelope in order to help with readers' woes, it would now inform them that individual replies could not be provided.

So, time to move on. I started scanning the local papers for jobs in the hope that I could avoid a daily commute on the tube.

The local authority was advertising for Day Care Social Workers at a newly-opened day centre for people with learning disabilities. It had very similar ambitions to Beechcroft. This seemed perfect – not only would the job be within walking distance of home, I had all the experience that would be needed to make something of it.

Of course, when I made my application all the old smooth talk came flowing out and the manager, Danny Lee, gave me the job at the Cowgate Day Centre in Greenford.

The council at that time seemed to have money coming out of its ears and the new, purpose-built centre was equipped with everything needed to make it a success. This included a large, enthusiastic young staff team and lots of therapists – speech, art, physio. The service users who would be coming here would be very lucky and have the best of opportunities.

As with Beechcroft, Cowgate's team was very easy to love. The optimistic atmosphere that all these thoughtful young people created was energising. There were high hopes of helping many of the people who would be attending to eventually get a life of their own in the community.

I spent twenty-two happy and very rewarding years there.

~ *68* ~

Being in a stable and secure job, having a happy home life and finding an outlet for my creative impulses was great. The *Gay Times* Mediawatch column had become one of the most popular features of the magazine and that's because there was absolutely no shortage of strong material to fill it.

The two and a half decades that I spent as a contributor to *Gay Times* turned out to coincide with the most important period of reform in the history of gay rights in Britain. And I had the privilege to be on the front line reporting it. I got through five editors before finally reaching the one who wanted to "try something else."

There were all kinds of issues that sprang up during this period of huge upheaval. Mrs Thatcher's election had galvanised the gay community when she introduced the notorious Section 28, aimed at outlawing the "promotion of homosexuality". It prompted huge demonstrations in London and Manchester. Then a group of lesbians managed to get into the BBC and invade the studios of the Nine o'Clock News. Sue Lawley and Nicholas Witchell, the newsreaders, tried to carry on as though nothing was happening even though the lesbians had chained themselves to the desks and were attempting to disrupt the bulletin. Heavies were trying to keep them quiet by sitting on them and putting their hands over their mouths. "I do apologise for the noise," Sue Lawley says, ever so calm and collected and sounding a bit like Lady Bracknell, "We seem to have been somewhat invaded."

The newspapers were playing a huge role in creating the anti-gay atmosphere that had made this disgusting legislation possible. They were increasingly using vile and abusive terminology and seeking out "gay scandals" that would bring the Labour party in disrepute.

They had discovered a small book called *Jenny Lives with Eric and Martin* in a library in the London borough of Harringey. It was meant to reassure children who might live with a gay parent and to perhaps educate those with whom they came into contact.

But the newspapers worked it up into what appeared to be the biggest gay scandal since the trial of Oscar Wilde. The struggle for gay rights had now become a political tool and by the time the Fleet Street propaganda had reached its zenith, Mrs Thatcher had no problem getting Section 28 on to the statute book.

Many of the Labour-controlled local authorities around the country were trying to improve life for their gay constituents. In Camden, the council had established a Lesbian and Gay Unit to consult with the local community. This set off another storm of "loony-left" anti-gay vituperation.

In the *Daily Star* there was a particularly toxic columnist called Ray Mills, who was the paper's deputy editor. His approach was to write the most outrageous copy, sometimes overtly racist and definitely sexist and homophobic. In one of his columns he wrote about Camden's L&G Unit:

"They employ four full-time woofter apologists... Mills has a positive view to offer: These filthy degenerates should be kicked up their much-abused backsides and locked up in their closets"

Of course for the men of the tabloid press this was all good fun. They had no conscience about the fact that they were referring to real people who might consequently suffer violence or discrimination on the back of the stuff they were writing.

Then came AIDS - another stick with which to beat gay men. The approach of the tabloids to this human catastrophe was frightening and callous. Not only were they creating hostility towards people who were terminally ill, they were spreading disinformation and lies about the nature of the disease.

It was just too easy for them to foment suspicion against an already unpopular (in their opinion) minority. Their behaviour was despicable and I was becoming increasingly alarmed about where all this was leading.

While the newspapers were doing their best to create hatred, TV was doing its bit to give at least a modicum of information. Admittedly at the time, at the height of the panic, few people knew where this would lead. There had been nothing quite as uncontrollable as this for a hundred years. It was a situation that required a calm approach and reassurance.

Instead, the tabloid press went in the opposite direction with headlines that became more and more extreme, with one in the *Sun* quoting some mad vicar saying that he would shoot his son if he found he had AIDS.

This was too much for me and I decided to make a complaint to the Press Council.

The Council was set up in 1953 and its stated purpose was to protect the freedom of the British Press but also to hold it accountable if it fell below the highest "professional and commercial" standards.

I said in my complaint that the *Sun*'s report was fear-mongering and likely to cause distress and alarm. Not only that, but the medical "facts" quoted in the article untrue and misleading.

Part of the Press Council's interminably long complaints process involved trying to conciliate a conclusion without the need to adjudicate. They would first write to one of the parties and then ask the other party to respond to it. And then that party would have to respond and so on *ad infinitum*.

Using this method, complaints could be strung out over many months.

Trying to keep this complaint going in the face of these endless exchanges of letters (email had not been invented at the time) was almost impossible, and the Press Council knew this. They would not entertain phone calls or faxes, it all had to be done through the post.

I pointed out many times that the Council was a self-regulatory body, manned and funded by the newspapers themselves. It soon became clear to me that its real purpose was not to resolve complaints but to deflect them. Only the most tenacious complainant could get to the end of this convoluted process.

I was one such complainant who was not going to be worn down and eventually, after the Press Council had taken seven months to reach a decision (long enough for the original story to have been long-forgotten), they rejected the complaint.

When celebrities began to succumb to AIDS, there was more opportunity for the tabloids not only to trash these people's reputations but to create even more loathing for gay men in general.

When the pop singer Freddie Mercury died, the tabloids poured vitriol on his memory. Then Rock Hudson, Kenny Everett, John Curry and many others fell victim. N each case, sensationalism was rife, fear-mongering common and homophobia ubiquitous.

It seemed that every day there was some new gay story that the tabloids turned into a hatefest. The words "poofs", "poofters", "woofters" and "queers" appeared daily on front pages.

There had to be a challenge or something terrible might happen.

~ *69* ~

How to be a Happy Homosexual was published and I was amazed at the amount of publicity it generated, not only in the gay press but also in the agony columns. Turnaround had made a good job of distribution and because of the unique appeal of the book, quite a lot of regular bookshops had decided to stock it too.

Sales began to climb and I was thrilled to see it as number one non-fiction book in Gay's the Word's weekly list of bestsellers that was published in *Capital Gay* newspaper. It stayed there for several weeks running.

Keith and I took a stall at the Gay Pride Festival to sell signed copies and I was overwhelmed by the demand for it. We sold literally hundreds that day and I felt like a bit of a celebrity, signing each copy.

It was at that event that I realised how much of an impact the Mediawatch column was having and how widely it was being read. People were coming up to the stall egging me on to continue, not to let the bastards get away with it.

In fact, I was now being regarded as a bit of a gay spokesperson, which led to me being frequently invited on to radio and TV programmes. Mostly these were live news broadcasts and it was always unpredictable as to what the approach would be when you got into the studio. Would they be sympathetic or hostile? My stage fright often ruined these opportunities and ensured that I was never going to be a TV personality. Each of these appearances stressed me out to the point that it took days to recover. But I felt obliged to do them because if there was an opportunity to put the other side of the story it ought to be put.

Of course, the more you do this kind of thing, the easier it gets and the more relaxed you become. But the road to that nirvana can be a long one – it was for me, anyway. After literally hundreds of broadcast interviews, I can now mostly keep my nerve and a clear head.

Quite often on these programmes I was up against some clergyman arguing against any advance in gay rights. It is the nature of TV talk shows that they want argy-bargy and so often these religious people were extreme. All this did nothing to enhance my regard for religion of any kind.

I took every opportunity to plug the book. When a Tory councillor in Kingston in Surrey called *How to be a Happy Homosexual* "scandalous" and had it banned from the teenage section of the local library, it was like manna from heaven. There is nothing like banning a book to get people wanting to read it.

I had an exchange of correspondence with this councillor, Owen Gardner, Mr Gardner wrote to me:

"I am not a prude but do feel very strongly that schoolchildren must be protected from the adult world for as long as possible in order for them to make their own decisions at a mature age.

"Homosexual activity, while a fact of life, is in my view not natural and children must be protected from its influence for as long as possible."

I responded that Mr Gardner was being short-sighted. I wrote:

"A large part of the book is taken up with giving information about how to avoid AIDS. The Government's slogan in its AIDS education campaign is "Don't Die of Ignorance" – but if this is the way the council in Kingston carry on, some of their teenagers may do just that."

The ban on the book was supported by the Liberal members of the council, which stirred up even more controversy.

The story was splashed not only in the local paper in Kingston but also all through the gay press and in one or two other outlets. It also resulted in a couple of radio interviews. By banning it, Councillor Gardner brought the book to the attention of more people than he could have ever imagined.

~ *70* ~

Poofter' is an Australian slang word so it wasn't really surprising that its use in the British press was pioneered in *The Sun*, owned by the "Dirty Digger", Rupert Murdoch. The paper also introduced other charming epithets for gay men and lesbians: 'nancy', 'fairy', .pansy', 'kharzi cruiser,' 'iron hoof' 'lesboes'.

These aren't unfamiliar words to most gay people, but they are usually encountered in the school playground or in the tap room of some low dive – or as a prelude to a gay bashing. You don't expect to see them in your morning paper.

The use of this language was an attempt to diminish and dehumanise gay people and the sheer ubiquity of the abuse in the tabloids was becoming dangerous. So, again, I decided that I would try to use the Press Council to calm it down.

But the Press Council had no real power. It had no mechanism for punishing recalcitrant newspapers or holding to account repeat offenders. It was all done on a voluntary basis and in reality the PC was more a chocolate fireguard than a ferocious watchdog.

If anyone managed to get through the lengthy complaints procedure they could expect nothing but a tiny apology at the bottom of page 29 in five-point type. In 1990 the Press Council reported that it had received 1,870 complaints and only 142 had reached the adjudication stage. The rest had been withdrawn or the complainant had retired from exhaustion. And even at the end of the procedure, if the paper decided not to print an apology, the PC had no sanctions to force it.

Indeed, one complaint about the *Sunday Sport*, which had used the word "chinks" about Chinese people, was upheld and resulted in the headline "Bollocks to the Press Council".

I had been railing for some time in my Mediawatch column about the abusive language being used in newspapers against gay people, and now others began to make complaints to the Press Council. In 1988 four people complained about a story in the *Sun* headed "Pulpit poofs can stay" which concerned the Church of England's decision not to start a witch hunt against its gay vicars.

The complainants charged that the headline contained "an offensive expression likely to encourage hatred of homosexuals." The Press Council did not agree.

"The headline was vulgar and intended to shock. Its coarseness would offend many readers and be found insulting to homosexuals, but the Press Council is unable to say that it would encourage hatred of them."

This complaint was followed up soon afterwards by another I lodged objecting to a *Sun* headline: "Runcie backs ban on pulpit poofs". After a great deal of deliberation and the usual copious amounts of correspondence, the Council ruled:

"The words 'poof' and 'poofter' are commonly used, and their appearance in a newspaper story was not likely to encourage hatred of homosexuals, the Council said, rejecting a complaint over a report in the Sun."

But that sort of complacency was not good enough. The arrogant and irresponsible approach of the newspapers couldn't continue go unchallenged. Real people were being hurt and I was determined that I would keep pressing until something changed.

The next complaint, though, came from the head of the Wimbledon Area Gay Society, who complained about three headlines from the *Daily Star:* "The Poofter MPs", "Runcie Poofs Ban" and "Up, Up and a Gay – Council's free flying lessons for poofs". The complainant said that the words "poof" and "poofter" were derogatory and insulting to gay people. He said the newspapers would be roundly condemned if they used objectionable word like "nigger" or "yid" to describe black people or Jews and there was no reason why a similar approach should not apply to words which were insulting to gays.

The editor of the *Star* was consulted for his opinion and responded that the Oxford English Dictionary defined "poof" as an "effeminate homosexual man" (origin unknown). "Gay" was described as "light-hearted, sporty, mirthful" and then, colloquially, "homosexual". He said it seemed homosexuals had quite successfully hijacked the word "gay" and made it their own.

The Press Council's adjudication on this case was:

"The headline language was coarse and no doubt intended to be derogatory and insulting to homosexuals. However, whether to publish it, using a words which though offensive is in common parlance, was within the editor's discretion."

I was encouraging my *Gay Times* readers to make more and more complaints and the Press Council was coming under pressure. It was clear that it was provoking a debate inside the Council. An indication of this turmoil was contained in a letter to me from Raymond Swingler, then Assistant Director of the Council.

"You are quite correct in your view that the use of pejorative expressions for homosexuality are now commonplace in the tabloid press: personally I find such use wholly unacceptable and although many on the Council share this view, it is, regrettably, not the common view of the body."

This indicated to me that we had created a fissure at the Council – with many of its members fed up with the loutish behaviour of tabloid editors. It was a crack that we could work on widening.

~ 71 ~

The first edition of *How to be a Happy Homosexual* sold out, but there was still a demand for it, so I decided to produce a second edition. This time I got a new cover designed and made a few tweaks to the text, taking into account some of the suggestions that the critics had made about the first edition.

Another 3,000 copies were ordered from the printer and Turnaround was doing brisk trade with an increasing number of bookshops placing orders. I was thrilled one day to see it in the shop window of a major book retailer in Covent Garden.

The book had been such a success that I thought maybe there was the possibility of another self-help title going into some of the areas in more detail. I thought perhaps a book about relationships, because I'd been reading more and more about the difference between gay and straight relationships and thought it warranted deeper investigation. So I started my research and found a great deal of information from the USA, where social enquiry into gay life was much more advanced than in the UK.

This research might help those gay people who were starting out on a relationship to keep it going. There was a widespread myth that gay relationships are, by their very nature, short-lived and unsatisfactory. It was a myth that religious opponents were always keen to promulgate. I knew from my own experience that it isn't universally true and that many gay couples were prepared to put in the legwork to make their relationships work and endure.

There were (and are) particular problems facing gay couples who want to stay together, and different challenges for same-sex partners. The book would be fascinating to write and I set down to get it on paper, and then into book form.

And so *Making Gay Relationships Work* was conceived.

~ *72* ~

In *Gay Times* I had invented a comic character called Doreen Potts whose fictional correspondence satirised the ignorant heterosexual approach to gay life. She meant well, but she was a fount of all the prejudices she had absorbed from the tabloid papers. When something is absurd – and ignorant expressions of homophobia often are - it can be effectively challenged with satire and mockery as well as political agitation.

The character was so popular that it became a series and eventually Doreen was adapted for the stage by a small theatre group who brought her to the Lesbian and Gay Centre in London.

It was a small-scale thing, but I enjoyed hearing my writing being acted out and hearing the audience laughing. After that I collected Doreen's belles-lettres together with some of my more whimsical articles and published them as *The Potts Correspondence*. Later on, there would be a follow-up in the form of a comic novel, *The Potts Papers*.

The list for the Otherway Press was growing, and after *Making Gay Relationships Work* I produced *Assertively Gay* and then *A Stranger in the Family: how to cope if your child is gay.* This was a guide for the parents of gay children who were struggling with the news. It was particularly apposite as Coming Out was now a right-of-passage for many young gay people, and some message of support was necessary for mum and dad.

The A-Z of Gay Sex was the Other Way Press's final title. The old adage that sex sells anything wasn't quite true of that book, which was the least successful of the lot.

But that didn't matter because it led to a commercial publisher, Carlton Books, commissioning me to write *The Gay Man's Kama Sutra*. This was an interesting project, trying to make an ancient Indian manual for living a successful and satisfying life into a guide for the modern gay man.

Most people think the Kama Sutra is simply a list of exotic sexual positions, but it is much more than that – it contains an ethical code which, with a bit of imagination, I was able to adapt for the modern man. My version of this book sold tens of thousands of copies around the world after it was translated into French, Spanish, German and Serbo-Croat.

I had also been commissioned to write a book for Cassell publishers based on the Mediawatch column in *Gay Times*.

Now I had nine books under my belt and a popular column in the leading gay magazine. I was happy.

~ *73* ~

One of the extra articles I had written for *Gay Times* was about Marlene. I hadn't written anything about her for years, not since *Gay News* in 1972. It was time to revisit her story in the light of new information that had emerged.

After the article was published, I received a phone call from a chap in Huddersfield called David Bret.

David is an interesting character. He is a writer, too, specialising in biographies of film stars, singers and other celebrities. He is of French origin but was adopted as a small child by a Yorkshire family and was raised not far from where I was.

He had read the article in *Gay Times* and told me that he knew Marlene Dietrich personally and was in regular contact with her. I was taken aback by this, and didn't know whether to believe it. This was someone with a pronounced Yorkshire accent who lived in a council house in the industrial north of England. What would the reclusive, secretive and uber-sophisticated Marlene Dietrich want with him?

He told me it had started when he was writing a book about the French music hall and had wanted to quote something that Dietrich had said about one of its stars. David had approached her agent in London, but he had told him "Don't ask me, ask her." This man had obviously been scalded by Dietrich's hot temper in the past and wasn't in a hurry to repeat the experience. So undaunted David wrote to Marlene at her Paris apartment.

She had been impressed by his honesty in at least asking permission, but was always wary of people who might be journalists trying to get the much sought-after exclusive access to the legend. Anyway, she had called him out of the blue one evening and found that his knowledge of her career, and of many of the people she had known in France during her early days, made conversation easy.

After that, she had called him almost every night at 6pm for a chat.

This all sounded very unlikely and he could hear the doubts in my voice. He used to that. Very few people believed him.

So he then played me a small extract from a tape he had made of one of the conversations. The voice was unmistakable – like the one in the Maximillian Schell film, only older and frailer. "David, it's Marlene," she was saying.

This was either a very good impersonation by somebody or it was true. And the more he told me about it, the more I came to see that it was true. There was nothing in it for him to lie.

He had sent her a copy of his first book, a biography of Edith Piaf, who had been a friend (maybe even a lover) of Marlene's. She had enjoyed it and so the conversations continued.

He said he had taped all the calls without her knowledge and she had eventually given him permission to write a book about her to be published only after she was dead. It was published as *Marlene, My Friend* by Robson Books.

After that, David would ring me from time to time to bring me up to date with his friendship with Marlene. He would tell me of her temperamental nature, how talking to her was like walking on eggshells – one wrong word and down would go the phone. But she would then call again the following day as though nothing had happened. Such was the unpredictable nature of la Dietrich that sometimes I think David rang me for counselling after a particularly fiery confrontation.

I was always happy to hear about this new contact with Marlene. David said he had sent the *Gay Times* article to her to read and she had said: "It's very good, but tell your friend he's too nice about me."

I loved hearing about the latest outrageous comment she had made about someone (she had a mean streak when talking about her contemporaries and even more contempt for the new generation of stars. Madonna had an obsession with her, but Marlene was dismissive in return).

This went on until I read an article in the *Sunday Times* about Dietrich's daughter, Maria Riva, planning to publish a biography of her mother. By all accounts it would be a tell-all opus that would not spare Marlene's blushes. Apparently Riva had undertaken not to publish this book until after her mother's death. I rang David and told him about this and he subsequently called Marlene.

He told me later that she had dropped the phone in disbelief.

However, Marlene died in May 1992, at the age of 91, a few months before the book came out, so she was spared the lurid spite that her daughter had heaped upon her.

The book was massive, running to nearly 800 pages, as you would expect for a life as long and crowded as Marlene's, but in the end, it revealed as much about the daughter as it did about the mother.

Maria Riva accused Marlene of neglecting her as a child, she threw cold water over Marlene's splendid war record, she belittled and insulted the many gay friends Marlene had cultivated over the years – even Noel Coward. She seems to suggest at one point that her mother deliberately placed her with a paedophile nanny who then abused her. She concludes by saying that she admired Dietrich the star and the public property, but she didn't care much for her mother.

Nevertheless, if you can screen out the personal acrimony, you find a book full of fascinating personal detail that only someone who had been with Dietrich throughout her life could know. It did seem that Marlene shared a little more about her love life with her daughter than most mothers would.

There are several other movie star biographies written by revenge-seeking daughters, notably those about Joan Crawford and Bette Davis. Whereas Cristina Crawford's book about her mother had been called "Mommie Dearest", Maria Riva's book was dubbed "Mommie Queerest" by some wag.

Yes, indeed, Marlene had a taste for the ladies and was as happy abed with a woman as a man. She was also, Maximillian Schell had revealed, an outspoken atheist. "If there is a God," she had told Schell, "then he's crazy."

So that was something else we had in common.

I read the Riva book avidly with a mixture of repulsion and fascination, wondering how she could remember all this detail from so long ago. I know my own memory has been tested writing *this* book and although I've tried my best to verify dates and places and names, I am not at all certain that every jot and tittle is accurate and that everything is in the correct order of occurrence.

But to recount someone else's life in such intimate detail and get it 100% right must be even harder. But Marlene had made it a little easier – she was an avid letter-writer and hoarder of absolutely everything. After she died there were two huge aircraft hangar-sized storage lockers packed with stuff she had accumulated. Nothing, but nothing, had been thrown away.

There would have been many clues there if you could find your way around it.

So now Marlene was finally gone. Even though I'd never met her, I had been in love with her so long, it seemed like a strangely personal bereavement.

~ 74 ~

The campaign to get the Press Council to criticise or restrain the tabloid press's use of abusive language continued.

It had reached such a pitch that it prompted the journalist Bernard Levin to write in *The Times*:

"Homosexuals are being portrayed – portrayed literally as well as metaphorically – as creatures scarcely human; they are being abused not just in the old mocking way but in the foulest terms, meant with deadly seriousness; they are experiencing an increasing discrimination over a wide range of situations; already voices have been raised demanding the 'cleansing' of schools as they have been for purging the church."

Then a new Chairman was appointed to the Press Council, the liberal lawyer Louis Blom-Cooper QC. The Council was formulating a new code of practice for journalists and, despite repeated requests, it had made clear that it did not intend to include homosexuality in the clause dealing with discrimination.

A report in *Capital Gay* said that the Council's director, Kenneth Morgan, had "considered the issue of homosexuality many times", but he had stated that the Review Committee, which was considering amendments to the code of practice, decided to limit itself to 'race and colour' in its discrimination clause. Morgan accepted that there was a widespread view that unnecessary references to race and colour should not be introduced into newspaper reports "irrelevantly in any prejudicial context" but he said there was "not, as yet, a sufficiently general view about such references to sex or sexuality to warrant these being prohibited by the code as well."

Recognising that there was an increasing sense of fear and alarm within the gay community about where all this hatemongering was leading, Louis Blom-Cooper agreed to meet a delegation from CHE and I was also invited to participate. The meeting took place at the Press Council's headquarters in Salisbury Square in January 1990.

Blom-Cooper said that although the Council had consistently ruled against any restriction on abusive words in the past, it was not beyond possibility that this could change. There were no promises or commitments, but the underlying message was clear, keep those complaints coming.

I waited until I found examples so egregious that I thought them indefensible before testing my suspicion that Mr Blom-Cooper was waiting for the opportunity to make a change.

Eventually I cited articles by Garry Bushell, *The Sun*'s TV critic, containing the words "woofter" and "poofter" used in such a way that could only be described as gratuitously insulting. I was happy to base the complaint on Garry Bushell's column because he was a particularly nasty example of the laddish columnist who thought it was funny to heap vile abuse on those who had no recourse. His column had been a source of irritation for years. His constant insulting comments about gay people and his ruthless use of AIDS as a political battering ram was causing distress and fury throughout the gay community. In fact, at one point during an Outrage! demonstration he was burned in effigy, something he subsequently professed made him proud.

Following the complaint, the usual long exchange of correspondence began between myself, the Press Council and various people on *The Sun*. Garry Bushell maintained, rather unconvincingly:

My attacks have not been on homosexuals but on:

1.The use of TV programmes to promote homosexuality which are nothing more than thinly disguised propaganda on behalf of the homosexual lobby.

2.The promotion of individual homosexuals on the basis of their sexual orientation rather than their talents. Many gay entertainers are so poor, I can think of no other reason for their success.

I make no apology for the language I use. It is the language of The Sun *readers and, indeed, the majority of British people.*

245

I responded by saying:

"Mr Bushell says that his attacks have 'not been on homosexuals'. This is disingenuous when seen in the light of comments he made in his column in The Sun *dated 21 March 1990 which read: "It must be true what they say about nobody being all bad.... Even STALIN banned poofs!"*
Mr Bushell says that TV programmes are used to 'promote homosexuality'. It seems that any mention of the subject angers Mr Bushell and thus constitutes – in his opinion – 'promotion'."

It was a long and winding road, but eventually the Press Council issued its adjudication on 14 May 1990. To my astonishment and delight, it upheld the complaint.

"Although the words "poof" and "poofter" are in common parlance they are so offensive to male homosexuals that publishing them is not a matter of taste or opinion within a newspaper editor's discretion.

"Upholding a complaint that The Sun *had used words of unnecessary crude abuse in three articles about television, the Council said newspapers should publish offensive language only where it was necessary for a proper understanding of an item. Nothing in the articles complained of made it necessary.*

"When Mr Terry Sanderson complained at the word 'poof' and 'woofter', the managing editor, Mr William Newman said they were in everyday use for homosexuals whose activities were repellent to the vast majority of people including Sun writers and readers. Mr Sanderson said it was fallacious to say the words could appear just because readers used them. They created contempt and violence against innocent individuals."

The Press Council's conclusion:

"Words describing an identifiable class of people, which are not merely coarse or intended to be derogatory, but are plainly insulting, should not generally appear in a newspaper.

"The words 'poof' and ;poofter'... while no doubt used in common parlance, were so offensive to male homosexuals as not to be a matter of taste or opinion within the editor's discretion.

"Newspapers should publish offensive language only where its use is necessary for the purpose of proper understanding of the item in which the offensive words appear. There was nothing in any of the three items in The Sun *which made the use of the words 'poof' or 'poofter' necessary. The complaint against* The Sun *is upheld."*

It was a major breakthrough and it was inevitable that the publication of this adjudication would create violent reaction in Fleet Street. That was an understatement, it created a positive tsunami of outrage. There were claims that free speech had been curtailed and political correctness had gone mad.

The Sun responded with an editorial headed: "You can't call 'em poofters", which read:

"In Alice in Wonderland the Queen of Hearts ordained that words meant what SHE SAID they meant. The Press Council has the same lordly manner over language. In their judgment today they seek to tell us which words we may or may not use. Our offence is that we spoke of homosexuals as poofs and poofters. The Press Council reached into the Shorter Oxford English Dictionary before reaching its conclusion. The Council's chairman Lord Louis Blom-Cooper QC knows a lot about the law. But we know a lot more about how ordinary folk think, act and speak. What is good enough for them is good enough for us.

"Incidentally, our dictionary defines gay as carefree, merry, brilliant. Does the Press Council approve of homosexuals appropriating such a fine old word?"

The usual cabal of right-wing columnists rushed to *The Sun*'s defence, using the opportunity once more to portray gay people as evil, debased and intolerable – and now the destroyers of free expression. Only the *Independent* came to our defence, with an editorial:

"The persecution of homosexuals is spiritually akin to anti-Semitism. Hitler proved the point by despatching homosexuals as well as Jews and gypsies to his concentration camps. It is intolerable that people should be persecuted for not belonging to the same race as the majority. It is no less excusable that they should be vilified and assaulted because their sexual orientation differs from the norm."

There were a few childish attempts to break the ban in the weeks that followed, but generally the yahoos that passed themselves off as journalists on the tabloid papers got the message that what they were doing didn't belong in a civilised society.

Nowadays, of course, they would be taken to court for writing the sort of stuff that they did then. Hatemongering against gays is now prohibited by law and the likes of Garry Bushell and Ray Mills have to curb their desire to spit hate in the faces of those they have a prejudice against.

Which is not to say that all criticism of homosexuality is off-limits. I would defend anybody's right not to approve of my sexuality, so long as they express their opinions in a way that is not likely to increase hatred and hostility to an identifiable minority. Violence and terror against gay people is on the rise, it does not need any encouragement from journalists.

~ 75 ~

How to be a Happy Homosexual went from strength to strength. For the fourth edition I handed it over to The Gay Men's Press, thinking they might have better distribution and could get it into more hands. But when the time came to renew the contract, I took it back and published a fifth edition through The Otherway Press. And still it kept on selling.

The problem was that gay life was changing so quickly that each new edition soon became outdated. It needed constant revision – to include new legal changes, to give the latest thinking on AIDS and safe sex and to take into account a new confidence that was arising among the younger generation of gay people.

Societal attitudes had changed beyond recognition since the first edition had been published. Young people no longer had the same equivocal attitudes to their gay friends that their parents had. Many young gays were totally accepted by their straight friends and the very concept of a "gay community" was being seen by some as outmoded. Many in this new generation were completely laid back and didn't see it as an issue at all.

One weekend, when I went back to Maltby to visit Mi Mam, I saw two girls walking hand in hand down the High Street without a care in the world. And on another visit, a gaggle of schoolgirls, with one very obviously gay boy in tow, were looking at photos on a mobile phone. They were sniggering at something and the boy said: "He's gorgeous – I'd have had his pants down in no time if it had been me."

At Cowgate I had a couple of colleagues – two young men who were straight but unfazed by their gay friends – who had decided to go to the Pride parade. They wanted to show solidarity they said, but mostly it was to join the party and see the pop acts. On their way there on the bus, they had been cornered by a group of West Indian youths who had identified them as "batty boys" – which was their slang for gay men.

My two colleagues came into work on the Monday morning sporting black eyes and broken noses. They had been queer-bashed and they weren't even queer! I thought that was the ultimate injustice and that they would be very resentful, but they shrugged it off as though it was an everyday occurrence.

If it had happened to me I would have been traumatised for months.

I had also sold translation rights to *Happy Homosexual* in Greece and Spain *(¿Entiendes o qué?* it was called there*)* and then was approached by a TV production company, Tiger Aspect, asking if the TV rights were available. They had got it into their heads to somehow make a drama out of it. They had a writer, they said, and Channel 4 were interested.

I couldn't imagine what a fictionalised version would consist of, but who was I to argue? They were prepared to pay a delicious amount of money for the rights and even more was promised when and if the programme was made.

And all I had to do was sign a contract. Maybe all they really wanted was the title – the one that Sheldon Press had dumped.

This contract was renewed for each of the subsequent four years, each time bringing another little windfall for doing absolutely nothing. In the end they decided that the project wasn't working, but I was laughing all the way to the bank. TV production is very wasteful but also very lucrative if you can break into it.

~ 76 ~

Keith's career in high finance was coming to an end. I could see that the constant stress of these high-powered jobs was getting to him and he thought the time had come for a change of direction.

At that moment a vacancy had arisen at the National Secular Society for a "general secretary". We were both members of the NSS and interested in the issues it covered. Keith was very tempted to apply for this as "something completely different." It might have been considered as downsizing to some, but it turned out to be one of the best things he ever did. Far from relieving him of stress, this job brought him into the national spotlight. But this was the kind of stress that he thrived on.

The National Secular Society was established in 1866 by a radical MP, Charles Bradlaugh.

Bradlaugh had been a very high profile atheist and when he was elected as MP for Northampton he was refused his seat in Parliament because his fellow MPs would not allow him take the oath, which then had to be on the Bible, because they knew he was an atheist.

A long struggle ensued in which Bradlaugh was refused his seat, then re-elected at a by-election, then refused, then re-elected. Eventually after much political controversy and parliamentary shenanigans, he overcame his enemies and took his seat on the fifth time in the House of Commons, where he became a very active Parliamentarian.

The NSS had survived into the twentieth century and had been deeply involved in the great reforms of the 1960s on abortion, homosexuality and racial equality. It had accumulated quite a lot of money over the years from large legacies and donations, but by the time Keith became involved, it had become little more than a historical society, constantly basking in the glory of battles long-since fought and mostly forgotten.

There were new battles now and old battles that needed to be revisited with the aid of modern technology. At one point it had seemed that secularism had won and religious power had been depleted. But then aggressive and politicised Islam began to stir and in its wake Christianity pulled back from what had seemed an inevitable decline. Suddenly religious power-seeking was everywhere.

The National Secular Society was needed once more to stand up against the privileges and power-seeking of a religion that few observed any more.

We needed to bring the NSS into the modern world. Keith felt he could help that process and so he was given the job and set about updating and reviving the organisation.

It was a long and gruelling process to get the NSS back into the political arena, but eventually it began to recruit new council members with good ideas and to start seriously campaigning on contemporary issues.

We are still proud of the history, but the war with power-hungry religion that we thought was won had actually only been a hiatus. Religion was becoming more extreme and dangerous than ever.

There were plenty of areas in need of reform that still hung over from previous generations – even previous centuries. "Faith schools" was one – indeed, that was the issue that almost everyone who joined the NSS was concerned about.

Then there was the blasphemy law that was still extant and which had been used by Mary Whitehouse against *Gay News* twenty-five years previously. There were many such religious privileges including Anglican bishops sitting in the House of Lords as of right – with England being the only country in the world that permits Christian clerics into its Parliament in this way.

Secularism, when partnered with democracy, can help keep the worst instincts of religion under control. It works to an extent in America, but even there the Christian right are energetically pursuing a programme of lies, obfuscation and manipulation of the media to impose their views, claiming that God's law is higher than the constitution or the supreme court.

Now we see all around the world what does happen when there are no restraints and one religion takes temporal power in

252

a society. It becomes a theocracy and the first job of any theocracy is to crush all opposition.

Secularism - if freely chosen by the people - can halt the ambitions of theocrats. Those who long for a religious dictatorship will always oppose the secular state because they know that while it exists, they cannot achieve the total control they desire.

Secularism does not want to destroy religion or inhibit its practice. It just seeks to ensure that everyone is safe from persecution by other faiths whatever religion they choose for themselves. Or, indeed, if they choose no religion at all.

I saw the value of secularism in protecting gay rights. Religion is the greatest opponent of justice for homosexuals and when laws are made according to religious principles, as they are in much of the Islamic world, then homosexuals become criminalised, persecuted and in constant peril. Punishments under religious law are harsh, even including death. When religious law is the law of the land, gay people can expect no mercy.

I wanted to be involved in this prootion of secularism and so, many years after Keith had been appointed, joined the Council of management.

One of our first big campaigns was to support Peter Tatchell who, in 1998, had climbed into the pulpit at Canterbury Cathedral to interrupt the Archbishop of Canterbury, George Carey, in mid-sermon to demand he address the issue of gay rights, which he had studiously avoided.

Tatchell was arrested and charged under the Ecclesiastical Courts Jurisdiction Act 1860, which was itself derived from a much older law, the Brawling Act of 1551. This made it an offence to cause a commotion in a church or church yard. There was a potential prison sentence attached to this law.

The NSS called for the Act to be scrapped and organised a petition signed by such luminaries as the writer Alan Bennett and the former Labour leader Michael Foot. We stated our concern that the Act gives the church a unique degree of protection, and an immunity to criticism which no other

253

institution enjoys. In the end, when the case came to court, the magistrate seemed to agree and showed his contempt by saying that this was equivalent to a minor public order offence, and fined Mr Tatchell £18.60 – one penny for each of the years in the Act's title.

Secularism, it seems to me, is the issue of the century. With a growing constituency of non-believers in Britain and an increasing number of minority religions, it is impossible to justify an established Church – particularly one like the Church of England which had been all-powerful once but is now a much diminished institution with a rapidly dwindling membership. It is consumed with arguments about whether it should accept or reject gay relationships. Any institution that is engaged in such a battle has my enmity.

I had thought through all the arguments about whether religious claims were true or not. I had read endlessly about the contradictions in the Bible and the evil history of the churches – not to mention what seemed to me the sheer silliness of other religious claims. What I had discovered was that attacking beliefs, however bizarre, had very little effect on the people who hold them. In fact, attacking people's religion just seems to make it stronger.

When the Catholic Church began to dramatically lose support in Britain, one of its bishops said that "a bit of persecution would be very handy" for creating a revival. Of course, any kind of criticism – however justified - was thenceforward defined as persecution.

The better approach, surely, is not to try to rob people of their faith but to try to take away the churches' political power. When the Anglican Bishops in the House of Lords use their privileged position to try to derail progressive legislation, they should be challenged. It is no good telling them that what they believe is ludicrous nonsense, they are immune to such jibes, and I have a sneaking feeling some already know that anyway, what we need to do is get them out of Parliament altogether and back into their cathedrals where they belong. There they can inflict their strange archaic rules on those who want them and not on those who don't.

Mind you, the bishops very rarely these days invoke biblical objections when they are opposing progressive legislation. They know that they will be laughed at if they try to create law based on Christian dogma and "God's law". In earlier times Christians in Parliament would not hesitate to invoke the name of the Lord as justification for their bigotry, nowadays they try to invent arguments that sound rational. Parliament nowadays has more than its fair share of religious MPs, but only a few try to legislate from a theocratic perspective.

So, although when Keith and I arrived, most members of the NSS were full-blown and convinced atheists, the constant harping on Biblical or Koranic truth, or lack of it, was getting us nowhere.

Many young people were coming to the conclusion themselves that what they were being told about religion was nonsense. Religious leaders could no longer control all sources of information as they had in the past. They could no longer censor or ban books and they certainly couldn't control the internet or social media.

When Richard Dawkins published his book *The God Delusion* it made him into an international celebrity and sold in its tens of millions. That book put the other side of the story and many young people read it and were reassured that their doubts about "faith" were legitimate.

The Church had employed the blasphemy law in the past to ensure that their beliefs and claims were not contradicted – and if you failed to respect them you could expect a hefty jail sentence. Indeed, many of the people who had fought for the NSS in the nineteenth and early twentieth century had been imprisoned for daring to challenge the religious hegemony. Many of them had received savage sentences, sometimes with hard labour. Charles Bradlaugh himself only narrowly escaped jail sentences on several occasions for daring not to be a Christian and for advocating for birth control.

But the efforts of these early pioneers, hard as they had been, were not in vain, and gradually the churches were stripped of their power to punish those who defied them.

There were still some hangovers from those days of church power, which was massive up until just around the time the NSS was formed. The Church had its own courts (sometimes called bawdy courts), and even prisons. The Church dealt with probate of wealthy estates. The NSS was formed to co-ordinate the numerous vigorous secular groups extant all over the country, many with their own halls, built because the Church would pressurise hall owners not to let them out to secularists. One of the last of the secular halls is still standing in Leicester.

The blasphemy law – the common law offence of blasphemous libel –survived into the 21st Century, a disgraceful reminder of a shameful history. It hadn't been used since the *Gay News* case in 1972, and was considered to be a dead letter. But, then again, it had been considered a dead letter when Mary Whitehouse had been on the rampage and she had managed to breathe life into it. It would be safer to finally kill it so it could never be revived again.

So, now that Keith had got the NSS moving again and made it relevant to the times we were living in, I decided to get involved more closely myself and soon became a Vice-President.

As I saw it, recruiting members was a priority. The membership roll had fallen into the hundreds and we needed to strengthen that. The only way to do that was to let people know that the NSS was still alive and that it was fighting for changes on issues that affected everyone.

In 2002, the NSS and several other organisations and individuals, staged a reading of *The Love that Dares to Speak its Name* – the poem that had got *Gay News* prosecuted - on the steps of St Martins in the Field Church in central London. The idea was that each verse would be read individually by a celebrity – an MP, a jazz singer or whatever – so that if the police decided to prosecute, they would not be able to prosecute an individual, they would have to haul everyone into court. Realising this, they didn't arrest anyone at the event or even take names and addresses.

Meanwhile, fundamentalist Christian activists gathered around the demo, including a man in a cowboy hat, carrying a menacing eight foot wooden cross over his shoulder, and playing hymns very loudly with a powerful amplifier. The Christians effectively drowned out the reading with their noise.

We had naively wondered why the police insisted on penning us into an enclosure of metal barriers. It gradually dawned on us that this was for our own protection. The Christians in huge numbers were clearly trying to intimidate us, and to an extent they succeeded. We ended up being grateful for the barrier, without which I am sure there would have been injuries. Gentle Jesus? Not that day.

We were only permitted to use a small megaphone, but it didn't really matter that no-one had been able to hear the poem, the symbolic act of defiance had taken place. As a result, a huge amount of publicity was generated, drawing attention to the law that everyone had thought was long gone.

In May that year, the House of Lords appointed a select committee "to consider and report on the law relating to religious offences". The committee's first report was published in April 2003. It concluded that any prosecution brought under the blasphemy law as it stood would not succeed. They could not agree whether a new blasphemy law was needed, but if Parliament decided that it was, it should apply to all religions. We at the NSS were determined that there would be no replacement. The dangers of making blasphemy prosecutions available to even more religious zealots were obvious – to us, at least.

The Home Secretary at the time, David Blunkett, then brought forward plans to criminalise incitement to religious hatred, which became the Racial and Religious Hatred Act 2006, and he suggested the blasphemy law might be repealed once the new law was in force.

The NSS believed that although it was right that religious individuals should be protected from discrimination and violence, their beliefs should not. It was extremely dangerous to make criticising religion an offence. It would become a *de facto* blasphemy law, but a much more threatening one than the one it would abolish. Surely human rights were for humans, not for ideas?

The NSS argued at every stage of the Parliamentary progress of the Bill that if it were to be brought on to the statute book, it should be modified to clearly protect free speech.

Keith was working incredibly hard on all these campaigns and making useful contacts in Parliament and in the media. He, too, was honing his skills as a campaigner and would soon far outflank me in effectiveness. Our partnership was noticed, of course, by those of a theocratic temperament, who thought the NSS was the devil's workshop, and they tried hard to use our gayness against us. But times have changed, and inciting hatred and fear of homosexuals is not as easy as it used to be – even among the religious - and much more likely to rebound on the inciter.

In 2005, the BBC had decided to broadcast the controversial musical *Jerry Springer – the Opera* which had run for over 600 performances in theatres. Theatrical performances have special protections to ensure that they are not restricted. But television, because it comes directly into our living rooms, is answerable for what it broadcasts to various regulatory bodies. The plan to broadcast a recording of *Jerry Springer – the Opera* drew the attention of a Christian extremist called Stephen Green. Seeing an opportunity, Green immediately began a campaign to have the programme cancelled.

Mr Green was a depressingly familiar opponent. He ran a small pressure group called Christian Voice which served as a platform for his extremist ideas. He had been a long-time opponent of gay rights and had written a rather obsessive book criticising gay lifestyles called *The Sexual Dead-End*. I had been up against him on many radio and TV programmes. He was a truly unpleasant man, but expressing views that were so extreme that he actually came across as something of a clown.

That very extremism ensured her got a regular media platform. In many of the radio debates where I had opposed him, I had stayed almost silent throughout. The producer would whisper in my ear: "Why don't you say something?" but Stephen Green was much better at bringing Stephen Green into disrepute than I could ever be. By far the best approach was to give him enough rope.

The Jerry Springer controversy was an issue that fundamentalist Christian groups had been waiting for – something that they could rally round and campaign on and which allowed them to present themselves as victims.

The show, which was co-written by comedian Stewart Lee, was a satire on the exploitative TV talk show genre, using Jesus as a "victim" of the Jerry Springer show. It was awash with four-letter words and sexual imagery. Mr Green claimed it was "blasphemous", even though he had never seen it.

An orchestrated campaign among Christians – most of whom had taken Mr Green's word that the show was anti-religious – resulted in 55,000 complaints being received by the BBC. The BBC said it usually expects no more than 20 complaints about even its most provocative programmes, so such an inflated protest was almost certainly non-spontaneous.

The NSS stepped in to defend the BBC's right to show the programme. We encouraged the Corporation to stick to its artistic guns and let viewers make up their own minds about it. There would be warnings before and during the programme to ward off those who didn't want to see it, and there were many other channels they could watch as an alternative.

But this wasn't about their desire not to see it, it was their instinctive desire to stop anybody seeing it.

The controversy grew and grew and I was doing one radio programme after another. The membership of the NSS was going up as a result. People wanted to do something positive to resist the rise of religious fundamentalism and supporting the NSS was their answer.

One radio programme that I was participating in was coming from the old Television Centre in White City. During the show, the presenter had heard that a big protest had arrived outside the doors of the building, and he insisted that we take our microphones and go outside to see what it was all about. When we got there we found a bus load of people from the controversial Peniel Pentecostal Church in Brentwood, Essex. The protest consisted of dozens of strangely glassy-eyed women being led by their "Bishop" Michael Reid.

Mr Reid had a foghorn-type preaching voice, much in the mould of Ian Paisley, and was shouting about insults to the Lord and an end to the blasphemers. I challenged his *bona fides* as a "Bishop" – asking who had anointed him thus?

He yelled that his followers intended to burn their TV licences in protest and would never watch the BBC again He then produced a bucket into which his Stepford Wife-style acolytes each put a piece of paper, purporting to be their TV licence, but on closer examination was actually a photocopy. They were then burned.

The whole thing was bizarre in the extreme but it was fascinating to see the hold Bishop Reid seemed to have over his female followers.

The "bishop" had made claims that he had seen miracualous healings in his church and used this in his recruitment advertisements. The Advertising Standards Authority were unable to find any evidence for such claims.

He was eventually kicked out of the Penniel church for repeated sexual misdemeanours but he hasn't gone away and continues to claim miraculous healings.

Stephen Green, in the meantime, tried to prosecute BBC executives, attempting to emulate Mary Whitehouse and revivify the blasphemy law. However, his attempts were thwarted by the courts who rejected his appeals. They opined that in the light of the Human Rights Act – which had now been written into law – blasphemy legislation was defunct and a prosecution could no longer succeed. As his campaign grew more desperate, Mr Green also irresponsibly published the home addresses of the BBC executives, one of whom subsequently received death threats.

On the day before the show was to be broadcast, I was invited by the *Sunday Telegraph* to a pre-screening, in which critics of the programme would also be present. These included the ghastly Mr Green and another extremist Christian, Anne Atkins, well known for her anti-gay and right-wing views which she spouted regularly on the BBC's *Thought for the Day* programme (from which non-religious voices are banned).

I was seated next to Anne Atkins in the preview room and the programme was shown. It was, as we knew it would be, peppered with expletives. I had not realised that Ms Atkins had a slight hearing impediment and she wasn't catching all the dialogue. She kept turning to me and asking: "What did he say?"

At one point I was able to reply: "Fuck you, Anne. He said 'fuck you'." It gave me great pleasure -and I am sure I spoke for many - when I was able to whisper those word into her ear.

Incidentally, Stephen Green was later accused by his ex-wife Caroline of beating her and their children. She described him in a newspaper interview as "controlling, spiteful and self-righteous, delusional and completely uncontrollable" and that living with Green "was almost like living in a cult."

It wasn't until 2008, during the passage of the Criminal Justice and Immigration Bill, that the Government announced that it would consider supporting the abolition of the blasphemy laws.

They checked that it was all right with the Church of England and other churches before reaching a decision – an indication of the political clout that these institutions still command.

The move had been prompted by a letter written to *The Daily Telegraph* at the instigation of MP Evan Harris and the National Secular Society that was signed by leading figures including Lord Carey, former Archbishop of Canterbury, who urged that the laws be abandoned.

On May 8, 2008, the Criminal Justice and Immigration Act abolished the common-law offences of blasphemy and blasphemous libel in England and Wales, with effect from 8 July 2008.

~ 77 ~

This was a major triumph for the NSS, which had been struggling to overturn the blasphemy law for almost a century and a half.

Naturally we had to have a celebratory party, which we called 'Bye Bye Blasphemy'. Among those attending were Stewart Lee of *Jerry Springer - the Opera* fame, Nigel Wingrove, whose film *Visions of Ecstasy*, about the sex maniac St Teresa of Avila had been banned by the Film Classification Board on the grounds that it *might* be blasphemous, Tony Reeves, who had drawn the illustration for the *Gay News* poem and Sir Ian McKellen who read *The Love that Dares to Speak its Name* to the assembled multitude.

This seemed like a marvellous revenge for what Mary Whitehouse had tried to do to the gay community all those years previously and I was just sorry that she was no longer alive to see it.

By this time I had become the eleventh President of the National Secular Society, following in the footsteps of some very illustrious predecessors. In many ways this was a no more popular a role than had been my time as convenor of Rotherham CHE. There were people who were outraged that the NSS even existed, and many people – particularly Christians – who were determined to do it down.

But I was very happy that the blasphemy law had been abolished on my watch and now we would see what else could be achieved. Over the coming years we had other extraordinary experiences.

In 2010 I received a phone call from a reporter at the Press Association who told me that Josef Ratzinger (stage name Pope Benedict XVI) was going to pay a state visit to Britain – did we intend to do anything about it? Impetuously and full of hubris I said: "Of course, we will mount a large-scale protest during the visit."

In his 2012 Christmas message, Ratzinger called gay and transgendered people a "bigger threat to mankind than even the destruction of the rainforests," and so naturally any opportunity to make life difficult for such a man would have to be taken.

The following day my braggadocio was splashed all over the papers. It was now beholden upon me to make it happen. But I had never organised a large-scale proper protest before, not one that involved parading through the streets of London. I had no idea how to go about it.

We decided to call a meeting of all interested groups and individuals and I hoped that someone among them would have the skills needed to organise this march and rally.

Fortunately, a young man called Marco Tranchino was there and he thought that he could take charge of that. He would negotiate with the police, arrange the banners, the loudspeakers and so on. He took his task very seriously and spent many weeks negotiating with an obstructive Scotland Yard to finalise the route and the rallying point. I will be eternally grateful for his input.

Now it was up to me to get people to come along.

This was where my previous campaigning and public relations experience came in handy. I had discovered in many of my gay confrontations how to create controversy in order to gain publicity. And such was the interest in this visit, and so unpopular was this Pope, that it wasn't going to be difficult.

We centred the campaign round the news that the taxpayer would be stumping up a minimum of £10 million for this visit. We argued that the state should not be spending such sums on any religion, but particularly not on a man who promoted policies that were anathema to most British people. As the visit approached it became clear that £10 million was a gross underestimate of how much it was really going to cost.

We organised a press conference of survivors of abuse by Catholic priests, which attracted journalists from all over the world. I put on a festival of films critical of the Catholic Church, exposing its corruption and its cruelty. One was about child abuse by priests, one was about the Magdalene Laundries and another was about the corrupt influence of their priests in South America.

On the day of the protest, 18 September 2010, it is estimated that 20,000 people took part at various stages. I was among those who was slated to make a short speech to this huge crowd. It was a daunting prospect to see so many faces looking up and waiting for you to say something inspiring. I managed to splutter a few words about "Pope – go home!" and then gratefully climbed down from the podium to allow much more interesting people – like Richard Dawkins and Geoffrey Robertson - to say more cogent things.

The Catholic Church pooh-poohed the protest. They tried to make out it had been an utter failure, as – predictably – did the BBC and much of the printed media, so much of which still inexplicably kow-tows to religion. Yet our demonstration stretched the whole length and most of the breadth of Piccadilly, from Hyde Park Corner to Piccadilly Circus. Unforgettable.

But the propagandists could not deflect attention from the fact that it was the Pope's visit that had failed to make much impact despite, in the end, having cost many tens of millions of pounds. The visit had enjoyed blanket coverage on radio and TV but even so, an opinion poll commissioned by the Catholic Church itself a year afterwards showed that hardly anyone remembered it and it had certainly not had any influence on what they thought or how they behaved. More people remembered our protest than any of the events organised by the Vatican.

In the run up to the visit, the Church had staged a huge counter-propaganda campaign, some of which was outright lies. It opened my eyes to how the Vatican operates when it receives criticism, and it is ruthless. But quietly and reluctantly, the Church had to admit that this had been the largest protest against a Pope that it had ever known.

Although the Protest the Pope campaign was dismissed and misrepresented by religious apologists, there is no denying that Pope Benedict was a disaster for the Vatican. His unyielding strictures on abortion, contraception, homosexuality and women's rights had caused millions of Catholics to abandon the

Church, calling it inhumane. And he had presided over the (mis)handling of child abuse for decades before becoming pope, even further centralising the Churches control over it.

Keith had spent a great deal of effort in acquainting the United Nations with all of this, and their verdict, when they considered it, was unbelievably damning. It spawned condemnatory and unprecedented worldwide publicity.

Ratzinger's unsmiling and slightly prissy persona lacked any kind of warmth or charisma. During the controversy a book had been published with the title *The Pope is Gay*. Whether or not that was true, I don't know, but it wouldn't surprise me. I had learned over the years that some of the most frothing homophobes are themselves gay.

In 2013 Mr Ratzinger announced that he was "resigning" from the papacy – the first Pope to do so since 1415. The truth is more likely to be that he was sacked. Booted out. The Church has an unerring instinct for self-preservation, and Benedict had to go. I like to think that our protest played a small part in that.

Later, on a holiday in Rome, Keith and I walked along the street that leads away from the Vatican and saw all the shops selling the kind of vulgar and schmaltzy souvenirs in which the Catholic Church specialises. But one thing was very obvious: for all the Pope propaganda that flooded the shops, including the . plethora of images of the new Pope Francis and many of his more popular predecessors, there was no sign of Benedict. Not a postcard, not a figurine, not a lurid drawing, nothing.

He seemed to have been edited out of the story. Best forgotten.

On this, and only this, I agreed with the Vatican.

Another big story that the NSS generated concerned the habit of some local authorities to open their council meetings with prayers. We had no objection to the councillors praying if they wanted to, but we argued it should not be part of the official agenda. When councillors are summoned to meetings, they should not be expected to pray as part of their duties – that is not what they were elected for and the council chamber is not a church. We had already seen arguments among councillors from different religions when prayers from a different faith didn't suit them.

The Christians, of course, were reluctant to give up this privilege. But when a councillor from Bideford in Devon, Clive Bone, approached us and said that he was an atheist and resented having to sit through prayers conducted by a local vicar, we decided to take up his case.

The upshot was that the matter reached the High Court and the judge ruled in our favour. Prayers should not be part of a council agenda, he said.

This decision prompted thousands of headlines around the world and also brought us many new members. It also resulted, some years later, in an evangelical Christian member of the government, Eric Pickles (now Sir Eric Pickles) fast-tracking a new Bill relating to local authorities that he claimed would override the court decision. But our legal advisors were clear that the new Bill, which became the Localism Act, did not do what Mr Pickles said it did.

Undeterred, other Christians in the House of Commons brought forward a dedicated Bill to return the right of councils to restore prayers to their agendas. This sneaked through Parliament at times when hardly anyone was in the chamber, and was a clear illustration of how Christian MPs misuse their power to promote the interests of religion.

But we had made our point. Many local authorities had removed prayers from their meetings and despite now having the right to put them back, few seem to have availed themselves of the opportunity.

For someone who fought so hard to protect gay people from public abuse, it may seem strange that I also joined a campaign to protect street preachers from being arrested when they quoted biblical condemnations of homosexuality. I got a lot of criticism from gay people who thought it was right that these extremists should be stopped from spouting what they saw as "poison" in the streets.

In some instances, when these rackety preachers were shouting their literalist interpretation of the Bible's demand that homosexuals should be stoned to death, hostile crowds had

266

gathered and the preachers had been stopped for their own protection. But sometimes they were stopped or even arrested by the police because someone *might* object to what they were saying.

I don't like what they say either. But, then again, they don't like what I say. Suppose the tables were turned and preachers had the power to stop gay people advocating for fairer treatment. They've done it in the past – with blasphemy laws and Section 28. But free speech is so precious that we must overcome our desire to gag our critics and instead let them have their say and then argue with them if we don't agree. And we must demand the same tolerance from them.

There is a difference between inciting hatred and merely being critical or satirical. If a preacher were to say to his followers: "Go out and kill all homosexuals" (as some Muslim imams have done), then he would deserve to have his collar felt and face the full might of the law. But if he simply says what's in the Bible, then we have to let him say it and engage him in conversation. If we don't want to do that, just let him have his say and ignore it.

We know there are religious fanatics that will not tolerate any dissent and are prepared to kill their critics – as the horrors of Charlie Hebdo in Paris and many others have illustrated. We also know that there are Islamist preachers in Britain who do, indeed, advocate killing homosexuals. Until recently they have been able to get away with it, but things are changing and the Government is acting at last to challenge the maniacs. The NSS has been urging them to do this for decades, as we have been urging them to tackle (mainly Muslim, but not entirely) extremism in schools.

The NSS also fought hard to protect the new Equality legislation from exemption demanded by religious groups. Evangelical Christian groups such as Christian Concern and the Christian Institute have brought numerous cases to court aimed at diminishing the protections from discrimination for gay people. So far they have not succeeded. Indeed, one of the cases resulted in one Judge, Lord Justice Laws, commenting:

"We do not live in a society where all the people share uniform religious beliefs. The precepts of any one religion — any belief system — cannot, by force of their religious origins, sound any louder in the general law than the precepts of any other. If they did, those out in the cold would be less than citizens, and our constitution would be on the way to a theocracy, which is of necessity autocratic."

That seems to me to summarise secularism, and why I am now so enthusiastic about the idea. But that does not mean that attacks on the equality law have gone away. Far from it.

One of our greatest victories concerned four evangelical Christian employees who claimed they had been discriminated against at work. Two said they didn't want to provide services to gay people and two claimed that their employer had forbidden them from wearing a crucifix work. Domestic courts in the UK had rejected these claims, rightly concluding that they had no merit. So they had taken them to the European Court of Human Rights, claiming their religious freedoms had been violated by the UK Courts.

One of the complainants was Lillian Ladele, an Islington (north London) registrar, who refused to officiate at gay civil partnerships on grounds of her "Christian conscience". Another was Gary McFarlane who expressed discomfort at providing psychosexual counselling to same sex couple for his employers, Relate. Both organisations had strong equal opportunity policies that neither of the claimants wanted to observe.

Nurse Shirley Chaplin had been asked by her employer to remove jewellery – which happened to be a cross hanging round her neck on a chain – on grounds of health and safety. Nadia Eweida who worked for British Airways was similarly asked to remove jewellery which did not conform to the company's uniform policy. The press consistently, despite being corrected, portrayed this as a ban on crucifixes.

The NSS was the only organisation to oppose all four cases and was exceedingly fortunate in being permitted by the European Court to intervene. Anthony Lester QC, who is practically the father of UK's human rights law fronted our intervention. He agreed with our contention that if these cases had succeeded it would have, at a stroke, almost destroyed human rights law in Europe by creating a hierarchy of rights with religion at the top.

Both the gay-related appeals were rejected in their entirety by the court. On the bans on jewellery, the Eweida case was upheld on a technicality and the Chaplin case was rejected. It is widely thought that our interventions were crucial to the Court's decision. So it may be that European equality law survives in its present effective form because of our decision to intervene and the excellent work done by our legal team.

But the Christians have not gone away and their attacks on equality remain and are now presented as persecution against Christians (the 'reasoning' being that if you are prevented from persecuting other people, you are being persecuted yourself.)

It is, they tell us, an infringement of religious liberty to stop them firing gay people from jobs, kicking them out of their homes and refusing them services. If they had their way, we would be back in the 1950s and all progress in gay equality would be erased.

We need to watch them carefully.

~ 78 ~

It is at this point that I will close the story. There is much more to tell about my foray into secularism, and the drama continues to unfold as Islamist fanaticism grows stronger and threatens us all. We are seeing with our own eyes what happens when theocracies arise. They are as bloody and merciless now as they have been throughout history.

The Islamists make new sport of throwing gay men from the rooftops of tall buildings, and if that does not kill them, pelting them with stones until the job is finished.

In the United States a large-scale movement to theocratise the nation has infiltrated the Republican Party. There is a huge push to remove separation of church and state from the constitution. So far it has made little progress, but it is a determined and very rich campaign - and the world is changing fast, but hopefully not in their favour.

Secularism offers some answers to containing this growing psychosis, but we are in dangerous new territory and once more gay people are on the front line. The need for activism is not over and, I suspect, it never will be.

Gay legal rights in Britain have reached their zenith, with most of the aims we thought would never be achieved now under our belts. I would never have guessed that all this could have happened within my lifetime – a bloodless revolution of the best kind, the sort that is achieved democratically and with consent. From complete illegality to gay marriage, all in the space of living memory. It's incredible.

But it is that very speed that makes me worry that all is not as solid and settled as I would like it to be.

Laws can be repealed, public attitudes can change very quickly. Homophobia lurks not far below the surface in Britain, as we see in the rising incidences of gay-bashing. We must be ever vigilant and watch particularly for the rise of extremism of all sorts, but particularly of the religious kind.

Nowadays I'm referred to as a "veteran gay rights campaigner" and "leading secularist" which pleases me.

Whenever I am asked to speak at an event, someone invariably comes up afterwards and asks: "Are you the Terry Sanderson who wrote *How to be a Happy Homosexual*? I just want to tell you how much it helped me when I was young and just starting out."

This always gives me a warm glow and I'm happy that they're happy.

To the next generation of gay people, I say enjoy your life. Live it on your own terms, in your own way.

But be vigilant. There are forces at work that would like you to suffer in the way that the generations who have gone before have suffered. It will be up to you to resist.